# Buenos Aires

## a Lonely Planet city guide

## by Wayne Bernhardson

D0038990

**Buenos Aires**
1st edition

**Published by**
  Lonely Planet Publications
  Head Office:  PO Box 617, Hawthorn, Vic 3122, Australia
  Branches:    155 Filbert St, Suite 251, Oakland,
               CA 94607, USA
               10 Barley Mow Passage, Chiswick,
               London W4 4PH, UK
               71 bis rue du Cardinal Lemoine,
               75005 Paris, France

**Printed by**
  Colorcraft Ltd, Hong Kong
  Printed in China

**Photographs by**
  **Front cover:** Dave G Houser

**First Published**
  May 1996

**Although the author and publisher have tried to make the information as accurate as possible, they accept no responsibility for any loss, injury or inconvenience sustained by any person using this book.**

National Library of Australia Cataloguing in Publication Data

Bernhardson, Wayne
  Buenos Aires.

  1st ed.
  Includes index.
  ISBN 0 86442 337 3.

  1. Buenos Aires (Argentina) – Guidebooks.
  I. Title. (Series: Lonely Planet city guide).

  918.2110464

# Wayne Bernhardson

Wayne Bernhardson was born in Fargo, North Dakota, grew up in Tacoma, Washington, and earned a PhD in geography at the University of California, Berkeley. He has traveled extensively in Mexico and Central and South America, and lived for extended periods in Chile, Argentina, and the Falkland (Malvinas) Islands. His other LP credits include two editions of *Argentina, Uruguay & Paraguay*, the 3rd edition of *Chile & Easter Island*, the 5th edition of *South America on a Shoestring*, the 3rd edition of *Baja California*, the 5th edition of *Mexico*, and the 1st edition of *Rocky Mountain States*. Wayne currently resides in Oakland, California, where his Alaskan malamute Gardel smiles every bit as charismatically as his legendary porteño namesake.

# From the Author

Special mention to Fito and Mary Massolo of Olavarría, Buenos Aires province, my Argentine family for so many years. Also in Olavarría, thanks to Juan Marcelo and María Estela Peruilh, and to Rodolfo (hijo) and Viviana Massolo.

Many others in Buenos Aires were exceptionally helpful and hospitable in the process of pulling this all together. The list could be even longer, but special mention goes to the following Buenos Aires residents: Federico Kirbus, Joaquín Allolio, Hebe Alicia Blanco, Adrián Harari and Cristina Messineo, and Conrado Etchebarne Bullrich; Eduardo Tapia of the Centro Cultural Recoleta; Julio Sapollnik of the Palais de Glaçe; Carlos Reboratti and Perla Zusman at the Instituto de Geografía at the Universidad de Buenos Aires; Nicholas Tozer, Michael Soltys, and Andrew Graham-Yooll of the *Buenos Aires Herald*; Diego Curubeto of *Ambito Financiero*; Mario Banchik of Librerías Turísticas; Monique Larraín of the *Guía Argentina de Tráfico Aéreo*; Alán Rodrigué of the *Guía Internacional de Tráfico*; Kevin Michael O'Reilly of the political section of the US embassy; and Armando Schlecker of the *Guía Latinoamericana de Transportes*. A huge and special thanks to Georges Helft of San Telmo for a crash course in contemporary Argentine art, and for his willingness to permit photography of his extraordinary collection.

For help outside the capital, I should add Guillermo Botarques of the Dirección de Turismo in the city of La Plata, Buenos Aires province. In Uruguay, I appreciate the help from Manuel Pérez Bravo of the Asociación de Hoteles y Restaurantes del Uruguay, and Juan Carlos

Migues and Jorge Herrera of the Ministerio of Turismo in Montevideo.

In Oakland, California, thanks to Peter Grace and María Laura Massolo, the latter for permission to adapt material from her contribution to LP's *Travel with Children*. Thanks also to Miguel Helft of Berkeley and Out There Trekking. Guy Mellet and Patricia Magnin of Geneva, Switzerland, were entertaining and informative companions in Buenos Aires and elsewhere.

Thanks again to Tony and Maureen Wheeler for keeping me employed these several years, and a special thanks to everyone in Melbourne who treated me like royalty during the 21st anniversary travel summit there.

## From the Publisher

Kate Hoffman combed the manuscript and maps. Cyndy Johnsen created the maps and performed layout magic. Carolyn Hubbard polished the text, and Alex Guilbert corrected the maps. Hugh D'Andrade selected the photos and designed the cover.

## Thanks to Readers

Our thanks to readers and travelers who wrote in with suggestions, many of whose names appear in the 2nd edition of *Argentina, Uruguay & Paraguay – a travel survival kit*. Other readers include: Nicola Ansell (UK), Ragnhild and Antoon Beyene-Pille (Belgium), Eric Gagnon (Canada), Lars Heitmann and Gunter Quaißer (Germany), Armin Howald (Australia), Erica Linden (Netherlands) and Bermond Lucien (France).

## Warning & Request

Things change – prices go up, schedules change, good places go bad and bad places go bankrupt. So if you find things better or worse, recently opened or long since closed, please write and tell us and help make the next edition better!

Your letters will be used to help update future editions and, where possible, important changes will also be included as a Stop Press section in reprints.

All information is greatly appreciated and the best letters will receive a free copy of the next edition or any other LP book of your choice.

# Contents

# Introduction

One of Latin America's key cities, Buenos Aires was once arguably its greatest. The region's first city to have a million inhabitants, the sprawling Argentine metropolis, sometimes known as the 'Paris of the South', retains many aspects of the Gran Aldea (Great Village) of the late 19th century in its intimate *barrios*. Among many *porteños* (as inhabitants of the port capital are known), there survives a remarkable and reassuring local spirit, encouraging a pride of place that could provide lessons for troubled cities elsewhere.

Since the restoration of democracy in 1984, Buenos Aires is once again a lively place despite lingering economic problems. Political and public dialogue are freewheeling, the publishing industry has rebounded, and the arts and music flourish within the limits of economic reality. Buenos Aires may have seen better days, but it survives to offer the visitor a rich and unique urban experience.

Buenos Aires' attractions are manifold. Beyond the bustling downtown, with its soaring hotels and theater district, lie the colonial quarter of San Telmo; the colorful working-class neighborhood of La Boca; the chic barrio of Recoleta with its sumptuous restaurants; the spacious parks and open spaces of Palermo and the riverside Costanera; and the suburban grace of Belgrano.

Only a few hours outside Buenos Aires by car, bus, train or boat are some intriguing towns and cities perfect for daytrips and weekends. To the north, porteños head to the waterways of the Paraná Delta and Tigre to escape the frenetic pace of city life. From Tigre, travelers can hop a ferry to Isla Martín García, a peaceful island offering historic attractions and scenic trails. To the southeast of Buenos Aires, the grandiose public buildings of La Plata, the provincial capital, line streets patterned after those of Washington, DC.

Sixty-five km west of Buenos Aires, Luján attracts thousands of pilgrims seeking the intercession of La Virgen, an image housed in a neo-Gothic basilica. Another 50 km west lies the gaucho capital of San Antonio de Areco. East of Buenos Aires, Colonia and Montevideo (the capital of Uruguay) are only a short ferry ride across the Río de la Plata.

The sophistication of Buenos Aires and the allure of easy daytrips in any direction should keep visitors happily preoccupied for weeks, or months, on end.

# Facts about Buenos Aires

## HISTORY

Buenos Aires dates from 1536, when Spanish explorer Pedro de Mendoza camped on a bluff above the Río de la Plata, possibly at the site of present-day Parque Lezama. Mendoza's oversized expedition of 16 ships and nearly 1600 men arrived too late in summer to plant crops, and the area's few Querandí Indian hunter-gatherers responded violently when the Spaniards forced them to seek food. The expedition struggled without adequate provisions and faced incessant Querandí opposition, which led part of the expedition to sail up the Río Paraná, where it founded the city of Asunción among the more sedentary and obliging Guaraní peoples. Within five years, despite some reluctance, the Spaniards completely abandoned Buenos Aires to the Querandí.

Nearly four decades passed before an expedition from Asunción, led by Juan de Garay, definitively reestablished Spain's presence on the west bank of the Río de la Plata in 1580. At the terminus of a cumbersome supply line stretching from Madrid via Panama and Lima, Buenos Aires was clearly subordinate to Asunción. The Spaniards in Buenos Aires survived but did not flourish (Garay himself died at the hands of the Querandí only three years later).

Over the next two centuries, Buenos Aires grew slowly but steadily, profiting from the enormous herds of wild cattle and horses that had proliferated on the lush pastures of the surrounding Pampas. One factor in this population growth was the importation of slaves from Africa, who constituted nearly a third of the city between 1778 and 1815. As local frustration at Spain's mercantile restrictions grew, merchants began to smuggle contraband from Portuguese and British vessels on the river. In 1776 Spain promoted Buenos Aires to capital of the new Virreinato del Río de la Plata (Viceroyalty of the River Plate), which included the famous silver district of Potosí, a palpable recognition that the adolescent city was outgrowing Spain's parental authority.

In late colonial times, the British invasions of 1806 and 1807 were a major turning point, as forces of *criollos* (American-born Spaniards) first seemed to cooperate with British forces but then repelled them. Only three years later, influential criollos, on the pretext that

Facts about Buenos Aires

Spain's legitimate government had fallen, confronted and deposed the viceroy. As described by American diplomat Caesar Rodney, the architects of the revolution and the people of the city showed remarkable restraint and maturity:

At some periods of the revolution, when the bands of authority were relaxed, the administration actually devolved into the hands of the inhabitants of the city. Hence, it might have been imagined, endless tumult and disorder would have sprung up, leading directly to pillage and bloodshed. Yet no such disturbances ever took place; all remained quiet . . . . The people have in no instance demanded victims to satisfy their vengeance; on the contrary, they have sometimes, by the influence of public opinion, moderated the rigor with which their rulers were disposed to punish the guilty.

Six years later in Tucumán, the Provincias Unidas del Río de la Plata (United Provinces of the River Plate) declared independence but failed to resolve the conflict between two elite sectors: the 'Federalist' landowners of the interior provinces, concerned with preserving their autonomy and economic privileges, and the 'Unitarist' porteños of Buenos Aires (not yet the capital), who maintained an outward orientation toward overseas commerce and European ideas. After more than a decade of violence and uncertainty, Federalist *caudillo* Juan Manuel de Rosas asserted his authority over Buenos Aires.

When Charles Darwin visited Buenos Aires in 1833, shortly after the ruthless Rosas took power, he was impressed that the city of 60,000 was

large; and I should think one of the most regular in the world. Every street is at right angles to the one it crosses, and the parallel ones being equidistant, the houses are collected into solid squares of equal dimensions, which are called quadras. On the other hand the houses themselves are hollow squares; all the rooms opening into a neat little courtyard. They are generally only one story high, with flat roofs, which are fitted with seats, and are much frequented by the inhabitants in summer. In the centre of the town is the Plaza, where the public offices, fortress, cathedral, &c., stand. Here also, the old viceroys, before the revolution had their palaces. The general assemblage of buildings possesses considerable architectural beauty, although none individually can boast of any.

Rosas' reign lasted nearly another three decades, during which time (ironically) Buenos Aires' influence grew despite his perhaps opportunistic Federalist convictions. His overthrow opened the city to European immigration, and the population grew from 90,000 in 1854 to 177,000 in 1869 to 670,000 by 1895. By the turn of the century, Latin America's largest city boasted more than a million inhabitants.

In the 1880s, when the city became the official federal capital, the indignant authorities of Buenos Aires province moved their government to a new provincial capital at La Plata. Still, as agricultural exports boomed and imports flowed into the country, the port city became even more important. In the words of British diplomat James Bryce, none of the leaders of Glasgow, Manchester or Chicago 'shewed greater enterprise and bolder conceptions than did the men of Buenos Aires when on this exposed and shallow coast they made alongside their city a great ocean harbour'.

Immigration and growth brought serious social problems, as families crowded into substandard housing, merchants and manufacturers suppressed wages, and labor became increasingly militant. In 1919, under pressure from landowners and other elite sectors, the Radical government of President Hipólito Yrigoyen ordered the Army to suppress a metalworkers' strike in what became known as La Semana Trágica (the Tragic Week), setting an unfortunate precedent for the coming decades.

In the 1930s, ambitious municipal administrations undertook a massive downtown modernization program, where broad avenues like Santa Fe, Córdoba and Corrientes obliterated narrow colonial streets. Since WWII, sprawling Gran Buenos Aires (Greater Buenos Aires) has absorbed many once-distant suburbs. Now home to more than a third of the country's population, the capital remains Argentina's dominant economic, political and cultural center.

Like the rest of the country, Buenos Aires suffered during the succession of military coups and dictatorships that culminated with the so-called Proceso de Reorganización Nacional of 1976 – 1983, which resulted in the notorious deaths and disappearances of the Guerra Sucia (Dirty War). Widespread corruption during the Proceso resulted in massive public works projects, many of them never completed, the funding for which most commonly lined the pockets of those who solicited loans from international development agencies. At the same time, the dictatorship neglected the capital's physical and social problems, so that a city that once prided itself on European sophistication and standards of living now shares the same dilemmas as other Latin American megacities – pollution, noise, decaying infrastructure and declining public services, unemployment and underemployment, and spreading shantytowns.

Not all signs are negative, though. Economic reforms have improved communications (at very high cost) through privatization; the current administration has reduced a bloated public sector and devised an effective tax collection system to support public services; and certain sectors of the economy, most notably finance and services, are prospering. The country's continuing economic difficulties make the future unpredictable, but Buenos Aires remains a vibrant combination of international capital, with all the cultural diversity that implies, and traditional barrio life.

## GEOGRAPHY & CLIMATE

At the continental edge of Argentina's Pampas heartland, an almost completely level plain of loess (gray, wind-blown deposits of fine-grained silt) and river-deposited sediments once covered by lush native grasses is now occupied by grain farms and ranches. Low-lying Buenos Aires sprawls along the west bank of the Río de la Plata, which discharges its thick sediments here and far out into the South Atlantic Ocean. The highest elevation in the city is barely 25 meters, and much of the city is barely above sea level.

Buenos Aires' climate is humid, with an annual rainfall of 900 mm spread fairly evenly throughout the year.

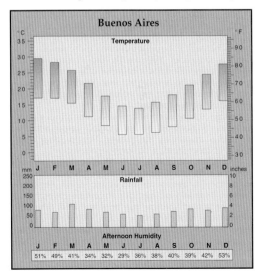

The changeable spring, hot summer and mild autumn resemble their counterparts in New York City, but the proximity of the South Atlantic moderates winter temperatures in a city where the relatively low latitude of 34° 37' S is more comparable to Northern Hemisphere locations like Los Angeles, Atlanta and Gibraltar, or Southern Hemisphere counterparts like Sydney and Cape Town. Frosts are exceedingly rare – the lowest temperature ever recorded is -5.4° C, while snow has only fallen once this century, in 1918. It is unlikely to fall again, or at least to stick, because of the urban heat island effect of the densely built city.

The warmest temperature ever recorded was 43.3° C, but much lower temperatures can seem oppressive when humidity is high. Occasional *pamperos* (cold fronts out of the southwest) can cause the ambient temperature to fall dramatically. From the other direction, the occasional *sudestada* (southeasterly) combines with high tides and heavy runoff in the estuary of the Río de la Plata to flood low-lying areas like La Boca.

# ECOLOGY & ENVIRONMENT

Buenos Aires' dense concentration of population and industry in a very small area has caused serious environmental problems. The single most palpable example is the visible contamination of waterways like the Riachuelo in the barrio of La Boca, but the concentration of industrial chemicals and heavy metals in the sediments beneath the surface is even more serious than floating oil slicks. Supposedly the Riachuelo is the Menem administration's number one environmental priority, but nobody takes seriously environment secretary María Julia Alsogaray's pledge to swim in the river when the cleanup finally ends.

Thanks to diesel-spewing buses, countless private vehicles and fleets of taxis, the capital's dense traffic has the usual impact on air quality. The frequent rains, however, clear the air with some regularity.

Like other world megacities, Buenos Aires long ago outgrew local energy resources; despite Argentina's self-sufficiency in petroleum and abundant (if sometimes remote) hydroelectric capacity, Argentine governments have promoted nuclear power since 1950. The 344-megawatt Atucha I reactor in the vicinity of Buenos Aires has supplied energy to the capital since 1974, but it operated only at half-capacity through the 1980s because cheaper hydroelectricity made nuclear power less competitive.

# GOVERNMENT & POLITICS

Buenos Aires, like Washington, DC, and Mexico City, is a federal district administratively distinct from Argentina's other 23 provinces (unlike Washington, however, Buenos Aires enjoys voting representation in the Argentine Congress). Traditionally, local government consists of a mayor, appointed by the president of the country, and a 60-member Concejo Deliberante elected by barrio. In late 1995, the Concejo consisted of 24 Radicals (a middle-class party with a misleading name),

WAYNE BERNHARDSON
Anti-wallowing graffiti

19 Peronists, and 17 members of lesser parties, including the left-leaning Frepaso (many of them ex-Peronists) and the extreme right-wing Modin.

Almost everyone admits that the concentration of political and economic power in the capital is undesirable, but residents of the provinces, especially those from large and important cities like Córdoba and Rosario, are the ones that most vigorously criticize the capital's primacy.

Even so, when the recent Radical government of President Raúl Alfonsín proposed moving the seat of government to the small northern Patagonian city of Viedma in Río Negro province, powerful opposition soon forced him to abandon the plan. The project probably would have been at least as costly and as unsuccessful as Brazil's attempt to reduce the influence of Rio de Janeiro and São Paulo by the creation of Brasilia, but Alfonsín's failure vividly illustrated Buenos Aires' persistent dominance.

An anticipated constitutional reform would permit the popular election of the mayor in 1996.

# ECONOMY

Relating the tale of a relative who found an unusable 'treasure' of 10 billion old pesos in the mountains of Córdoba, a character in Osvaldo Soriano's recent novel *Shadows* remarks that 'a country where finding a fortune is a waste of time isn't a serious country'. Indeed, Argentina's inability to achieve its potential, despite its abundant natural resources, and highly literate and sophisticated population, has mystified outside

WAYNE BERNHARDSON

Demonstrations such as this one by a theater union
are common in Buenos Aires' streets.

observers for decades. Burdened with a monstrous foreign debt unlikely ever to be repaid, its middle class is
shrinking, while the working class and the poor have
little hope of advancement. Despite the recent stability of
the Menem administration, it is difficult to find any
Argentine truly optimistic about the country's future.

With a per capita GDP of nearly US$6800 (a figure
exaggerated by an overvalued peso), Argentina is one of
Latin America's wealthiest countries, but its modern
economic history has been one of astronomical inflation
amid corruption and perpetual chaos. General Juan
Perón's rise to power after WWII demonstrated that
the export-oriented rural economy was inadequate for
broader prosperity, that Argentina needed to develop its
industrial base, and that workers needed to share in the
development of Argentine industry. At the time, there
was probably no alternative to state involvement in
industry, but its dominance over succeeding decades
outlived its usefulness, and many state enterprises
became havens for corruption.

Argentines refer to individuals who hold multiple
government jobs as *ñoquis*, after the traditional potato
pasta served in Argentine households on the 29th of
each month – the implication being that they appear on
the job just before their monthly paychecks are due.
The presence of such 'ghost employees' contributed to
inflation rates often exceeding 50% per month, but the

Menem administration has broken the inflationary spiral, at least temporarily, by reducing excessive public sector employment, selling off inefficient state enterprises, and restricting labor union activities. The key measure, however, has been economy minister Domingo Cavallo's 'convertibility' law, which pegs the peso at parity with the US dollar – in effect establishing a gold standard as the government would print no more pesos than its hard currency reserves. An inflation figure for 1994 of less than 4%, astonishingly low by Argentine standards, reflected the success of Cavallo's measures. In March 1995 there was a virtually unprecedented *deflation* of -0.4%.

Selling off state assets like Aerolíneas Argentinas, the state petroleum enterprise YPF, and the phone company ENTel was a one-time bonanza that reduced or eliminated short-term budget deficits, but increased productivity and a more efficient tax system will have to do so in the future. The legacy of state domination has fostered a large informal sector that operates parallel to the official economy in providing goods and services. One study claimed that only 40% of Argentina's workers functioned in the 'official' economy – the remainder labored independently, were often paid in cash, and avoided taxes entirely.

The reduction of the state sector has also brought costs that often do not fit into conventional accounting systems. In April 1995, for instance, the privatized YPF dumped waste oil into the Río de la Plata near Buenos Aires' popular Reserva Ecológica beyond the port, on the rationale that 'we had to get rid of the waste somehow and this looked like the only solution'. A state-controlled YPF might not have done things any differently, but this intentional discharge also came at a time when the company had contracted to clean up the area's waters.

Whether the 'rationalization' of the Argentine economy envisaged by Menem and Cavallo will be successful is uncertain, but similar measures over the last 15 years have failed many times. One of the side effects of privatization has been increasing unemployment that the government sees as an essential structural adjustment but that ordinary people worry may be a more enduring problem. As of mid-1995, official unemployment figures hit 12.2%, with a probable undercount in rural areas, and then rose to nearly 20% as the economy contracted in the aftermath of President Menem's re-election. The legal monthly minimum wage is only US$200 in a country where living expenses are not much less than in Europe or North America.

The economy of the Capital Federal remains largely administrative and financial, supporting the export-oriented rural economy. There is a large service-oriented sector as well, but the industrial suburbs of Gran Buenos Aires, like Avellaneda, are the primary sources of blue-collar jobs. The tourist trade is a major contributor to the relative prosperity of Buenos Aires, where unemployment and underemployment are considerably lower than in the provinces.

## POPULATION & PEOPLE

More than a third of Argentina's 32.3 million people reside in Gran Buenos Aires (Greater Buenos Aires), which includes the Capital Federal and nearby suburbs in Buenos Aires province. From the mid-19th century, a trickle of European immigrants became a flood, as Italians, Basques, Welsh, English, Ukrainians and immigrants of other nationalities inundated Buenos Aires as they did New York. Italian surnames are even more common than Spanish, though Italo-Argentines do not constitute a cohesive, distinctive group in the way that Italian-Americans do in many North American cities.

Some immigrant groups, most notably the Anglo-Argentines throughout the country, have retained a distinctive cultural identity. Buenos Aires' flourishing Jewish community of about 400,000, the world's eighth-largest, has drawn international attention in the wake of the bombings of the Israeli embassy in 1992 and the Asociación Mutua Israelita Argentina (AMIA) in July 1994, which killed at least 86 people in leveling the Jewish cultural center.

Middle Eastern immigrants, though not numerous, have political influence disproportional to their numbers – their most prominent figure is President Carlos Menem, who is of Syrian ancestry. Argentines refer indiscriminately to anyone of Middle Eastern ancestry (except Jews or Israelis) as a *turco* (Turk), sometimes but not always with racist connotations.

The Buenos Aires suburb of Escobar has a conspicuous Japanese community, but non-European immigrants have generally not been welcome – despite the upheavals in Asia over the past decade-plus, a relative handful of immigrants from that region have entered the country. Nevertheless, scores of Chinese restaurants have opened in the past decade (there is a small 'Chinatown' in the barrio of Belgrano) and the common Korean surname Kim fills nearly a page in the Buenos Aires telephone directory. 'Coreatown' is around Av Cobo in the southern barrio of Nueva Pompeya.

Some Bolivian highlanders have come to Buenos Aires, where they mainly work in the construction industry and live around Nueva Pompeya's Av Fernández de la Cruz; many Paraguayans and Uruguayans also reside permanently in Argentina. Like many US and Canadian cities, Buenos Aires has a small and barely visible population of urban Indians, in this case from the Andean Northwest and from Patagonia.

# ARTS

In the 19th and early 20th centuries Buenos Aires self-consciously emulated French cultural trends in art, music and architecture, thereby earning the nickname the 'Paris of the South'. Many Argentine intellectuals have been educated in European capitals, particularly Paris, and many performers have made their mark outside the country's borders.

## Music & Dance

Music and dance are difficult to separate in Buenos Aires. The palatial Teatro Colón, home of the Buenos Aires opera, is one of the finest facilities of its kind in the world. Classical music and ballet, as well as modern dance, appear here and at similar venues like the Teatro Avenida.

**Tango & Folk** Probably the best known manifestation of Argentine popular culture is the tango, both as music and dance, with important figures like the legendary Carlos Gardel, the late Julio Sosa and Astor Piazzola, and contemporaries like Susana Rinaldi, Eladia Blásquez, and Osvaldo Pugliese. Tango is constantly on the radio, tops the bill at the capital's finest nightclubs, and is even heard in the streets.

The late Atahualpa Yupanqui was a giant of Argentine folk music, which takes much of its inspiration from the northwestern Andean region and the countries to the north, especially Bolivia and Peru. Contemporary performers include Mercedes Sosa of Tucumán, Suna Rocha of Córdoba, Tarragó Ross, Leon Gieco (modern enough to adopt and adapt a rap style at times) and the Conjunto Pro Música de Rosario.

**Rock & Pop** Rock musicians such as Charly García (formerly a member of the important group Sui Generis) and Fito Páez (dismissed by some as excessively commercial) are national icons. García performed a version of the Argentine national anthem much along the lines

## Gardel & the Tango

In June 1935, a Cuban woman committed suicide in Havana, while a woman in New York and another in Puerto Rico tried to poison themselves, all over the same man whom none of them had ever met. The man whose smiling photograph graced their rooms had himself just died in a plane crash in Medellín, Colombia. On his body's long odyssey to its final resting place in Argentina, Latin Americans thronged to pay him tribute in Colombia, New York, Rio de Janeiro and Montevideo. Once in Buenos Aires, his body lay in state at Luna Park stadium before a horse-drawn carriage took him to Chacarita Cemetery. The man was tango singer Carlos Gardel, *El Zorzal Criollo*, the songbird of Buenos Aires.

WAYNE BERNHARDSON

Carlos Gardel singlehandedly legitimized tango.

Originating around 1880, only a decade before Gardel's birth, the tango was the vulgar dance and music of the capital's *arrabales* or fringes, blending gaucho verse with Spanish and Italian music. Gardel created the *tango canción*, the tango-song, taking it out of the brothels and tenements to New York and Paris. Only after Gardel had won over audiences in those cities did the Argentine elite deign to allow it into their salons.

It was no accident that the tango grew to popularity when it did. In the late 19th century, the *Gran Aldea* (Great Village) of Buenos Aires was becoming an immigrant city where frustrated and melancholic Europeans displaced gaucho rustics, who retreated gradually to the ever more distant countryside. The children of those immigrants would become the first generation of porteños, and the tango-song summarized the new urban experience.

Permeated with nostalgia for a disappearing way of life, the melancholic tango-song expressed the apprehensions and anxieties of individuals. Its themes ranged from mundane pastimes like horse racing and other popular diversions to more profound feelings about the changing landscape of neighborhood and community, the figure of the mother, betrayal by women, and friendship or other personal concerns. English musician Robert Fripp would later compare the relation of Argentines and tango to that of North Americans and the blues.

The inevitable transformations of La Boca's 'Caminito' mirrored the changes in Gardel's own life:

| | |
|---|---|
| *Caminito que entonces estabas* | Caminito of what you once were |
| *bordeado de trébol y juncos en flor* | bordered by clover and flowering rushes |
| *una sombra ya pronto serás* | a shadow you soon will be |
| *una sombra, lo mismo que yo . . .* | a shadow just like me . . . |

Though born in France, Gardel came to epitomize the porteño. When he was three, his poor and single mother brought him to Buenos Aires, where he passed his formative years in a neighborhood near the Mercado de Abasto (a central produce market near which porteños now board the Subte at Estación Carlos Gardel). In his youth, he worked at a variety of menial jobs but also entertained neighbors with his singing. His performing career began after he befriended Uruguayan-born José Razzano. They formed the popular duo Gardel-Razzano, which lasted until Razzano lost his voice.

From 1917 onward, Gardel performed solo. His voice, his singing and his personal charisma made him an immediate popular success in Argentina and other Latin American countries, although the Argentine elite still despised the music and what it stood for – the rise of a middle class that challenged its monopoly on power. Building on this popularity, Gardel sang regularly on the radio and soon became a recording star. To broaden his appeal, he traveled to Spain and France, where widespread acceptance finally made him palatable even to the elite sectors of Argentine society, which once were scandalized by the tango's humble origins and open sensuality. Later he began a film career that was cut short by his death.

In a sense, Gardel's early death rescued him from aging and placed him in an eternal present, allowing his iconic figure to dominate Argentine popular culture. One measure of this immortality is the common saying that 'Gardel sings better every day'. Photographs of Gardel, with his unmistakably charismatic smile, are everywhere – one photo lab in Buenos Aires sold more than 350,000 pictures in the first two decades after his death. The large, devoted community of his followers, known as *ardelianos*, cannot pass a day without listening to his songs or watching his films.

Daily, a steady procession of pilgrims visit his plaque-covered tomb in Chacarita Cemetery where, often, a lighted cigarette rests in the hand of his life-size statue. On December 11, 1990, the centenary of his birth, it was smothered in floral tributes.

For an excellent account of Gardel's life in English, see Simon Collier's *The Life, Music and Times of Carlos Gardel*, a serious biography that refrains from the most romantic exaggerations of the singer's fanatical devotees.

of Jimi Hendrix's 'Star-Spangled Banner'; after a judge dismissed a lawsuit that alleged García lacked 'respect for national symbols', the *Buenos Aires Herald* editorialized that García's defense was a victory over 'extremist nationalist sectors' which had too long 'imposed their warped and often authoritarian views on the rest of society'.

Les Luthiers, an irreverent group who build many of their unusual instruments from scratch, satirize those sectors in the middle class and the military. Many performers are more conventional and derivative, but before you report an Elvis sighting in Buenos Aires, make sure it isn't Sandro, a living Argentine clone of the King. The advent of Sandro impersonators in the raucous *boliches* (nightclubs) of La Boca sends a backhanded compliment to the man known to his devotees as 'El Maestro'.

Increasingly popular Argentine groups playing 'rock nacional' include Soda Stereo, Los Divididos, Los Fabulosos Cadillacs and especially Los Ratones Paranóicos, who opened for the Rolling Stones on their spectacularly successful five-night stand in Buenos Aires in February 1995 (longtime Stones associate Andrew Loog Oldham has produced one of the Ratones' albums). Also on the bill with the Stones were Las Pelotas and local blues artist Pappo.

Blues are currently fashionable in Buenos Aires. Porteño blues band Memphis La Blusera has worked with North American legend Taj Mahal. Las Blacanblus, a female group, performs humorous, nearly a cappella versions of blues standards.

Singer Patricia Sosa's closest counterparts in the English-speaking world would be Janis Joplin or, today, perhaps Melissa Ethridge. The appropriately named group Dos Minutos emulates the Ramones, who themselves have played Buenos Aires several times.

# Painting & Sculpture

Like much of Argentine culture, the visual arts express a tension between the European derivative and criollo originality – the European influence has been so powerful that porteño art critic Jorge Glusberg has argued that the 'colonial period' in Argentine art lasted into the mid-20th century, when it was severed only by WWII. Nevertheless, there exists a thriving alternative and unconventional art scene, only grudgingly acknowledged, if at all, by the arbiters of official taste, who tend to be middle class and conservative. Many of the most innovative artists must go abroad, usually to Europe or North America, to make a living.

Early Argentine painting can pride itself on figures like self-taught Cándido López, a 19th-century military officer who lost his right hand in the war against Paraguay but rehabilitated himself enough to paint more than 50 extraordinary oils, with both artistic and historiographical value, on the conflict. The many Argentine artists who studied in France or Italy produced work with demonstrably European themes, but some local manifestations of their work are memorable, such as the restored ceiling murals of Antonio Berni, Lino Spilimbergo and others in the Galerías Pacífico shopping center on Florida. The late Benito Quinquela Martín, who put the working-class barrio of La Boca on the artistic map, painted brightly colored oils of life in the factories and on the waterfront.

Contemporary painting has eschewed the romantic without abandoning its regard for the countryside. Tucumán-born Víctor Hugo Quiroga's paintings, for instance, deal with provincial rather than porteño themes, but they successfully reflect the impact of modern global developments on criollo life. Porteño painter Guillermo Kuitca makes an imaginative use of cartographic images by integrating them with events like the genocide against European Jews in works like *Kristallnacht II*. Graciela Sacco is a multi-media artist who incorporates audio and video narratives into her arrangements of readymade objects like plastic spoons and barcodes.

Given its French origins, official public art tends toward hero worship and the pompously monumental, expressed through equestrian statues of military figures like José de San Martín, Justo José Urquiza and Julio Argentino Roca. A welcome exception is the work of the late Rogelio Yrurtia, some of whose works deal sympathetically with the struggles and achievements of working people – see his *Canto al Trabajo* on the Plazoleta Olazábal on Av Paseo Colón at Av Independencia in San Telmo.

An even stronger counterpoint to nationalist idolatry are modern works by individuals like sculptor Alberto Heredia, whose work ridicules the solemnity of official public art and even figures like national icon San Martín. Heredia's powerful and controversial statue *El Caballero de la Máscara* depicts a 19th-century caudillo as a headless horseman. During the military dictatorship of 1976–1983, the sculpture could not be exhibited under its

WAYNE BERNHARDSON
Anti-Vietnam War sculpture
by Leon Ferrari, Helft
Collection

WAYNE BERNHARDSON
Sculpture by Yoel
Novoa, Centro Cultural
San Martín

original title *El Montonero*, which implied associations
with guerrilla forces that had nothing to do with the
artist's theme. Heredia has also dealt with environmental issues in works like the ghostly *Chernobyl*.

Another overtly political sculptor is Juan Carlos Disté-
fano, whose disconcerting *El Rey y La Reina* (The King
and the Queen), an image of two figures shot to death in
the front seat of an automobile, actually appeared in a
gallery on Calle Florida during the dictatorship. For
comic relief, the surrealistic junk sculptures of Yoël
Novoa are accessible to audiences of almost any age or
political persuasion.

Buenos Aires has a multitude of art galleries, most of
which are very conventional but some of which deal
with audacious modern art; for suggestions on which
merit a visit, see the Shopping chapter. The biweekly
freebie *Arte al Día*, widely distributed in areas frequented by tourists around the city, is a guide to current
events in the art world.

For a brief survey of modern Argentine art in English,
look for Glusberg's *Art in Argentina* (Giancarlo Politi
Editore, Milan, 1986). Readers who understand Spanish
can try Rafael Squirru's *Arte Argentino Hoy* (Ediciones de
Arte Gaglianone, Buenos Aires, 1983), a selection of
work from 48 contemporary painters and sculptors
illustrated in color.

## Architecture

Buenos Aires' reputation as the 'Paris of the South' would lead travelers to expect European styles, and in fact many of the capital's turn-of-the-century buildings would not be out of place across the Atlantic. There may be a better representation of early 20th-century Western European styles here than in many parts of Europe, since the latter suffered the devastation of WWII (Buenos Aires, by contrast, has experienced erosion through economic decline). Many public buildings, like the landmark Palacio de Aguas Corrientes on Av Córdoba, are remarkable examples of a European style that, despite features like French mansard (two-tier) roofs, does not seem out of place here. Others, however, such as the new Biblioteca Nacional in Palermo, are pharaonic monuments to the corruption and excesses of military dictatorships.

Buenos Aires retains a sample of valuable colonial and

DAVE HOUSER

DAVE HOUSER

WAYNE BERNHARDSON

Sausage house,
San Telmo

WAYNE BERNHARDSON

Palacio de Aguas
Corrientes

post-independence architecture in the barrio of San Telmo, one of the city's best walking areas. There is also a wide variety of vernacular architecture, ranging from the *casas chorizos* (sausage houses) of San Telmo, so-called for their long narrow, shape (some have only two meters frontage on the street), to the brightly painted corrugated metal-clad dwellings that give the barrio of La Boca much of its unique personality.

The best easily accessible guide to the capital's architecture is *Buenos Aires: Guía de Arquitectura de la Ciudad*, published jointly by the Spanish Junta de Andalucía and the Municipalidad de la Ciudad de Buenos Aires, which includes eight extensive walking tours with detailed accompanying text, diagrams and outstanding B&W photographs. Even those with limited Spanish will find it a useful resource.

## Literature

Mostly porteños, Argentine writers of international stature include Jorge Luis Borges, Julio Cortázar, Ernesto Sábato, Manuel Puig, Osvaldo Soriano, Adolfo Bioy Casares, and Victoria Ocampo, much of whose work is readily available in English translation.

Borges is a world literary figure, best known for his short stories but also for his poetry. His erudite language and references sometimes make him inaccessible to readers without a solid grounding in the classics, even though his material often deals with everyday porteño and rural life. Sábato's *On Heroes and Tombs* is a psychological novel that explores people and places in Buenos Aires. Originally published in 1961, it was a cult favorite among Argentine youth. Also try *The Tunnel*, Sábato's engrossing novella of a porteño painter so obsessed with his art that it distorts his relationship to everything and everyone else.

Although an expatriate in Paris, Cortázar nevertheless emphasized clearly Argentine characters in novels such as the experimentally structured *Hopscotch* and *62: A Model Kit*. The landmark 1960s film *Blow-Up* was based on one of his short stories. Manuel Puig's novels, including *Kiss of the Spider Woman*, *The Buenos Aires Affair* and *Betrayed by Rita Hayworth*, focus on the ambiguous role of popular culture in Argentina.

Bioy Casares' hallucinatory novella *The Invention of Morel* also deals with an inability or unwillingness to distinguish between fantasy and reality; it was a partial inspiration for the highly praised film *Man Facing Southeast*. Casares' *Diary of the War of the Pig* is also available in translation.

Osvaldo Soriano, perhaps Argentina's most popular contemporary novelist, wrote *A Funny Dirty Little War*, later adapted into a film, and *Winter Quarters*. In Soriano's *Shadows*, the English translation of *Una Sombra Ya Pronto Serás* (the title of which is the lyric of a popular tango), the protagonist is lost in an Argentina where the names are the same, but all the familiar landmarks and points of reference have lost their meaning. A film version has recently appeared.

Far fewer women writers have appeared in English translation than their male counterparts, but Doris Meyer's biography *Victoria Ocampo: Against the Wind and the Tide* contains a selection of Ocampo's essays for English readers. Ocampo's literary magazine *Sur* was a beacon for Spanish-language writers in the first half of the century and also proved influential among writers in other languages, including England's famous Bloomsbury group.

A guide to Buenos Aires bookshops appears in the Shopping chapter.

# Film

Despite the limited resources available to directors, Argentine cinema has achieved international stature, especially since the end of the military dictatorship of 1978 – 1983. Many Argentine films, both before and after the Dirty War, are available on video.

María Luisa Bemberg, one of Argentina's best-known contemporary directors, died of cancer in mid-1995. Her historically based films often illuminate the Argentine experience, particularly the relationship between women and the Church. *Camila* (nominated for an Oscar as best foreign film in 1984) recounts the tale of Catholic socialite Camila O'Gorman, who ran away from Buenos Aires with a young Jesuit priest in 1847, an act that incited Rosas' government to hunt them down and execute them. Bemberg's English-language film *Miss Mary* (1986), starring Julie Christie, focuses on the experience of an English governess of upper-class Argentine children. Her last directorial effort, *I Don't Want to Talk About It* (1992), is an unusual love story starring Marcelo Mastroianni; filmed in the Uruguayan city of Colonia (see the Excursions chapter), across the river from Buenos Aires, it metaphorically explores issues of power and control in a provincial town.

Director Luis Puenzo's *The Official Story* deals with the delicate and controversial theme of adoption of the children of missing people by those responsible for their disappearance during the military dictatorship's

Dirty War of 1976 – 1983; it stars Norma Leandro, a popular stage actress who has also worked in English-language films in the US. A truly creepy, English-language film, *Apartment Zero* depicts many amusing aspects of porteño life as it follows an Anglo-Argentine film buff who takes a morbid interest in his mysterious North American housemate. Eliseo Subiel's *Man Facing Southeast* (1986) takes part of its inspiration from Adolfo Bioy Casares' novella *The Invention of Morel*.

Héctor Babenco directed *Kiss of the Spider Woman*, set in Brazil but based on Manuel Puig's novel, an intricate portrayal of the way in which the police and military abuse political prisoners and exploit informers. *Las Locas de la Plaza de Mayo* is a documentary tribute to the mothers and grandmothers who defied the Proceso by marching every Thursday in front of the Casa Rosada. *The Night of the Pencils* also deals with the Dirty War.

Argentina has also left its mark on Hollywood and vice-versa. Carlos Gardel flashed his smile in several Spanish-language films, including *El Día Que Me Quieras*, and Hollywood used Argentina as a location under forced circumstances. When Juan Perón's economic policies prohibited American studios from exporting their profits, some made a virtue of a necessity by using their money to film in Argentina; the epic *Taras Bulba*, for instance, was filmed partly around Salta. Fay Dunaway's salary probably accounted for 90% of the budget in the truly atrocious *Eva Perón*, a 1981 NBC-TV miniseries now trying to recover costs in video release.

Readers who know Spanish may enjoy *Ambito Financiero* film critic Diego Curubeto's *Babilonia Gaucha* (Editorial Planeta, Buenos Aires, 1993), an entertaining exploration of the relationship between Hollywood and Argentina. For video versions of Argentine films, check Alquileres Lavalle (☎ 476-1118) at Lavalle 1199, or Blakman Video No Convencional at Ayacucho 509. Note that Argentine videos use the European system and may be incompatible with North American video format.

## Theater

Buenos Aires has a vigorous theater community, equivalent in its own way to New York, London or Paris. It began in colonial times, a few years after the city became the viceregal capital, but it really took off through the artistic and financial efforts of the Podestá family, whose name graces theaters in Buenos Aires and La Plata, and playwrights like Florencio Sánchez, Gregorio de Laferrere and Roberto Payró. Legendary performers include

Luis Sandrini and Lola Membrives; famous European writers like Federico García Lorca and Jean Cocteau have explored the Buenos Aires theater scene. Probably Argentina's most famous contemporary playwright is Juan Carlos Gené, who is also director of the Teatro General San Martín.

Av Corrientes is the capital's Broadway or West End, but throughout the city are large and small theater venues and companies, some very improvisational and unconventional – some rent houses to stage their performances, others act in plazas and parks, and one 'underground' company literally performs in subway stations. Generally, the difference between official and unconventional theater is the quality of production rather than the actors, who are very professional at all levels. The number of companies and the proliferation of those offering acting lessons seems extraordinary, though participation can be an exercise in therapy – Buenos Aires is renowned for the concentration of shrinks in its so-called 'Barrio Freud'. Many of the capital's most popular shows move to the provincial beach resort of Mar del Plata for the summer.

Unlike stage actors in some countries, those in Argentina seem to move seamlessly among stage, film and television. Perhaps performers like Norma Leandro, Federico Luppi, and China Zorrilla feel less self-conscious about moving among the various media, since the Argentine public is smaller and work opportunities fewer than in global communications and entertainment centers like London, New York and Los Angeles. Some 150 Argentine plays have passed from the theater to film since the silent era.

# SOCIETY & CONDUCT

English-speaking visitors may find Argentina more accessible than other Latin American countries because of its superficial resemblance to their own societies. In contrast to countries like Peru and Bolivia, with their large indigenous populations, foreign travelers are relatively inconspicuous and can more easily integrate themselves into everyday life. Argentines are gregarious and, once you make contact, much likelier to invite you to participate in their regular activities than is, say, a Quechua llama herder in Bolivia.

Sport is extremely important to Argentines. Most visitors will be familiar with Argentine athletes through its World Cup champion soccer teams, featuring players like Diego Maradona and Daniel Passarella (the latter now coach of the national team), and with tennis stars like Guillermo Vilas and Gabriela Sabatini, but rugby, polo, golf, skiing and fishing also enjoy great popularity. Soccer, though, is the national obsession – River Plate (from the elite barrio of Núñez) and Boca Juniors (based in the working-class immigrant barrio of La Boca) are nationwide phenomena.

# Traditional Culture

One traditional activity, which visitors should never refuse, is the opportunity to *tomar un mate*, drink *yerba mate* (pronounced MAH-tay). Also known as Paraguayan tea, mate is an important ritual throughout the River Plate region, but especially so in Argentina, where it serves as a social glue that transcends class.

## Mate

No other trait captures the essence of *argentinidad* ('argentinity') as well as the preparation and consumption of *mate* (pronounced MAH-tay), perhaps the only cultural practice that transcends barriers of ethnicity, class and occupation. More than a simple drink like tea or coffee, mate is an elaborate ritual, shared among family, friends, and coworkers. In many ways, sharing is the whole point.

*Yerba mate* is the dried, chopped leaf of *Ilex paraguayensis*, a relative of the common holly. Also known as 'Paraguayan tea', it became commercially important during the colonial era on the plantations of the Jesuit missions in the upper Río Paraná. Europeans quickly took to the beverage, crediting it with many admirable qualities. The Austrian Jesuit Martin Dobrizhoffer wrote that mate 'provokes a gentle perspiration, improves the appetite, speedily counteracts the languor arising from the burning climate, and assuages both hunger and thirst'. Unlike many American foods and beverages, though, mate failed to make the trip back to Europe. After the Jesuits' expulsion in 1767, production declined, but it has increased dramatically since the early 20th century.

Argentina is the world's largest producer and consumer of *yerba mate*. Argentines consume an average of five kg per person per year, more than four times their average intake of coffee, although Uruguayans consume twice as much *yerba mate* per capita as Argentines. It is also popular in parts of Chile, in southern Brazil and in Paraguay.

Preparing mate is a ritual in itself. In the past, upper-class families even maintained a slave or servant whose sole responsibility was preparing and serving it. Nowadays, one person takes responsibility for filling the mate (gourd) almost to the top with yerba, heating but not boiling the water in a *pava* (kettle) and pouring it into the vessel. People sip the liquid from a *bombilla*, a silver straw with a bulbous filter at its lower end that prevents the leaves from entering the tube.

The *asado*, the famous Argentine barbecue, is as much or more a social occasion as a meal. An important part of any meal, whether at home or in a restaurant, is the *sobremesa*, dallying at the table to discuss family matters or other events of the day. No matter how long the lines outside, no Argentine restaurateur would even dream of nudging along a party that has lingered over coffee long after the food itself was history.

# Dos & Don'ts

During the military dictatorship of 1976 – 1983, Argentina was a forcibly conformist culture – police or military who saw a man or boy with hair they thought too long would abduct him to shave it off – at best.

Gourds can range from simple calabashes to carved wooden vessels to the ornate silver museum pieces of the 19th century. Bombillas also differ considerably, ranging in materials from inexpensive aluminum to silver and gold with intricate markings, and in design from long straight tubes to short, curved ones.

There is an informal etiquette for drinking mate. The *cebador* (server) pours water slowly near the straw to produce a froth as he or she fills the gourd. The gourd then passes clockwise and this order, once established, continues. A good cebador will keep the mate going without changing the yerba for some time. Each participant drinks the gourd dry each time. A simple *gracias* will tell the server to pass you by.

There are marked regional differences in drinking mate. From the Pampas southwards, Argentines take it *amargo* (without sugar), while to the north they drink it *dulce* (sweet) with sugar and *yuyos* (aromatic herbs). Purists, who argue that sugar ruins the gourd, will keep separate gourds rather than alternate the two usages. In the summer, Paraguayans drink mate ice-cold.

An invitation to mate is a sign of acceptance and should not be refused, even though mate is an acquired taste and novices may find it bitter and very hot at first. On the second or third round, both the heat and bitterness will diminish. It is poor etiquette to hold the mate too long before passing it on. Drinking it is unlikely to affect either your health or finances despite Dobrizhoffer's warning that

> by the immoderate and almost hourly use of this potation, the stomach is weakened, and continual flatulence, with other diseases, brought on. I have known many of the lower Spaniards who never spoke ten words without applying their lips to the gourd containing the ready-made tea. If many topers in Europe waste their substance by an immoderate use of wine and other intoxicating liquors, there are no fewer in America who drink away their fortunes in potations of the herb of Paraguay. ∎

Thankfully, in the aftermath of the Proceso, unconventional appearance barely raises eyebrows, and many Argentine men of all ages now sport ponytails (even pierced body parts are not unusual). Still, being polite goes a long way in any encounter with Argentine officialdom – or with any ordinary Argentine for that matter. Do not forget to preface any request for information with the appropriate salutation *buenos días* (good morning), *buenas tardes* (good afternoon), or *buenas noches* (good evening), and use the formal mode of address *usted* unless you are certain that informality is appropriate.

While Argentines dress casually for most recreational activities, informal dress is normally inappropriate for business, some restaurants, casinos and events like performances by the symphony or opera. Some places that are informal by day may become very formal by night.

# RELIGION

Inattention to the role of religion will limit any visitor's understanding of Argentine society. Roman Catholicism is the official state religion, but as in many other Latin American countries, evangelical Protestantism is making inroads among traditionally Catholic believers. Even within the Catholic religion, popular beliefs diverge from official doctrine – one of the best examples is the cult of the Difunta Correa, based in San Juan province, to which hundreds of thousands of professed Catholics make annual pilgrimages and offerings despite an aggressive campaign by the Church hierarchy against her veneration.

WAYNE BERNHARDSON

Tomb of Madre María Salomé, Cementerio de Chacarita

Spiritualism and veneration of the dead have remarkable importance in a country that prides itself on European sophistication – novelist Tomás Eloy Martínez has observed that Argentines honor national heroes like San Martín not on the anniversary of their birth but of their death. Visitors to Recoleta and Chacarita cemeteries in Buenos Aires – essential sights for comprehending

Argentine culture – will see steady processions of pilgrims communicating with icons like Juan and Evita Perón, psychic Madre María, and tango singer Carlos Gardel by laying hands on their tombs and leaving arcane offerings.

Like other Argentine institutions, the Church has many factions. During the military dictatorship of the late 1970s and early 1980s, the official Church generally supported the de facto government despite persecution, kidnapping, torture and murder of religious workers. Most of these workers, adherents of the movement toward 'Liberation Theology', worked among the poor and dispossessed in both rural areas and the *villas miserias* (shantytowns) of Buenos Aires and other large cities. Such activism has resumed in today's more permissive political climate, but the Church hierarchy remains obstinate: The Archbishop of Buenos Aires, for example, has defended President Menem's pardon of the convicted murderers and torturers of the Proceso, and it appears that official chaplains acquiesced in the atrocities of the Dirty War by counseling the perpetrators.

# LANGUAGE

Spanish is the official language, but some immigrant communities retain their language as a badge of identity. Italian, as the language of the single largest immigrant group, is widely understood, but the importance of English outweighs the relatively small number of native speakers in the Anglo-Argentine community – many porteños study English as a second language, and it is widely understood in the tourist and financial sectors of the city's economy. German speakers are numerous enough to support a weekly newspaper, *Argentinisches Tageblatt*.

## Argentine Spanish

Spanish in Argentina, and the rest of the River Plate region, has characteristics that readily distinguish it from the rest of Latin America. Probably the most prominent are the usage of the pronoun *vos* in place of *tú* for 'you', and the trait of pronouncing the letters 'll' and 'y' as 'zh' (as in 'azure') rather than 'y' (like English 'you') as in the rest of the Americas. Note that in American Spanish, the plural of the familiar 'tú' or 'vos' is *ustedes* rather than *vosotros*, as in Spain. Argentines understand continental Spanish but may find it quaint or pretentious.

There are many vocabulary differences between European and American Spanish, and among Spanish-speaking countries in the Americas. The speech of Buenos Aires, in particular, abounds with words and phrases from the colorful slang known as *lunfardo*. Although you shouldn't use lunfardo words unless you are supremely confident that you know their *every* implication (especially in formal situations), you should be aware of some of the more common everyday usages. Argentines normally refer to the Spanish language as *castellano* rather than *español*.

Every visitor should make an effort to speak Spanish, the basic elements of which are easily acquired. If possible, take a brief night course at your local university or community college before departure. Even if you can't speak very well, Argentines are gracious hosts and will encourage your use of Spanish, so there is no need to feel self-conscious about vocabulary or pronunciation. There are many common cognates, so if you're stuck, try Hispanicizing an English word – it is unlikely you'll make a truly embarrassing error. Do not, however, admit to being 'embarrassed' *(embarazada)* unless you are in fact pregnant; see the list of 'false cognates' below for other usages to be avoided.

---

**Lunfardo**

Below are a few of the more common, and innocuous, lunfardo usages that you may hear on the streets.

| | | | |
|---|---|---|---|
| *guita* | money | *pibe* | guy, dude |
| *laburo* | work | *piola* | cool |
| *morfar* | to eat | *pucho* | cigarette |
| *palo* | ten pesos | | |

---

## Phrasebooks & Dictionaries

Lonely Planet's *Latin American Spanish phrasebook* by Anna Cody is a worthwhile addition to your backpack. Another exceptionally useful resource is the *University of Chicago Spanish-English, English-Spanish Dictionary*; its small size, light weight and thorough entries make it perfect for travel.

## Pronunciation

Spanish pronunciation is, in general, consistently phonetic. Speak slowly to avoid getting tongue-tied until you become confident of your ability.

**Cognates & Condoms**
False cognates are words that appear very similar but have different meanings in different languages; in some instances, these differences can lead to serious misunderstandings. The following is a list of some of these words in English with their Spanish cousins and their meaning in Spanish. Note that this list deals primarily with the River Plate region, and usages may differ in other areas.

| English | Spanish | Meaning in Spanish |
|---|---|---|
| actual | *actual* | current (at present) |
| carpet | *carpeta* | looseleaf notebook |
| embarrassed | *embarazada* | pregnant |
| introduce | *introducir* | introduce (as an innovation) |
| present (verb) | *presentar* | introduce (a person) |
| precise | *preciso* | necessary |
| preservative | *preservativo* | condom |
| violation | *violación* | rape |

**Vowels** Vowels are very consistent and have easy English equivalents.

**a** is like 'a' in 'father'.
**e** is like 'ai' in 'sail'.
**i** is like 'ee' in 'feet'.
**o** is like 'o' in 'for'.
**u** is like 'u' in 'food'. After consonants other than 'q', it is more like English 'w'. When the vowel sound is

modified by an umlaut, as in 'Güemes', it is also pronounced 'w'.

**y** is a consonant except when it stands alone or appears at the end of a word, in which case its pronunciation is identical to Spanish 'i'.

**Consonants** Spanish consonants resemble their English equivalents, with some major exceptions. Pronunciation of the letters *f*, *k*, *l*, *m*, *n*, *p*, *q*, *s* and *t* is virtually identical to English. Although *y* is identical in most Latin American countries when used as a consonant, most Argentines say 'zh' for it and for *ll*, which is a separate letter. *Ch* and *ñ* are also separate letters, with separate dictionary entries.

**b** resembles its English equivalent but is undistinguished from 'v'. For clarity, refer to the former as 'b larga', the latter as 'b corta' (the word for the letter itself is pronounced like English 'bay').

**c** is like the 's' in 'see' before e and i, otherwise like English 'k'.

**d** closely resembles 'th' in 'feather'.

**g** is like a guttural English 'h' before Spanish 'e' and 'i', otherwise like 'g' in 'go'.

**h** is invariably silent. If your name begins with this letter, listen carefully when immigration officials summon you to pick up your passport.

**j** most closely resembles English 'h' but is slightly more guttural.

**ñ** is like 'ni' in 'onion'.

**r** is nearly identical to English except at the beginning of a word, when it is often rolled.

**rr** is very strongly rolled.

**v** resembles English, but see 'b', above.

**x** is like 'x' in 'taxi' except for very few words for which it follows Spanish or Mexican usage as 'j'.

**z** is like 's' in 'sun'.

**Diphthongs** Diphthongs are vowel combinations forming a single syllable. In Spanish, the formation of a diphthong depends on combinations of 'weak' vowels ('i' and 'u') or strong ones ('a', 'e', and 'o'). Two weak vowels or a strong and a weak vowel make a diphthong, but two strong ones are pronounced as separate syllables.

A good example of two weak vowels forming a diphthong is the word *diurno* (during the day). The final syllable of *obligatorio* (obligatory) is a combination of weak and strong vowels.

**Stress** Stress, often indicated by visible accents, is very important, since it can change the meaning of words. In general, words ending in vowels or the letters 'n' or 's' have stress on the next-to-last syllable, while those with other endings have stress on the last syllable. Thus *vaca* (cow) and *caballos* (horses) both have accents on their penultimate syllables.

Visible accents, which can occur anywhere in a word, dictate stress over these general rules. Thus *sótano* (basement), *América* and *porción* (portion) all have stress on different syllables. When words appear in capitals, the written accent is generally omitted but still pronounced.

---

### El Voseo

Spanish in the River Plate region differs from that of Spain and the rest of the Americas, most notably in the familiar form of the second person singular pronoun. Instead of the *tuteo* used everywhere else, Argentines, Uruguayans and Paraguayans commonly use the *voseo*, a relict 16th-century form requiring slightly different endings. Both regular and most irregular verbs differ from *tú* forms; regular verbs change their stress and add an accent, while irregular verbs do not change internal consonants but add a terminal accent. This is true for -ar, -er and -ir verbs, examples of which are given below, with the tú forms included for contrast. Imperative forms also differ, but negative imperatives are identical in both the tuteo and the voseo.

In the list below, the first verb of each ending is regular, while the second is irregular; the pronoun is included for clarity, though most Spanish-speakers normally omit it.

| Verb | Tuteo/Imperative | Voseo/Imperative |
|---|---|---|
| *hablar* (to speak) | tú hablas/habla | vos hablás/hablá |
| *soñar* (to dream) | tú sueñas/sueña | vos soñás/soñá |
| *comer* (to eat) | tú comes/come | vos comés/comé |
| *poner* (to put) | tú pones/pon | vos ponés/poné |
| *admitir* (to admit) | tú admites/admite | vos admitís/admití |
| *venir* (to come) | tú vienes/ven | vos venís/vení |

Note that some of the most common verbs, like *ir* (to go), *estar* (to be) and *ser* (to be) are identically irregular in both the tuteo and the voseo, and that Argentines continue to use the possessive article *tu* (¿Vos tenés tu lápiz?) and the reflexive or conjunctive object pronoun *te* (¿Vos te das cuenta?).

An Argentine inviting a foreigner to address him or her informally will say *Me podés tutear* (you can call me 'tú') rather than *Me podés vosear* (you can call me 'vos'), even though the expectation is that both will use 'vos' forms in subsequent conversation. ■

## Greetings & Civilities

In their public behavior, Argentines are very conscious of civilities, sometimes to the point of ceremoniousness. Never, for example, approach a stranger for information without extending a greeting like *buenos días* or *buenas tardes*.

| | |
|---|---|
| yes | *sí* |
| no | *no* |
| thank you | *gracias* |
| you're welcome | *de nada* |
| hello | *hola* |
| good morning | *buenos días* |
| good afternoon | *buenas tardes* |
| good evening | *buenas noches* |
| good night | *buenas noches* |
| goodbye | *adiós, chau* (informal) |
| I don't speak much Spanish. | *Hablo poco castellano.* |
| I understand. | *Entiendo.* |
| I don't understand. | *No entiendo.* |

## Useful Words & Phrases

| | |
|---|---|
| and | *y* |
| to/at | *a* |
| for | *por, para* |
| of/from | *de, desde* |
| in | *en* |
| with | *con* |
| without | *sin* |
| before | *antes* |
| after | *después* |
| soon | *pronto* |
| already | *ya* |
| now | *ahora* |
| right away | *en seguida* |
| here | *aquí* |
| there | *allí* |
| Where? | *¿Dónde?* |
| Where is/are . . . ? | *¿Dónde está/están . . . ?* |
| When? | *¿Cuando?* |
| How? | *¿Cómo?* |
| I would like . . . | *Me gustaría . . .* |
| coffee | *café* |
| tea | *té* |
| beer | *cerveza* |
| wine | *vino* |
| How much? | *¿Cuanto?* |
| How many? | *¿Cuantos?* |
| Is/Are there . . . ? | *¿Hay . . . . ?* |

# Countries

The list below contains only countries whose spelling differs significantly in English and Spanish.

| | |
|---|---|
| Denmark | *Dinamarca* |
| England | *Inglaterra* |
| France | *Francia* |
| Germany | *Alemania* |
| Great Britain | *Gran Bretaña* |
| Ireland | *Irlanda* |
| Italy | *Italia* |
| Japan | *Japón* |
| Netherlands | *Holanda* |
| New Zealand | *Nueva Zelandia* |
| Peru | *Perú* |
| Scotland | *Escocia* |
| Spain | *España* |
| Sweden | *Suecia* |
| Switzerland | *Suiza* |
| United States | *Estados Unidos* |
| Wales | *Gales* |

# Getting Around

| | |
|---|---|
| airplane | *avión* |
| train | *tren* |
| bus | *colectivo, micro, omnibus* |
| ship | *barco, buque* |
| ferry | *barca de pasaje* |
| hydrofoil | *aliscafo* |
| car | *auto* |
| taxi | *taxi* |
| truck | *camión* |
| pickup | *camioneta* |
| bicycle | *bicicleta* |
| motorcycle | *motocicleta* |
| hitchhike | *hacer dedo* |
| I would like a ticket to . . . | *Quiero un boleto/pasaje a . . .* |
| What's the fare to . . . ? | *¿Cuanto cuesta el pasaje a . . . ?* |
| When does the next bus leave for . . . ? | *¿Cuando sale el próximo ómnibus para . . . ?* |
| Is there a student/ university discount? | *¿Hay descuento estudiantil/ universitario?* |
| Do you accept credit cards? | *¿Trabajan con tarjetas de crédito?* |
| first/last/next | *primero/último/próximo* |
| first/second class | *primera/segunda clase* |
| single/return (roundtrip) | *ida/ida y vuelta* |
| sleeper | *camarote* |
| left luggage | *guardería, equipaje* |

## Accommodations

Below you will find English phrases with useful Spanish equivalents for Argentina, most of which will be understood in other Spanish-speaking countries.

| | |
|---|---|
| hotel | *hotel, pensión, residencial* |
| single room | *habitación para una persona* |
| double room | *habitación doble, matrimonio* |
| How much does it cost? | *¿Cuanto cuesta?* |
| per night | *por noche* |
| full board | *pensión completa* |
| shared bath | *baño compartido* |
| private bath | *baño privado* |
| too expensive | *demasiado caro* |
| discount | *descuento* |
| cheaper | *mas económico* |
| May I see it? | *¿Puedo verla?* |
| I don't like it. | *No me gusta.* |
| the bill | *la cuenta* |

## Around Town

| | |
|---|---|
| tourist information | *oficina de turismo* |
| airport | *aeropuerto* |
| train station | *estación de ferrocarril* |
| bus terminal | *terminal de ómnibus* |
| bathing resort | *balneario* |
| post office | *correo* |
| letter | *carta* |
| parcel | *paquete* |
| postcard | *postal* |
| airmail | *correo aéreo* |
| registered mail | *certificado* |
| express mail | *puerta a puerta* |
| stamps | *estampillas* |
| person to person | *persona a persona* |
| collect call | *cobro revertido* |

## Toilets

The most common word for toilet is *baño*, but *servicios sanitarios* (services) is a frequent alternative. Men's toilets usually bear a descriptive term like *hombres, caballeros* or *varones*. Women's restrooms have a *señoras* or *damas* sign.

## Numbers

Should hyperinflationary times return, you may have to learn to count in very large numbers.

## Facts about Buenos Aires

| | | | |
|---|---|---|---|
| 1 | *uno* | 70 | *setenta* |
| 2 | *dos* | 80 | *ochenta* |
| 3 | *tres* | 90 | *noventa* |
| 4 | *cuatro* | 100 | *cien* |
| 5 | *cinco* | 101 | *ciento uno* |
| 6 | *seis* | 102 | *ciento dos* |
| 7 | *siete* | 110 | *ciento diez* |
| 8 | *ocho* | 120 | *ciento veinte* |
| 9 | *nueve* | 130 | *ciento treinta* |
| 10 | *diez* | 200 | *doscientos* |
| 11 | *once* | 300 | *trescientos* |
| 12 | *doce* | 400 | *cuatrocientos* |
| 13 | *trece* | 500 | *quinientos* |
| 14 | *catorce* | 600 | *seiscientos* |
| 15 | *quince* | 700 | *setecientos* |
| 16 | *dieciseis* | 800 | *ochocientos* |
| 17 | *diecisiete* | 900 | *novecientos* |
| 18 | *dieciocho* | 1000 | *mil* |
| 19 | *diecinueve* | 1100 | *mil cien* |
| 20 | *veinte* | 1200 | *mil doscientos* |
| 21 | *veintiuno* | 2000 | *dos mil* |
| 22 | *veintidós* | 5000 | *cinco mil* |
| 30 | *treinta* | 10,000 | *diez mil* |
| 31 | *treinta y uno* | 50,000 | *cincuenta mil* |
| 40 | *cuarenta* | 100,000 | *cien mil* |
| 50 | *cincuenta* | 1,000,000 | *un millón* |
| 60 | *sesenta* | | |

## Time

Telling time is fairly straightforward. Eight o'clock is *las ocho*, while 8:30 is *las ocho y treinta* (literally, eight and thirty) or *las ocho y media* (eight and a half). However, 7:45 is *las ocho menos quince* (literally, eight minus fifteen) or *las ocho menos cuarto* (eight minus one quarter). Times are modified by morning *de la mañana* or afternoon *(de la tarde)* instead of am or pm. Transportation schedules commonly use the 24-hour clock.

## Days of the Week

| | |
|---|---|
| Monday | *lunes* |
| Tuesday | *martes* |
| Wednesday | *miércoles* |
| Thursday | *jueves* |
| Friday | *viernes* |
| Saturday | *sábado* |
| Sunday | *domingo* |

# Facts for the Visitor

## WHEN TO GO

For residents of the Northern Hemisphere, Argentina offers the inviting possibility of enjoying two summers in the same year, but the country's great variety can make a visit in any season worthwhile. In the southern winter or spring, the heat and humidity are less oppressive. However, Buenos Aires' urban attractions transcend the seasons.

## ORIENTATION

At first glance, Buenos Aires seems as massive and imposing as New York or London, but a brief orientation suffices for the city's compact downtown grid and most frequented *barrios* (boroughs or neighborhoods).

The Capital Federal, bounded by the Río de la Plata and its tributary the Riachuelo, plus the ring roads of Av General Paz and Av 27 de Febrero, consists of 47 distinct barrios, some of them very small and others quite large. These barrios have clearly defined limits, but informal boundaries are rarely congruent and often contradictory – the line between Palermo and Recoleta, for instance, is often indistinct, while the Av Córdoba boundary between Balvanera and Recoleta/Barrio Norte so rigidly demarcates two very distinct parts of the city that every porteño who crosses the street recognizes the division.

Other factors complicate the geographical organization of the city. Porteños barely acknowledge the downtown barrio of San Nicolás as such, often using the term *microcentro* for the area north of Av de Mayo and east of Av 9 de Julio, a sector that includes the Florida and Lavalle *peatonales* (pedestrian malls), Plaza San Martín and the important commercial and entertainment areas along Avs Corrientes, Córdoba and Santa Fe. In fact, this also comprises parts of the barrio of Retiro and the area popularly known as Congreso, which overlaps the barrio of Balvanera. Barrio Norte, for that matter, is not a formal barrio but rather a neighborhood that comprises mostly residential parts of Recoleta and Retiro.

Consequently, the limits indicated for the maps in this book have as much to do with convenience as strict geographical correctness, about which even porteño sources disagree. The major divisions are the microcentro and Av de Mayo (part of the barrio of Monserrat, also known

## Law of the Indies

Perceptive visitors to Buenos Aires and other Latin American cities will immediately notice their structural similarity. Except in the great indigenous empires of Mexico and the Andes, where the Spaniards adapted pre-Hispanic cities to their own ends, the colonial *Leyes de Indias* (Law of the Indies) decreed the imposition of a regular grid pattern traceable back to Roman times.

The Spaniards were largely an urban people and drew on their European experience to build the new colonial settlements. In Spain, the slow-growing medieval city had resulted in dispersal of major urban institutions like the cabildo (town council), the church and the market, but in the colonies all of these clustered around the central plaza. Because of the plaza's defensive functions on the frontier, settlers often called it the 'Plaza de Armas'. As the leading Spanish citizens settled near the institutions of power, the plaza became the city's economic and social center.

There were exceptions to the rule, of course. Officials were directed to choose town sites in open, level areas, but the spontaneous development and irregular topography of many ports and mining towns discouraged the uniform application of the system. Nevertheless, the rectangular grid system became the template for urban development throughout the region. Especially in Argentina, where many contemporary cities have little or no colonial past, this legacy greatly simplifies the task of orientation for visitors. ■

sometimes as Catedral al Sur), Congreso and Corrientes (comprising parts of the microcentro and the barrios of Monserrat and Balvanera), San Telmo and Constitución, La Boca, Retiro, Recoleta and Barrio Norte, and Palermo and Belgrano (including the 'Costanera', which provides access to the Río de la Plata).

The capital's traditional focus of activity is the Plaza de Mayo, opposite the Casa Rosada presidential palace. Both the Catedral Metropolitana (cathedral) and portions of the original cabildo (colonial town council) are also here, at the east end of Av de Mayo. Street names change, and street numbers rise, on each side of Av de Mayo, while numbers on east-west streets rise from zero near the waterfront. Only outside the city's central grid does numbering become any more complex.

A pedestrian's nightmare, the broad Av 9 de Julio forms a second north-south axis, simultaneously encompassing Cerrito and Carlos Pellegrini north of Av de Mayo, and Lima and Bernardo de Irigoyen south of Av de Mayo. It runs from Plaza Constitución in San Telmo to Av del Libertador in Recoleta, which continues to the city's exclusive northern suburbs and their spacious parks.

# MAPS

Metrovías, the private operator of the Subte (subway), publishes a very good pocket-size map of the area it serves, within which most of the capital's tourist attractions fall; it's available for free from most public information offices. Covering a smaller area on a larger scale, Guías Taylor's *Plano Turístico de la Ciudad de Buenos Aires* focuses on the microcentro and San Telmo, Recoleta, La Boca and Palermo barrios. Widely available from kiosks along

JAMES LYON

Av Lavalle

Florida, it also contains a useful Subte diagram, but oversized symbols for some city landmarks detract from the map's readability.

For visitors spending some time in Buenos Aires, Lumi Transportes publishes *Capital Federal* and *Capital Federal y Gran Buenos Aires* maps in compact, ring-binder format, with all city streets and bus routes indexed. A similar worthwhile acquisition is the *Guía Peuser*.

For topographic maps, visit the Instituto Geografico Militar, at Av Cabildo 381 in Palermo (on the border of Belgrano), reached by bus No 152 and open 8 am to 1 pm. These maps are much more difficult to obtain outside the capital.

DAVE HOUSER

Plaza de Mayo, the heart of the microcentro

The Automóvil Club Argentino (ACA, ☎ 802-6061), Av del Libertador 1850 in Palermo on the border of Recoleta, publishes a *Carta Vial de Buenos Aires y Alrededores* which is useful beyond the city center; its detailed provincial road maps are imperative for motorists and useful for anyone else. (See the section on Cars & Motorcycles in the Getting There & Away chapter for more on ACA.) You may also find them at specialist bookstores like Edward Stanford's in London or in the map rooms of major university libraries. Members of foreign automobile clubs can purchase them at discount prices in Argentina. ACA has branch offices in Congreso (☎ 372-5283) at Av Belgrano 1749, in Palermo (☎ 771-9158) at Godoy Cruz and Demaría, and Belgrano (☎ 785-2934) at the corner of Av Cabildo and Virrey Arredondo.

# TOURIST OFFICES
## Local Tourist Offices

The Dirección Nacional de Turismo (☎ 312-2232), Av Santa Fe 883 in Retiro, is open weekdays from 9 am to 5 pm; there's a branch (☎ 480-0224) at Aeropuerto Internacional Ezeiza. Both have well-prepared English-speaking staff.

More convenient for most purposes are the municipal tourist kiosks on Florida between Av Córdoba and Paraguay, at the intersection of Florida and Diagonal Roque Sáenz Peña, and at the intersection of RM Ortiz and Av Quintana in Recoleta. These kiosks, which distribute excellent pocket-size maps in English and Spanish, as well as other brochures, are open weekdays from 8:30 am to 8:30 pm and Saturdays 9 am to 7 pm, except for the Recoleta branch, which is open from 10 am to 9 pm daily (except Sunday, when it's open noon to 8 pm).

For more detailed information on the city, visit the Dirección General de Turismo de la Municipalidad de Buenos Aires (☎ 476-3612, 371-1496), in the Centro Cultural San Martín, 5th floor, Sarmiento 1551 in Corrientes. This office also organizes free weekend guided walks of certain barrios at 5 pm Saturdays and Sundays in summer, and at 3 pm the rest of the year.

Readily available around town is the glossy bilingual (English-Spanish) *BA Guide*, which contains useful information on basic visitor services and current events in the city, despite the flagrant commercialism of its restaurant and shopping listings.

## Tourist Offices Abroad

The larger Argentine consulates, such as those in New York and Los Angeles, usually have a tourist representative in their delegation. Local representatives of Aerolíneas Argentinas often have similar information at their disposal.

**Australia**
1st floor, MLC Tower
Woden, ACT 2026
☎ (06) 282-4555

**Canada**
Suite 620, 90 Sparks St
Ottawa, Ontario
☎ (613) 236-2351

Suite 605, 1010 Saint
Catherine St West
Montréal, Québec
☎ (514) 866-3810

**UK**
53 Hans Place
London SW1 XOLA
☎ (0171) 589 3104

**USA**
1600 New Hampshire
Ave NW
Washington, DC 20009
☎ (202) 939-6411

12 W 56th St
New York, NY 10019
☎ (212) 603-0400

800 Brickell Ave
Penthouse 1
Miami, FL 33131
☎ (305) 373-1889

20 N Clark St, Suite 602
Chicago, IL 60602
☎ (312) 263-7435

Suite 1810
2000 S Post Oak Rd
Houston, TX 77056
☎ (713) 871-8935

Suite 1450
5005 Wilshire Blvd
Los Angeles, CA
☎ (213) 954-9155

# DOCUMENTS

Passports are obligatory for all visitors except citizens of bordering countries. Argentina presently enjoys civilian government and the police and military presence are subdued, but the police can still demand identification at any moment. In general, officials are very document-oriented and passports are essential for cashing traveler's checks, checking into hotels, and other routine activities.

## Visas

Argentina has eliminated visas for many but not all foreign tourists. In theory, upon arrival all nonvisa visitors must obtain a free tourist card, good for 90 days and renewable for 90 more. In practice, immigration officials issue these only at major border crossings, such as airports and on the ferries and hydrofoils between Buenos Aires and Uruguay. Do be careful with your card. However, should you lose it, immigration officials will provide immediate replacement at most exit points; that is, the bureaucracy may require you to fill one in even though you're leaving the country.

Nationals of the USA and most Western European countries, including Britons, do not need visas. Australians and New Zealanders, who do need visas, must submit their passports with a payment of US$30 and may need to show a return or onward ticket; ordinarily, the visa will be ready the following day.

Argentina has a wide network of embassies and consulates, both in neighboring countries and overseas. Some are very accommodating, while others (most notably those in Colonia, Uruguay, and La Paz, Bolivia) act as if your visit is a major nuisance. Renewing a nearly expired visa at a consulate other than the one which issued it can be nearly impossible; it is easier to get a new passport and then request a new Argentine visa.

Individuals born in Argentina, even of foreign parents, are considered Argentines and may encounter difficulties entering the country with non-Argentine documents – in one instance, officials harassed a retired US army colonel, who was born in Buenos Aires, for lacking proof of completing obligatory military service in Argentina. Argentine passports renewed overseas expire upon re-entry into Argentina, and renewing them with the Policía Federal can be a tiresome process on a short trip.

## Visa Extensions

Argentine tourist cards are valid for 90 days. For a 90-day extension, visit the Dirección Nacional de Migraciones (☎ 312-3288) at Av Antártida Argentina 1365 in Retiro or in provincial capitals, or at provincial delegations of the Policía Federal. There may be a nominal charge. In areas where the police are unaccustomed to dealing with immigration, the process can be tedious and time-consuming.

Travelers wishing to stay longer than six months will find it simpler to cross the border into a neighboring country for a few days and then return for an additional six months. Although it is possible to obtain residence, leaving the country then becomes problematic and you cannot take advantage of tourist regulations with respect to Argentine customs and duties.

# Driver's License & Permits

Motorists need an International or Interamerican Driving Permit to complement their national or state licenses, but drivers should not be surprised if police at the numerous roadside checkpoints do not recognize it or, worse, claim it is invalid and try to exact a bribe. Politely refer them to the Spanish translation.

# Hostelling International Card

Sponsored by UNESCO, the nonprofit Asociación Argentina de Albergues de la Juventud (☎ 476-1001) is the local affiliate of Hostelling International. On the 2nd floor at Talcahuano 214 in Congreso, it's open weekdays 11 am to 7 pm. It sponsors hostels in Buenos Aires and many provincial towns.

The Hostelling International Card is cheaper to acquire overseas than in Argentina, where the initial year's membership costs anywhere from US$48 to US$60, depending on the age of the member. Renewal is half-price.

# Student & Youth Cards

The International Student Identity Card (ISIC) may help travelers obtain discounts on public transportation, museum admissions and the like, but virtually any official-looking university identification is an acceptable substitute.

# Seniors' Cards

Travelers over the age of 60 may also obtain *tercera edad* (senior citizen) discounts on museum admissions and the like. Usually a passport with date of birth will be sufficient evidence of age.

DAVE HOUSER

Teatro Colón

# EMBASSIES & CONSULATES

Argentina has diplomatic representation throughout Latin America, North America, Western Europe and many other regions, including Australia. The following are most likely to be useful to prospective visitors. See also the Tourist Offices Abroad section above.

## Argentine Embassies Abroad

**Australia**
1st floor, MLC Tower
Woden, ACT
☎ (06) 282-4555

**Bolivia**
2nd floor, 16 de Julio 1486
La Paz
☎ 35-3089

**Brazil**
2nd floor
Praia de Botafogo 228
Rio de Janeiro
☎ 551-5198

8th floor, Rua Araújo 216
São Paulo
☎ 256-8555

**Canada**
Suite 620, 90 Sparks St
Ottawa, Ontario
☎ (613) 236-2351

2000 Peel St
Montréal, Quebec
☎ (514) 842-6582

**Chile**
Vicuña Mackenna 41
Santiago
☎ 222-8977

**Paraguay**
Banco Nación, España at
Perú, Asunción
☎ 21-2320, 21-2321

**UK**
53 Hans Place
London SW1 XOLA
☎ (0171) 584-6494;
consulate 589-3104

**USA**
229 Peach Tree St
Suite 1401
Atlanta, GA 30303
☎ (404) 880-0805

205 N Michigan Ave
Suite 4209
Chicago, IL 60601
☎ (312) 819-2610

1600 New Hampshire
Ave NW
Washington, DC 20009
☎ (202) 939-6411

12 W 56th St
New York, NY 10019
☎ (212) 603-0400

800 Brickell Ave
Penthouse 1
Miami, FL 33131
☎ (305) 373-1889

20 N Clark St
Suite 602
Chicago, IL 60602
☎ (312) 263-7435

Suite 1810
2000 S Post Oak Rd
Houston, TX 77056
☎ (713) 871-8935

Suite 1450
5005 Wilshire Blvd
Los Angeles, CA
☎ (213) 954-9155

**Uruguay**
Río Branco 1281
Montevideo
☎ 90-0897, 92-0667

# Foreign Embassies in Buenos Aires

Every European and South American country and many others throughout the world have embassies and consulates in Buenos Aires. The following partial list contains those most likely to be useful for travelers.

**Australia**
Villanueva 1400
in Belgrano
☎ 777-6580

**Belgium**
8th floor, Defensa 113
in Monserrat
☎ 331-0066

**Bolivia**
Av Belgrano 1670
in Congreso
☎ 381-0539

**Brazil**
5th floor,
Carlos Pellegrini 1363
in Retiro
☎ 394-5227, 394-5260

**Canada**
Tagle 2828
in Palermo
☎ 805-3032

**Chile**
9th floor, San Martín 439
in the microcentro
☎ 394-6582

**Denmark**
9th floor, LN Alem 1074
in Retiro
☎ 312-6901

**France**
3rd floor, Santa Fe 846
in Retiro
☎ 312-2409

**Germany**
Villanueva 1055
in Palermo
☎ 778-2500

**Ireland**
Suipacha 1380
in Retiro
☎ 326-2612

**Israel**
10th floor
Av de Mayo 701
in Monserrat
☎ 342-1465

**Italy**
MT de Alvear 1149
in Barrio Norte
☎ 325-6135

**Japan**
Paseo Colón 275
in Monserrat
☎ 343-2561

**Mexico**
Larrea 1230
in Recoleta
☎ 821-7170

**Netherlands**
Av de Mayo 701
in Monserrat
☎ 334-4000

**Norway**
3rd floor
Esmeralda 90
in Retiro
☎ 312-1904

**Paraguay**
Viamonte 1851
in Corrientes
☎ 812-0075

**Perú**
San Martín 969
in Retiro
☎ 311-7582

**Spain**
Guido 1760 in Recoleta
☎ 811-0078

**Sweden**
3rd floor, Corrientes 330
in the microcentro
☎ 328-3088

**Switzerland**
10th floor, Santa Fe 846
in Retiro
☎ 311-6491

**UK**
Doctor Luis Agote 2412
in Palermo
☎ 803-7070

**Uruguay**
Las Heras 1907
in Recoleta
☎ 807-3044

**USA**
Colombia 4300
in Palermo
☎ 774-4533

# CUSTOMS

Argentine customs officials are generally reasonable, but travelers who cross the border frequently and carry electronic equipment such as cameras or a laptop computer may find it helpful to have a typed list of equipment, including serial numbers, to be stamped by authorities. At Buenos Aires' Aeropuerto Internacional Ezeiza, officials often ask about such goods, which are much more costly in Argentina than overseas.

Depending on where you have been, officials focus on different things. Travelers southbound from the central Andean countries may be searched for drugs, while those from central Chile or from Brazil will have fruit and vegetables confiscated. *Never* carry firearms.

# MONEY

For visitors unaccustomed to hyperinflation and without sufficient zeros on their pocket calculators, Argentine money has traditionally presented real problems – when Argentine economists spoke hopefully of single-digit inflation, they meant *per month*. Since the institution of Domingo Cavallo's convertibility policy in early 1991, however, inflation has fallen to record lows, and the peso has remained at parity with the dollar. Still, given Argentina's history of financial instability, travelers should keep a close watch on exchange markets and current economic events; it is still not advisable to keep large amounts of cash in local currency.

## Cash

Cash can be exchanged at banks, cambios, hotels and some travel agencies, and often in shops or on the street. Travelers confident of their ability to carry cash safely will find it a much better alternative than traveler's checks, which often carry commission charges of up to 10% or more. Hard currencies other than US dollars will find a market in Buenos Aires, though they are less convenient; outside Buenos Aires, they are difficult to exchange.

## Traveler's Checks

Traveler's checks are easier to change in Buenos Aires than elsewhere in the country, but they are increasingly difficult to cash anywhere and specifically *not* recommended; an ATM card is a far better alternative. American Express, Arenales 707 near Plaza San Martín in Retiro, will change its own traveler's checks without commission.

## ATMs

While traveler's checks are problematical, *cajeros automáticos* (ATMs) are increasingly abundant and can also be used for cash advances on major credit cards like MasterCard and Visa. ATMs are so ubiquitous downtown that it would superfluous to mention any in particular; many but not all will dispense either US dollars or Argentine pesos.

## Credit Cards

The most widely accepted credit cards are Visa and MasterCard (the latter, affiliated with the local Argencard, is the most useful; travelers with UK Access should insist on their affiliation to MasterCard). American Express, Diner's Club and others are also valid in many places. Because lost or stolen credit cards are vulnerable to abuse, credit card holders should consider enrolling in a protection plan to insure themselves against serious financial loss.

Credit card users should be aware of two complications. In the first place, some businesses add a *recargo* (surcharge) of 10% or more to credit card purchases to recoup high bank charges and the loss of interest between the time of purchase and their own receipt of payment. The flip side of this practice is that some merchants give a discount of 10% or more for cash purchases.

Second, the actual amount customers pay depends upon the exchange rate at the time the purchase is posted to an overseas account, which can be weeks later. If the local currency is depreciating, the price may be a fraction of the dollar cost calculated at the time of purchase. On the other hand, a strong local currency may mean that the cost in dollars (or other foreign currency) will be significantly greater than expected. At present, this is not an issue for travelers whose overseas accounts are in US dollars, but those whose purchases are converted to other currencies should be wary of changes.

Holders of MasterCard and Visa can also get cash advances at most downtown banks between 10 am and 4 pm.

The following local representatives can help travelers replace credit cards and/or traveler's checks:

**American Express**
Arenales 707
☎ 312-1661

**Diner's Club**
Carlos Pellegrini 1023
☎ 815-4545

**MasterCard**
Hipólito Yrigoyen 878
☎ 331-1021, 331-2559

**Visa**
Corrientes 1437, 3rd floor
☎ 954-2000

## International Transfers

Travelers who have suffered lost cash and credit cards or had them stolen have found the American Express Money Gram a quick and efficient (if costly) means of transferring funds from their home country to Argentina. Amex has a major office in Buenos Aires and representatives throughout the country.

## Currency

The present unit of currency is the peso ($), which replaced the inflation-ravaged *austral* on January 1, 1992. (The austral had replaced the *peso argentino* in 1985, which had replaced the *peso ley* in 1978, which had replaced the ordinary *peso* some years earlier.) One new peso equals 10,000 australs, which is on a par with the US dollar.

Paper money comes in denominations of 1, 2, 5, 10, 20, 50 and 100 pesos. One new peso equals 100 *centavos*; coins come in denominations of 1, 5, 10, 25 and 50 centavos, but few merchants want anything to do with one centavo coins. Tattered, nearly shredded Argentine banknotes seem to stay in circulation for decades, but few banks or businesses accept torn, worn or defaced dollars.

At present, dollars are de facto legal tender almost everywhere, but it's wise to carry some pesos; institutions like the post office and some bus companies, as well as a few nationalistic merchants, refuse to accept US currency.

# Currency Exchange

Exchange rates can be volatile. For example, in mid-December of 1990 the dollar had sunk below 5000 australs until a minor economic crisis and intensified domestic demand by Argentines planning overseas holidays drove the rate up dramatically. By September 1991, the rate for the previous currency was just below 10,000 australs per US dollar.

| | | |
|---|---|---|
| Australia .....................A$1 | = | $0.74 |
| Bolivia ......................Bol$1 | = | $0.20 |
| Brazil .....................BraRl 1 | = | $1.07 |
| Chile ..................Chi$1000 | = | $2.60 |
| France ......................FFr1 | = | $0.21 |
| Germany ...................DM1 | = | $0.72 |
| Italy ......................It£1000 | = | $0.63 |
| Japan ..................Jpn¥100 | = | $1.14 |
| Paraguay .............Par 1000 | = | $0.51 |
| United Kingdom ...........UK£1 | = | $1.60 |
| United States ...............US$1 | = | $1 |
| Uruguay ...............Urg$1000 | = | $16 |

# Changing Money

While convertibility has reduced the need to change money, dozens of *casas de cambio* (exchange houses) still line Calle San Martín south of Av Corrientes, which is to Argentina what Wall Street is to the US. There are many more cambios north of Av Corrientes, along Av Corrientes itself, and on the Florida peatonal. Cambio hours are generally from 9 am to 6 pm weekdays, but a few are open Saturday mornings.

# Black Market

At present, there is no black market and there are few restrictions on changing money freely, but in times of crisis visitors should stay aware of the so-called *mercado paralelo* (parallel market). For the most up-to-date information, see *Ambito Financiero*, Argentina's counterpart to *The Wall Street Journal* or *Financial Times*, or the English-language daily *Buenos Aires Herald*.

# Costs

At times of economic instability, which is often enough, Argentines panic and buy US dollars, the exchange rate collapses, and the country can become absurdly cheap for the visitor with hard currency. At present, though, the economy is relatively stable due to the stringent convertibility policy, making Buenos Aires nearly as expensive as European or North American capitals. Inflation has remained relatively high in some sectors, so that prices for hotels, restaurants and similar travelers' services have increased more rapidly than others in the economy at large – in 1994, when the aggregate inflation rate was only 4%, transportation costs nevertheless increased by nearly 19%. Some Argentines even prefer to take their holidays in less expensive countries like the USA and have acquired the ironic nickname 'démedos' because, on their visits to Miami, they find consumer items so cheap that they tell the clerk to 'give me two'.

This does not make budget travel impossible. Certain costs, such as modest lodging, food and some transportation, will be lower than in Europe or North America even if they are higher than in surrounding countries. After overcoming the initial shock, travelers arriving from inexpensive countries like Bolivia should be able to spend a rewarding time in Argentina by adapting to local conditions. By seeking out cheaper lodging and dining selectively, judicious travelers can control costs. In particular, those accustomed to eating every meal in a restaurant in neighboring countries will not be able to do so in Argentina; consider sandwich fixings from the market and splurge on an occasional treat elsewhere.

Still, everyone but dedicated shoestring travelers should probably allow a minimum of US$35 to US$40 per day for food and lodging, and pat themselves on the back if they can get by on less. It's possible to spend much more, and prices in this book are subject to wild fluctuations.

## Tipping & Bargaining

In restaurants, it is customary to tip about 10% of the bill, but in times of economic distress Argentines frequently overlook the custom. In general, waiters and waitresses are ill paid, so if you can afford to eat out, you should be able to afford to tip. Even a small *propina* will be appreciated. Cinema ushers also receive a small tip.

Bargaining is not the way of life as it is in Bolivia or Peru, but artisans' markets and downtown shops selling leather and other tourist goods will consider offers.

## Discounts

Late in the evening, some hotels may give a break on room prices; if you plan to stay several days, they almost certainly will. Many better hotels give discounts up to 30% for cash payment. Students, teachers and senior citizens with appropriate identification may obtain discounts on long-distance buses and admission to museums.

## Taxes & Refunds

One of Argentina's primary state revenue earners is the 21% *Impuesto de Valor Agregado* (IVA or Value Added Tax). Under limited circumstances, foreign visitors may obtain IVA refunds on purchases of Argentine products upon departing the country. A 'Tax Free' (in English) window decal identifies participants in this program, but always verify the shop's status before making your purchase.

To obtain a refund on purchases of US$200 or more, present your passport and immigration card to the merchant, who must enter the amount of the refund on the reverse of the invoice and paste an equivalent quantity of stamps on the form, whose triplicate you will also receive. On leaving the country, keep the purchased items separate from the rest of your baggage; a customs official will check them and seal the invoice.

With this invoice, branches of Banco de la Nación at Buenos Aires' Aeropuerto Internacional Ezeiza, Aeroparque Jorge Newbery (for flights to some neighboring countries), and the capital's river ports at Dársena Norte and Dársena Sur will refund the money in pesos and then convert it to US dollars. These branch banks are open 24 hours daily.

## POST & COMMUNICATIONS

### Post

The distinctive Correo Central, Sarmiento 189, occupies an entire block along Av LN Alem between Av Corrientes and Sarmiento. It's open weekdays 9 am to 7:30 pm and is the only post office that offers international express mail service. US dollars are not accepted here.

For international parcels weighing over one kg, go to the Correo Internacional, on Antártida Argentina near the Retiro train station. Hours are weekdays 11 am to 5 pm.

Branch post offices are scattered throughout the city; one of the most central is beneath street level in the Galería Buenos Aires, on Florida between Av Córdoba and Paraguay. Another is at Solís and Hipólito Yrigoyen, near the Plaza del Congreso.

Send essential overseas mail *certificado* (registered) or *puerta a puerta* (express, literally 'door to door') to ensure its arrival. Mail is likely to be opened and the contents appropriated if it appears to contain money or anything else of value.

When writing to addresses in Buenos Aires, bear in mind that Argentines commonly refer to the city as the 'Capital Federal'. Porteños often shorten this term further to 'la capital'.

**Postal Rates** Argentina's postal rates are among the world's highest. Domestic letters weighing 150 grams or less cost US$0.75, while postcards cost US$0.50. International letters weighing 20 grams or less cost US$0.75 to bordering countries, US$1 elsewhere in the Americas, and US$1.25 outside the Americas. International express mail services are much more expensive but a better value because of their dependability.

Airmail packages are expensive, while surface mail is much cheaper but even less dependable.

**Receiving Mail** Travelers can receive mail via Poste Restante or Lista de Correos, both equivalent to general delivery, at any Argentine post office. Instruct correspondents to address letters clearly and to indicate a date on the envelope until which the post office should hold them; otherwise they will be returned or destroyed.

Post offices have imposed heavy charges, up to US$1.50 per letter, on Poste Restante services; to avoid this surprisingly costly and bureaucratic annoyance, arrange to have mail delivered to a private address such as a friend or a hotel.

**Private Mail Services** Correo Argentino (ex-Encotel) no longer has a monopoly on postal services, and private-run international and national services are considerably more dependable but much more expensive. Federal Express (☎ 325-6551) is at Maipú 753 in the microcentro, while DHL International (☎ 343-1687) is at Hipólito Yrigoyen 448, also in the microcentro. OCA (☎ 788-7777), which makes domestic connections for several international couriers, is at Echeverría 1238 in Belgrano. Private international mail services will accept US dollars.

## Telephone

Argentine telephone rates are very high, and travelers making overseas calls will find it much cheaper to use credit cards or to call collect. Callers to Germany cannot take advantage of this because Argentina and Germany have no reciprocal communications agreement.

Argentina's two phone companies, Telecom and Telefónica, have split the city down the middle at Av Córdoba; theoretically, everything north belongs to Telecom, while everything south is the responsibility of Telefónica, but occasionally there's overlap. Despite some improvements in service, the antiquated infrastructure bequeathed by the former state monopoly ENTel will probably plague the city for decades. In theory, local calls should be simple, but callers often find that, even if the call gets through, the person at the other end is unable to hear. Repairs can take weeks, and coordination between the two companies is very poor.

Most public telephones are now functional. To make a local call, purchase *cospeles* (tokens) or more convenient *tarjetas telefónicas* (phone cards) from almost any kiosk or newsstand, or from street vendors. Callers fortunate enough to get through will only be able to speak for about two minutes, so carry lots of cospeles. There are different types of cospeles for local and long-distance calls.

Long-distance offices are usually very busy, especially during evening (10 pm to 8 am) and weekend discount hours when overseas calls are more reasonable. At Telefónica's most convenient and efficient office, open 24 hours at Av Corrientes 701, booths with direct connections to operators in North America, Japan, Europe and neighboring countries greatly simplify collect and credit-card calls. Otherwise, an attendant will give you a priority number and, when that number is called, a cashier will give you a ticket for a booth. Once in the booth, you can either dial directly or ask for operator assistance. When you complete the call, pay the cashier.

Since the demise of ENTel, numerous other private *locutorios* have sprung up around central Buenos Aires, so it is usually not necessary to make a long trip out of your way simply to make a long-distance or overseas call, or to send or receive a fax. However, few locutorios care to handle collect or credit-card calls, which must be placed at Telecom or Telefónica offices, or from a private telephone. If you're calling from a private phone, use Discado Directo Internacional (International Direct Dialing), which provides direct access to home-country operators for long-distance collect and credit card calls.

Argentina's country code is 54; Buenos Aires' area code is 01. The Spanish term for area code is *característica*.

## Fax, Telegraph & Email

International telegrams, telexes and faxes can be sent from Encotel, still a state monopoly, at Av Corrientes 711 next door to the main Telefónica office. Many locutorios also offer fax services.

Netheads and other computer-oriented individuals will find Argentina frustrating because of the poor telephone system and bureaucratic controls on access – even many university researchers have to go through an official gatekeeper, who often works only a few hours a day. It's best to look for a friend or acquaintance with access to a line.

# BOOKS

There is a tremendous amount of literature on Argentina, much of it by porteño authors, so readers can afford to be selective. Many key writers, such as Jorge Luis Borges, Julio Cortázar, Adolfo Bioy Casares, Ernesto Sábato, Osvaldo Soriano and Manuel Puig have been translated into English. Buenos Aires is one of the Spanish-speaking world's major publishing centers and has many excellent bookstores on or near Av Corrientes, which is a delightful area to browse; for suggestions, see the chapter on Shopping.

## Lonely Planet

Other guidebooks can supplement and complement this one, especially for travelers visiting areas outside Buenos Aires or countries other than Argentina. Two obvious endorsements are the 2nd edition of *Argentina, Uruguay & Paraguay*. Also useful is the 6th edition of *South America on a Shoestring*, a collaborative effort by several LP authors. LP also has travel survival kits for Ecuador & the Galápagos Islands, Peru, Colombia, Venezuela, Bolivia, Brazil, and Chile & Easter Island, as well as the *Latin American Spanish phrasebook*.

## Other Guidebooks

The annually updated *South American Handbook*, published by Trade & Travel in the UK and Prentice Hall in North America, contains a substantial chapter on Buenos Aires. The *APA Insight Guides* series has separate volumes on Buenos Aires and Argentina which are excellent in cultural and historical analysis, and illustrated with superb photographs. However, they're weak on practical information and consequently much better for pre-trip familiarization than use on the road. Many typographical errors mar the Argentina volume.

Readers competent in Spanish will find *La Guía Pirelli, Buenos Aires, Sus Alrededores y Costas del Uruguay*

(Editorial Sudamericana, 1993) full of illuminating historical and cultural material on the capital and nearby areas, but the woefully incomplete maps are unsuitable even for orientation. It's also one of those books that seems to assume every visitor has a new BMW and stays in five-star hotels – by their standards, Hotel Plaza Francia rates as budget accommodations. Pirelli also publishes a guide to the entire country with the same strengths and shortcomings; both may be available in English, but the English language editions are less up-to-date than the Spanish versions.

Though selective rather than definitive in its coverage, the multi-authored *Buenos Aires: Guía de Arquitectura*, jointly published by the Municipalidad de la Ciudad de Buenos Aires and the Spanish Junta de Andalucía, is a superbly written and illustrated guide to the city's architecture, with superb B&W photographs. Eight suggested walking tours focus on some of the city's most notable buildings and public spaces. It also offers a representative selection of activities and places to dine. Although expensive at nearly US$40, it's highly recommended for travelers spending any length of time in the city.

For a distinct specialized audience, there's always Raquel Orella's and Marcela Osa's *Guía Erótica de Buenos Aires* (Ediciones Temas de Hoy, Madrid, 1994).

## History

James Scobie's *Argentina: A City and a Nation* has gone through many editions and is now a standard account of the country's Buenos Aires-biased development. More specialized is Scobie's *Buenos Aires: Plaza to Suburb, 1870 – 1910*, which focuses on the social evolution of the city during the period of its greatest growth.

The most up-to-date, comprehensive history of the country in English is David Rock's *Argentina 1516 – 1987: From Spanish Colonization to the Falklands War and Alfonsín*. Visitor's interested in the capital's sizeable Jewish community should acquire Víctor Mirelman's *Jewish Buenos Aires, 1890 – 1930: In Search of an Identity*. Mirelman did his research in the archives of the Asociación Mutual Israelita Argentina (AMIA), since destroyed by a terrorist bomb in 1994.

## NEWSPAPERS & MAGAZINES

Argentina is South America's most literate country, supporting a wide spectrum of newspapers and magazines despite unceasing economic crisis. Freedom of the press is far greater than under the military dictatorship of

WAYNE BERNHARDSON

1976 – 1983, but abuses still occur. For instance, the present administration has withheld official advertising from newspapers that have investigated official corruption too vigorously for its taste.

The thriving daily press in Buenos Aires displays unambiguous political tendencies. The most important porteño dailies are the venerable *La Prensa* and *La Nación* (the latter founded by President Bartolomé Mitre) and the centrist tabloid *Clarín*, which has an excellent Sunday cultural section. *Página 12*, which does not publish Mondays, provides a refreshing leftist perspective and often breaks important stories that mainstream newspapers are slow to cover.

The English language daily *Buenos Aires Herald* covers Argentina and the world from an Anglo-Argentine perspective, emphasizing commerce and finance, but its perceptive weekend summaries of political and economic developments are a must for visitors with limited Spanish; its Sunday edition now includes Britain's *Guardian Weekly* at no extra charge. *Argentinisches Tageblatt* is a German-language weekly that appears Saturdays.

## The *Herald* and Its History

Ever since its debut under Scottish founder William Cathcart in 1876, *The Buenos Aires Herald* has played a critical, activist role at times of crisis, when Argentina's Spanish-language press has often been timid or sycophantic. The *Herald* do this in part because it appears in English, but that did not insulate it against official and extra-official hostility – during the Dirty War of the late 1970s and early 1980s, the paper was so outspoken in condemning military, paramilitary, police and guerrilla abuses that editor Robert Cox and his family became the focus of threats that forced them into exile. Current editor-in-chief Andrew Graham-Yooll has experienced the same. Nationalist hysteria during the Falklands/Malvinas War of 1982 led Cox's successor James Neilson to move himself and his family across the river to Uruguay for the duration of the conflict, but the paper never backed off from its independent editorial stance.

These were not the paper's first encounters with external pressures. In the early 1950s, the government of Juan Perón forced the paper to sell its printing plant in an effort to control production, distribution, and (indirectly) editorial policy. By 1975, though, the paper had built new offices and a printing plant only a few blocks from the Casa Rosada presidential palace.

In the interest of being accessible to all Argentines, the *Herald* publishes its editorials in both English and Spanish. Several sections, including regular aviation and shipping features, reflect the commercial interests of the Anglo-Argentine community, though much of the paper's advertising also appears in Spanish. The current owner is the Charleston Publishing Company of South Carolina, USA, which purchased the paper in 1968 from the Italo-British Rugeroni family, who had owned it since 1925 and are still shareholders.

Most of the *Herald*'s staff are Argentines, from the secretarial staff and gofers to the editor-in-chief, and there's a scattering of other nationalities including British, American, and Australian. Attentive readers will notice irregularities and idiosyncrasies that set the paper apart from its overseas counterparts – the typesetting, for example, often reflects Spanish rather than English syllabification. ■

*Ambito Financiero*, the morning voice of the capital's financial community, also has an excellent entertainment and cultural section. *El Cronista Comercial* is its afternoon rival.

Monthlies like *La Maga* and *El Porteño* offer a forum for Argentine intellectuals and contribute greatly to the capital's cultural life. The monthly *Humor* caricatured the Argentine military during the Dirty War and even during the early nationalist hysteria of the Falklands conflict; in safer times, it has lost much of its edge but is still worth reading. Avoid its soft-porn spinoff *Humor Sexo*. In a country known for its conservative Catholicism and male machismo, downtown kiosks sell (or at least display) a surprising amount of gay pornography.

# RADIO & TV

In recent years, the end of government monopoly in the electronic media has opened up the airwaves to a greater variety of programming than in the past. The most popular station, the nationwide Radio Rivadavia, is a combination of top 40 and talk radio, and there are many other choices on the AM band. More than a dozen FM stations specialize in styles from classical to pop to tango.

Legalization of privately owned television and the cable revolution have brought a wider variety of programming to the small screen. To be sure, there are countless game shows, dance parties and soap-opera drivel *(novelas)*, but there is also serious public-affairs programming on major stations at prime viewing times such as on Sunday evening. Foreigners can tune to CNN for news and ESPN for sports. Spanish and Chilean stations are also available.

# PHOTOGRAPHY & VIDEO

Kinefot (☎ 374-7445), Talcahuano 248 in Congreso, has fast, high-quality developing of E-6 slide film, but it is not cheap. For prints, try Le Lab (☎ 322-2785) at Viamonte 624 or Laboclick at Esmeralda 444 both in the microcentro.

For minor camera repairs, visit Gerardo Föhse, in the basement at Florida 835, Local 37 (☎ 311-1139). For fast, dependable service on more complex problems, phone José Norres (☎ 326-0963), 4th floor, Oficina 403, Lavalle 1569, who accepts payment in US dollars only.

# TIME

For most of the year, Argentina is three hours behind GMT/UMT, but Buenos Aires observes daylight-saving time (summer time), even though most provinces do not. Exact dates for the changeover vary from year to year.

# ELECTRICITY

Electric current operates on 220 volts, 50 cycles. Calle Talcahuano, south of Av Corrientes, has a large concentration of shops specializing in appliance transformers and adapters.

# LAUNDRY

In recent years, laundries have become much more common in Buenos Aires, but they tend to be more expensive than their equivalent in the USA or Europe – figure about US$6 per load, washed, dried and folded. Some inexpensive hotels have a place where you can wash your own clothes and hang them to dry. In some places maid service will be reasonable, but agree on charges in advance.

# RECYCLING

Most beer and soft drink bottles purchased at markets and grocery stores are still reusable, and merchants collect a small deposit for them; they will usually only reimburse customers for bottles purchased from their own store, but will accept bottles from other sources. In downtown Buenos Aires at the junction of the Florida and Lavalle pedestrian malls, there are containers for reycling aluminum and colored glass.

# WEIGHTS & MEASURES

The metric system is universal and obligatory, but a few vernacular measures survive. Hands are used to measure horses, while carpenters often use English units. Tire pressure is commonly measured in pounds per square inch.

# HEALTH

Buenos Aires' Hospital Municipal Juan Fernández (☎ 801-5555) is at Av Cerviño 3356 in Palermo, but there are many others, including the highly regarded British Hospital (☎ 304-1081) at Perdriel 74, a few blocks northwest of the Constitución train station.

# TOILETS

In terms of cleanliness and sanitation, toilets are probably better than in most of the rest of South America, but there are still poorly maintained. For the truly squeamish, the better restaurants and cafés are good alternatives. Always carry your own toilet paper.

# WOMEN TRAVELERS

In Argentina, International Women's Day becomes yet another occasion to 'send her flowers', but for women traveling alone, the country is probably safer than Europe, the USA and most other Latin American countries. Still, Buenos Aires is notorious for annoyances such as unwelcome physical contact, particularly on crowded buses or trains. If you're physically confident, a slap or a well-aimed elbow should discourage any further contact. If not, a scream can be very effective.

Other nuisances include crude language and *piropos*. Crude language, generally in the presence of other males, usually emphasizes feminine physical attributes. If you respond aggressively ('Are you talking to me?'), you will probably shame the aggressor. One clever New Yorker found that a bogus wedding ring helped deter unwanted admirers.

As for piropos, there is no universally accepted definition, but most Argentine males consider it the masculine art of approaching a woman in public and commenting on her femininity or attractiveness. This is an idealized definition because piropos are most often vulgar, even though some are creative and even eloquent (one recently cited in the *Buenos Aires Herald* was 'Oh God, the sky is parting and angels are falling'). While verbal aggression can be irritating, it rarely becomes physical. On occasions when persistent suitors trail you for blocks, the best means of discouraging their pursuit is to completely ignore them.

Single women checking in at low-budget hotels may find themselves objects of suspicion, since prostitutes often frequent such places. If you otherwise like the place, ignore this and the suspicions will evaporate. You should interpret questions as to whether you are running away from parents or husband as expressions of concern.

# GAY & LESBIAN TRAVELERS

While Argentina is a strongly Catholic country and homosexuality is taboo to many (former military dictator Juan Carlos Onganía recently caused a furor by stating he would not have a homosexual friend), there are enclaves of tolerance in Buenos Aires (particularly Av Santa Fe and in Recoleta), the Paraná Delta and some other areas. Argentine males are often more physically demonstrative than their North American and European counterparts, so behaviors such as kissing (at least on the cheek in greeting) or a vigorous embrace may seem innocuous even to those who express unease with homosexuals. Lesbians walking hand-in-hand will attract relatively little attention, since Argentine women frequently do so, but this would be very conspicuous behavior for males. When in doubt, it's better to be discreet.

# DISABLED TRAVELERS

Travelers with disabilities will find things difficult at times. The wheelchair-bound in particular will find Buenos Aires' narrow, often broken sidewalks difficult to negotiate. Crossing streets is also a problem, since Argentine drivers can be a challenge to even world-class gymnasts. Nevertheless, Argentines with disabilities do get around – one of the most famous works of contemporary Argentine fiction is Ernesto Sábato's *On Heroes and Tombs*, part of which is an extraordinary 'Report on the Blind' based, in part, on the author's Buenos Aires observations (Sábato himself, however, is not blind).

# SENIOR TRAVELERS

Senior travelers should encounter no particular difficulties in Buenos Aires, where older citizens traditionally enjoy a great deal of respect; on crowded buses, for instance, most Argentines will readily offer their seat to an older person. Senior discounts on transportation and most other services are, however, virtually a thing of the past.

# BUENOS AIRES FOR CHILDREN

Despite the fact that it's a major megalopolis, Buenos Aires is remarkably child-friendly. Once children are old enough to cross the street safely and find their way back home, porteño parents don't hesitate to send unaccompanied preadolescents on errands or on visits to friends or neighbors. While most visiting parents are not likely to know the city well enough to feel comfortable doing this, they can still count on children's safety in public places.

Porteños are very helpful on public transport. Often someone will give up a seat for a parent and child, but if that does not occur, an older person may offer to put the child on his or her lap. Sometimes this is so spontaneous that foreigners find someone pulling the child out of their arms. This is also a country where people frequently touch each other, so your children may be patted on the head or gently caressed.

Basic restaurants provide a wide selection of food suitable for children (vegetables, pasta, meat, chicken, fish), but adult portions are normally so large that small children rarely need a separate order. Waiters are accustomed to providing extra plates and cutlery for children, though some places may add a small additional charge. Argentine ice cream, often of high quality, is a special treat for children. Breastfeeding in public is highly unusual, but mothers can always retreat into a café and cover themselves with a baby blanket during feedings.

Public bathrooms, often poorly maintained, may be a concern for some parents. Always carry toilet paper, which is rarely stocked. While a woman may take a young boy into the ladies' room, it would be socially unacceptable for a man to take a girl of any age into the men's room.

Buenos Aires' numerous plazas and public parks, many of which have playgrounds, are popular gathering spots for families; the most attractive are the wide open spaces of Palermo. Plaza Alemania, fronting on Av del Libertador between Cavia and Av Casares, is where porteño skateboarders go to show their moves; younger children also bicycle and in-line skate in the area.

*Ambito Financiero*, the capital's financial daily, publishes an excellent cultural section with listings of children's activities, including films, music and theater presentations. More of these activities take place during winter recess (early to mid-July), but they are also very crowded then.

# USEFUL ORGANIZATIONS

ASATEJ (☎ 311-6953, fax 311-6840), Argentina's non-profit student travel agency and an affiliate of STA Travel, is on the 3rd floor, Florida 835, 1005 Buenos Aires, in Retiro. The organization is eager to encourage low-budget travelers, and you need not be a student to take advantage of their services.

Contact the Asociación Argentina de Albergues de la Juventud (☎/fax 476-1001), 2nd floor, Oficina 6, Talcahuano 214, 1013 Buenos Aires, in Corrientes, for information on Argentine youth hostels. This office also serves as a travel agency, issues international student cards, and maintains a message board for travelers (mostly young Argentines) seeking companions for extended trips.

The Administración de Parques Nacionales (☎ 311-0303, ext 165), at Santa Fe 690 in Retiro, provides information on national parks and stocks a small number of publications of interest to conservationists and wildlife enthusiasts. Another address of interest to conservationists is the wildlife organization Fundación Vida Silvestre Argentina (☎ 331-4864), Defensa 245 just south of Plaza de Mayo. Membership starts at US$35 per year, and includes the Fundación's newsletter *Otioso*; US$60 memberships includes the group's magazine, *Revista Vida Silvestre*. Hours are 9:30 am to 6 pm weekdays.

Birding enthusiasts might contact the Asociación Ornitológica del Plata (☎ 312-8958) at 25 de Mayo 749, 2nd floor, in the microcentro. The Argentine affiliate of Greenpeace (☎ 962-2291) is at Mansilla 3046, a few blocks from the Agüero station on Línea D of the Subte (underground) in Palermo.

Buenos Aires has two AIDS-related support organizations. Cooperación, Información y Ayuda al Enfermo de SIDA (COINSIDA, ☎ 383-2788) is an information and assistance center for victims of AIDS and HIV in Talcahuano 309, 5th floor, Departamento 10 in Corrientes. Línea SIDA (☎ 922-1617) is at Zuviría 64 (Subte Av La Plata).

# DANGERS & ANNOYANCES

Violent crime is rare, and personal security is a lesser concern in Buenos Aires than in most other Latin American cities. Still, travelers cannot afford to be complacent with their possessions – pickpockets, purse-snatchers and the like certainly exist. Watch for common diversions like the 'inadvertent' collision that results in ice cream or some other substance being spilled on an unsuspecting visitor, who loses precious personal possessions while distracted by the apologetic perpetrator working in concert with a thief (one LP reader has eloquently called them 'mustard artists'). Some travelers have had similar problems with ambulatory street vendors at sidewalk cafés.

Porteño drivers, like most Argentines, jump the gun when the signal is about to change to green. Be especially wary of vehicles turning right; even though pedestrians at corners and crosswalks have legal right-of-way, almost nobody behind the wheel respects it. Other troublesome and even potentially deadly hazards include potholes and loose tiles on city sidewalks, which can also be very slippery when wet – people have died after falling and striking their heads.

US residents concerned with domestic travel conditions in Argentina or any other country can obtain recorded travel information from the US Department of State Bureau of Consular Affairs (☎ (202) 647-5225).

## Police & Military

Travelers may find the police, who are not above petty harassment, of more concern than common criminals.

For motorists, so-called safety campaigns often result in citations for very minor equipment violations that carry very high fines – up to US$200 for an inadequate hand brake. In most cases, corrupt officers will settle for less expensive *coimas* (bribes), but this requires considerable caution and tact. A discreet hint that you intend to phone your consulate may minimize or eliminate such problems – often the police count on foreigners' ignorance of Argentine law.

Avoid approaching military installations, which often display the warning 'No stopping or photographs – the sentry will shoot'. In the event of a military coup or other emergency, state-of-siege regulations suspend all civil rights; carry identification at all times, and make sure someone knows your whereabouts. Contact your embassy or consulate for advice.

## Fireworks

A recent cause for concern is the widespread availability of fireworks, which are high-powered, poorly regulated and very dangerous. Especially around holidays such as Christmas and New Year's, idiots set off firecrackers in the streets and even toss them from high-rise apartments (when these go off between tall buildings, the echo-chamber effect sounds like the bombing of Hanoi). It may be better to stay off the streets at these times.

## Terrorism

The state terrorism of the 1970s and 1980s has subsided, but deadly attempts on Jewish/Israeli centers in Buenos Aires have raised questions as to the government's commitment to public safety. In the months prior to the bombings, anti-Semitic incidents were increasingly common, and most Jewish community landmarks are now heavily fortified.

# Smoking

Many Argentines are heavy smokers, even though most will acknowledge the habit is unhealthy – if lung cancer death rates are not higher than they are, it's only because so many Argentines perish in traffic accidents first. In what might be the ultimate example of 'unclear on the concept', the author once saw a porteño jogger with a lighted *pucho* in his mouth.

Nevertheless, long distance and local buses, the Buenos Aires subway, and some other areas are legally smoke-free, even if enforcement is lax. Under recent municipal legislation, many restaurants and confiterías have set aside smoke-free areas. Travelers bothered by second-hand smoke in an inappropriate setting, such as a taxi, will find it more productive to appeal to common courtesy by pleading *alergia* (allergy) than to get indignant.

# BUSINESS HOURS & HOLIDAYS

Traditionally, business hours commence by 8 am and break at midday for three or even four hours, during which people return home for lunch and a brief siesta. After the siesta, shops reopen until 8 or 9 pm. This schedule is still common in the provinces, but government offices and many Buenos Aires businesses have adopted a more conventional 8 am to 5 pm schedule in the interests of 'greater efficiency' and, especially in the case of government, reduced corruption.

Government offices and businesses are closed on the numerous national holidays which include:

| | |
|---|---|
| January 1 | *Año Nuevo* (New Year's Day) |
| March/April (dates vary) | *Viernes Santo/Pascua* (Good Friday/Easter) |
| May 1 | *Día del Trabajador* (Labor Day) |
| May 25 | *Revolución de Mayo* (May Revolution of 1810) |
| June 10 | *Día de las Malvinas* (Malvinas Day) |
| June 20 | *Día de la Bandera* (Flag Day) |
| July 9 | *Día de la Independencia* (Independence Day) |
| August 17 | *Día de San Martín* (Date of San Martín's death) |
| October 12 | *Día de la Raza* (Columbus Day) |
| December 25 | *Navidad* (Christmas Day) |

# SPECIAL EVENTS

Visitors staying in Buenos Aires for an extended period should ask the Municipal Subsecretaría de Turismo for its annual booklet listing special events in the city; one section covers January through June, while the other covers July through December. It also lists congresses and conventions due to take place in the capital (probably only a handful of readers will be interested in events like the 25th annual plastic-surgery congress).

Restricted to a small area on Av de Mayo between Bolívar and Luis Sáenz Peña, Buenos Aires' annual Carnaval is a very modest celebration by Brazilian standards (even Montevideo's is more impressive), but can be worth a visit if you're in town.

Buenos Aires' annual book fair, the Feria del Libro, attracts more than a million customers during the first three weeks of April; most exhibitors come from Latin America, but by no means all – in 1995, there were displays from England, China, France, Ukraine, Norway, Armenia, and other countries. It takes place at the sprawling Centro Municipal de Exposiciones (☎ 374-1251, ext 208) at Av Figueroa Alcorta and Av Pueyrredón in Recoleta, and is important enough that the President of the country gives the opening address.

# WORK

It is not unusual for visiting travelers to work as English-language instructors in Buenos Aires, but wages are much lower than they would be in the US. Check the classified section of the *Buenos Aires Herald*. Residence and work permits are fairly easy to obtain, but the effort may not be worth it.

# Getting There & Away

Buenos Aires has a bewildering variety of transportation options. Space limitations preclude very detailed air and bus schedules, but information is fairly easy to come by. Most daily newspapers, including the English-language *Buenos Aires Herald*, publish lists of arriving and departing international flights. Bus services are very frequent to most major domestic destinations, and there are also ferry and hydrofoil services across the Río de la Plata to Uruguay.

## AIR

Buenos Aires' Aeropuerto Internacional Ministro Pistarini (commonly known as Ezeiza) has excellent connections from North America, Europe, the UK and Australia/New Zealand, plus feasible, if more costly, routes from southern Africa across the Atlantic via Brazil. Some regional flights use Aeroparque Jorge Newbery, a short distance from downtown Buenos Aires.

There are often significant seasonal discounts, so try to avoid peak travel times such as Christmas/New Year's or Holy Week. Advance purchase of a ticket for a given period of time, usually less than six months, usually provides the best, most flexible deal.

Advance Purchase Excursion (Apex) tickets must be bought well before departure, but they can be a good deal for travelers who know exactly where they will be going and how long they will be staying. Such tickets have minimum- and maximum-stay requirements, rarely allow stopovers, and are difficult or impossible to modify without incurring monetary penalties.

Valid for 12 months, economy-class (Y) tickets have the greatest flexibility within their time period. However, travelers who try to extend their stay beyond a year will have to pay the difference of any price increase in the interim.

Discount fares are often available from travel agents but are less common in Latin America; they do exist between Buenos Aires and Santiago, Chile, however. One of the cheapest means of getting to South America is via courier flights, in which travelers surrender all or part of their baggage allowance and accompany business equipment or documents in return for a highly discounted fare. The major drawbacks, in addition to being limited to carry-on baggage, are the relatively

72

short travel period and the very limited number of gateway airports in Europe and North America.

Some travelers take advantage of Round the World (RTW) fares to visit widely separated places (for example, in Asia and South America) on the same trip. For example, a Qantas-Aerolíneas Argentinas ticket lets travelers circle the globe with stops in New Zealand, Europe and Southeast Asia, but Aerolíneas has similar RTW agreements with Air New Zealand, British Airways, Cathay Pacific, KLM, Singapore Airlines, and Thai Airways International. The Aerolíneas-British Airways ticket allows one side trip in South America and another in Europe.

International passengers leaving from Ezeiza pay a US$13 departure tax, also payable in local currency. On flights of less than 300 km to neighboring countries, such as Uruguay, the tax is only US$5.

## Airline Offices

Many major international airlines have Buenos Aires offices or representatives. Most of the following serve Ezeiza for long-distance international flights, but a few from neighboring countries use Aeroparque.

**Aeroflot**
Av Santa Fe 816/822
☎ 312-5573

**Aerolíneas Argentinas**
Paseo Colón 185
☎ 343-2071, 343-2089
Perú 2
☎ 343-8551, 343-8559

**Aero Perú**
Av Santa Fe 840
☎ 311-6431

**Air France**
Av Santa Fe 963
☎ 327-0202

**Alitalia**
Suipacha 1111, 28th floor
☎ 321-8421

**All Nippon Airways**
Av Córdoba 679, 1st floor
Oficina 113
☎ 314-1600

**American Airlines**
Av Santa Fe 881
☎ 312-3640

**Avianca**
Carlos Pellegrini 1163
4th floor
☎ 394-5990

**British Airways**
Av Córdoba 650
☎ 325-1059

**Canadian Airlines International**
Av Córdoba 656
☎ 322-3732

**Cubana de Aviación**
Sarmiento 552, 11th floor

**Iberia**
Carlos Pellegrini 1163
1st floor
☎ 327-2739, 327-2752

**Japan Airlines**
Av Córdoba 836
11th floor
☎ 393-1896

**KLM**
Reconquista 559, 5th floor
☎ 480-9470

**Korean Air**
Av Córdoba 669, 3rd floor
Oficina B
☎ 311-9237

**Ladeco**
Av Santa Fe 920
☎ 326-9937

**LanChile**
Paraguay 609, 1st floor
☎ 311-5334

**Lapsa (Air Paraguay)**
Cerrito 1026
☎ 393-1527

**Lloyd Aéreo Boliviano**
Carlos Pellegrini 141
☎ 326-3595, 326-6411

**Lufthansa**
MT de Alvear 636
☎ 319-0600

**Malaysia Airlines**
Suipacha 1111, 14th floor
☎ 312-6971

**Pluna (Líneas Aéreas Uruguayas)**
Florida 1
☎ 342-4420

**Saeta**
Cerrito 1026
☎ 393-1527

**Swissair**
Av Santa Fe 846
☎ 319-0000

**TAP (Air Portugal)**
Cerrito 1146
☎ 811-0984

**Trans Brasil**
Florida 780
☎ 394-8424

**United Airlines**
Carlos Pellegrini 1165
5th floor
☎ 326-9111

**Varig**
Florida 630
☎ 329-9200, 329-9201

**Vasp**
Av Santa Fe 784
☎ 311-2699

**Viasa**
Carlos Pellegrini 1163
1st floor
☎ 326-5082

## To/From the USA

The principal gateways are Miami, New York and Los Angeles. Aerolíneas Argentinas is the national carrier, but other airlines serving Buenos Aires include All Nippon Airways, American Airlines, British Airways, Japan Airlines, Korean Air, Ladeco, Lloyd Aéreo Boliviano, United Airlines and Varig.

Líneas Aéreas Paraguayas (Lapsa or Air Paraguay, ☎ (800) 795-2772 in North America) is traditionally a budget carrier, but its recent acquisition by the Ecuadorian airline Saeta may alter this focus; US domestic carriers usually connect with Lapsa in Miami. As of mid-1995, it was still offering a US$545 roundtrip, valid for 45 days, between Miami and Buenos Aires.

AeroPerú (☎ (800) 777-7717 in North America) offers a Visit South America fare that includes a return flight from the US to Lima, and six coupons for flights within the continent to any of the following: Buenos Aires, Guayaquil, La Paz, Rio de Janeiro, Santiago and São Paulo. Valid for 60 days and available only in the USA, low-season tickets cost US$1099 from Miami, US$1299 from Los Angeles. High-season tickets (from July 1 to August 1 and December 15 to January 15) cost US$200 more.

Most major airlines have ticket 'consolidators' offering substantial discounts on fares to Latin America, but things change so frequently that even weekly newspaper listings are soon out of date. Among the best sources of information on cheap tickets are the Sunday travel pages of major US newspapers, such as the *New York Times*, *Los Angeles Times* or *San Francisco Examiner*. Travelers can also check the local affiliate of the Council on International Education & Exchange (CIEE or Council Travel) or the Student Travel Network (STA); student status is not necessary to take advantage of their services.

Council Travel (☎ (800) 226-8624 in the USA) has agencies are in the following cities:

**Berkeley, CA**
2486 Channing Way
☎ (510) 848-8604

**Boston, MA**
Suite 201, 729 Boylston St
☎ (617) 266-1926

**La Jolla, CA**
UCSD Student Center
B-023
☎ (619) 452-0630

**Los Angeles, CA**
10904 Lindbrook Drive
☎ (213) 208-3551

**New York, NY**
205 E 42nd St, 16th floor
☎ (212) 661-1450

**Pacific Beach, CA**
943 Garnett Ave
☎ (619) 270-6401

**San Francisco, CA**
530 Bush St
☎ (415) 421-3473

**Seattle, WA**
1314 NE 43rd St
Suite 210
☎ (206) 632-2448

Student Travel Network (STA, ☎ (800) 825-3001) has offices in the following cities:

**Boston, MA**
297 Newbury St
☎ (617) 266-6014

**Chicago, IL**
429 S Dearborn St
☎ (312) 786-9050

**Los Angeles, CA**
7202 Melrose Ave
☎ (213) 934-8722

**New York, NY**
10 Downing St
☎ (212) 627-3111

| | |
|---|---|
| **Philadelphia, PA** | **Seattle, WA** |
| 3730 Walnut St | 4341 University Way NE |
| ☎ (215) 382-2928 | ☎ (206) 633-5000 |
| | |
| **San Francisco, CA** | **Washington, DC** |
| 51 Grant Ave | 2401 Pennsylvania Ave |
| ☎ (415) 391-8407 | Suite G |
| | ☎ (202) 887-0912 |

In the USA, New York and Miami are the only choices for courier flights to South America. For the widest selection of destinations, try Now Voyager (☎ (212) 431-1616, fax 334-5253), 74 Varick St, Suite 307, New York, NY 10013; Air Facility (☎ (718) 712-0630) or Travel Courier (☎ (718) 738-9000) in New York; Linehaul Services (☎ (305) 477-0651) in Miami; or Discount Travel International (☎ (305) 538-1616) in Miami or (☎ (212) 362-3636, fax 362-3236), 169 W 81st St, New York, NY 10024.

For up-to-date information on courier and other budget fares, send US$5 for the latest newsletter or US$25 for a year's suscription from Travel Unlimited, PO Box 1058, Allston, MA 02134. Another source of information is the *Air Courier Bulletin* of the International Association of Air Travel Couriers (☎ (407) 582-8320), 8 South J St, PO Box 1349, Lake Worth, FL 33460; its US$35 annual membership fee includes the monthly newsletter *Shoestring Traveler* (not related to Lonely Planet).

## To/From Canada

Aerolíneas Argentinas, British Airways and Ladeco serve Montreal, while Aerolíneas Argentinas and Canadian Airlines International fly from Toronto.

Travel Cuts, the Canadian national student travel agency, is the Canadian counterpart of Council Travel and STA. Travel Cuts is located at 171 College St, Toronto, Ontario M5T 1P7 (☎ (416) 977-3703, fax 977-4796).

## To/From Mexico

Aerolíneas Argentinas and Ladeco serve Buenos Aires from Mexico City, and Ladeco also flies from Cancún. Aeroperú, American, Cubana and Lloyd Aéreo Boliviano provide less direct services.

## To/From the UK & Europe

Direct services to Buenos Aires are available with Aeroflot, Aerolíneas Argentinas, Air France, Alitalia, British Airways, Iberia, KLM, Lufthansa, Pluna, Swissair and TAP (Air Portugal).

London's so-called 'bucket shops' can provide the best deals; check out newspapers or magazines such as the Saturday *Independent* or *Time Out* for suggestions. Currently the cheapest fares from London to Buenos Aires run about £369 one-way, £599 return.

Since bucket shops come and go, it's worth inquiring about their affiliation with the Association of British Travel Agents (ABTA), which will guarantee a refund or alternative if the agent goes out of business. The following are reputable London bucket shops:

**Campus Travel**
52 Grosvenor Gardens
London SW1
☎ (0171) 730-3402

**Journey Latin America**
16 Devonshire Rd
Chiswick, London W4 2HD
☎ (0181) 747-3108

**Passage to South
America**
☎ (0171) 602-9889

**South American
Experience**
47 Causton St
London SW1
☎ (0171) 976-5511

**STA Travel**
86 Old Brompton Rd
London SW7
☎ (0171) 937-9962

117 Euston Rd
London NW1 2XF

**Trailfinders**
194 Kensington High St
London W8
☎ (0171) 938-3939

42-50 Earls Court Rd
London W8
☎ (0171) 938-3366

In Berlin, check out the magazine *Zitty* for bargain-fare ads. In Berlin and other European capitals, the following agencies are good possibilities for bargain fares:

**France**
Council Travel, 31 Rue
Saint Augustine
Paris 2ème
☎ 1-42.66.20.87

Council Travel, Rue des
Pyramides, Paris 1er
☎ 1-44.55.55.44

**Germany**
Alternativ Tours
Wilmersdorferstrasse 94
Berlin
☎ 030-881-2089

SRID Reisen
Bergerstrasse 1178
Frankfurt
☎ 069-43-01-91

**Ireland**
USIT Travel Office
19 Aston Quay
Dublin
☎ 01-679-8833

**Italy**
CTS, Via Genova 16
Rome
☎ 06-46 791

**Netherlands**
NBBS, Rokin 38
Amsterdam
☎ 020-642-0989

Malibu Travel, Damrak 30
Amsterdam
☎ 020-623-6814

**Spain**
TIVE, Calle José Ortega y
Gasset, Madrid
☎ 91-401-1300

**Switzerland**
SSR, Leonhardstrasse
5 & 10, Zürich
☎ 01-261-2956

The only apparent courier flights from Europe are to Rio de Janeiro; Courier Travel Service (☎ (0171) 351-0300), 346 Fulham Rd, London SW10 9UH charges £425 for a 28-day return fare.

## To/From Australia & New Zealand

The most direct service is Aerolíneas Argentinas' weekly transpolar flight from Sydney via Auckland, which is an obvious connection for buyers of the Qantas-Aerolíneas RTW fare. Otherwise, LanChile's trans-Pacific flights to Santiago have ready connections to Buenos Aires, but some travelers have found it cheaper to go via London or Los Angeles.

For travelers starting in Australia, the combined Qantas-Aerolíneas Argentinas ticket allows stopovers in Auckland, London, Paris, Bahrain, Singapore and other cities, but you must arrange the itinerary in advance. The price for the Aerolíneas-Qantas ticket is A$3000 in Sydney or US$3124 in Buenos Aires (the latter figure represents about 15% more than the former, so it is cheaper to buy in Australia).

STA Travel is a good place to inquire for bargain air fares; again, student status is not necessary to use their services.

**Adelaide**
Level 4, the Arcade
Union House
Adelaide University
☎ 08-223-6620, 08-223-6244

**Brisbane**
Shop 25 & 26
Brisbane Arcade
111-117 Adelaide St
Brisbane 4000
☎ 07-221-3722

**Canberra**
Arts Centre, GPO Box 4
ANU, Canberra 0200
☎ 06-247-0800

**Hobart**
Ground Floor
Union Building

University of Tasmania
Hobart 7005
☎ 002-243-496

**Melbourne**
220 Faraday St
Carlton 3053
☎ 03-9347-6911

**Perth**
1st Floor, New Guild
Building
University of West
Australia
Crawley 6009
☎ 09-380-2302

**Sydney**
1st Floor, 732 Harris St
Ultimo 2007
☎ 02-212-1255

## To/From Asia & Africa

Carriers serving Buenos Aires directly from Asia, usu-ally via North America, include All Nippon Airways (with Aerolíneas Argentinas), Japan Airlines and Korean Air. Varig and Vasp also have good connections via Rio de Janeiro or São Paulo.

Malaysia Airlines flies twice weekly from Kuala Lumpur to Buenos Aires via Cape Town and Johannes-burg. South Africa Airways flies weekly from Johan-nesburg to Buenos Aires via Rio de Janeiro or São Paulo.

## To/From Neighboring Countries

Air connections with Chile, Bolivia, Paraguay, Brazil and Uruguay are primarily but not exclusively via capital cities.

**Chile** Many airlines fly between Ezeiza and Santiago, a route on which discount tickets are available.

**Bolivia** La Paz is the principal destination, but some flights continue to Santa Cruz de la Sierra. Aerolíneas also flies to Santa Cruz via Córdoba and Salta. Lloyd Aéreo Boliviano flies to Santa Cruz and Cochabamba, and to Santa Cruz and La Paz.

**Paraguay** Asunción is Paraguay's only air connection with Buenos Aires; flights leave from both Aeropuerto Jorge Newbery (Aeroparque) and Ezeiza. The only direct carriers are Aerolíneas Argentinas and Lapsa, though many other South American airlines pass through Asunción.

**Brazil** From Ezeiza, Rio de Janeiro and São Paulo are the main destinations for many airlines, but Aerolíneas also offers flights from Ezeiza to Porto Alegre and Flori-anópolis. In addition, it flies from Aeroparque to Rio and São Paulo, both direct and via Córdoba.

**Uruguay** There are numerous flights from Aeroparque to Montevideo, while a few long-distance international flights continue from Ezeiza to Montevideo. From Aeroparque, the only other Uruguayan destinations are Punta del Este and Colonia del Sacramento.

## Domestic & Regional Air Routes

Argentine air traffic, routes and fares have undergone a major transformation since the privatization of Aero-líneas Argentinas, which handles domestic as well as international routes, and Austral, which handles domestic routes only. While these two airlines have the most extensive services, some existing secondary airlines have expanded routes, and others have come into existence, undercutting the very high existing fare structure of the established carriers. Apparently in response, Aerolíneas and Austral have introduced a supplementary fare system that offers cheaper alternatives with some restrictions.

Nearly all domestic and some regional flights leave from Aeroparque Jorge Newbery, a short distance north of downtown, but a few depart from Ezeiza. To Uruguay, in particular, services from Aeroparque are cheaper and more efficient than the major international airlines at Ezeiza.

Argentine domestic flights carry a departure tax of about US$3, which is not included in the price of the ticket.

**Aerolíneas Argentinas** This airline has extensive domestic and international routes. Paseo Colón 185 in Monserrat (☎ 343-2071, 343-2089) or Perú 2 also in Monserrat (☎ 343-8551, 343-8559).

**Austral Líneas Aéreas** Close partners Austral and Aerolíneas share an identical fare structure. Both serve nearly every major Argentine city between Bolivia and the Beagle Channel. Corrientes 485 in the microcentro (☎ 325-0777).

**Dinar Líneas Aéreas** This new airline flies to the northwestern Argentine destinations of Tucumán, Salta, and Jujuy. Fares are lower than Aerolíneas' or Austral's, but capacity is limited. Diagonal Roque Sáenz Peña 933 in Monserrat (☎ 326-0135).

**Líneas Aéreas del Estado (LADE)** The Air Force's commercial service serves Patagonian destinations exclusively. Perú 710 in San Telmo (☎ 361-0583).

**Líneas Aéreas de Entre Ríos (LAER)** This airline flies to Mesopotamia, Santa Fe, La Pampa, and coastal Buenos Aires province. 5th floor, Carlos Pellegrini 1055 in Retiro (☎ 328-3932).

**Líneas Aéreas Privadas Argentinas (LAPA)** LAPA has acquired many new planes and expanded routes to compete with Aerolíneas and Austral. Its capacity is still much smaller than its competitors, and flights are often booked far in advance. Also provides regional services to Colonia and Montevideo, Uruguay. MT de Alvear 790 in Recoleta (☎ 314-1005).

**Sapse Líneas Aéreas** This airline flies smaller planes to coastal Buenos Aires province and Patagonia. Fares are slightly more than half those of the larger airlines, but the limited number of flights are usually heavily booked. Tucumán 1920 (☎ 371-7066).

**Transporte Aéreo Costa Atlántica (TACA)** TACA flies small planes to Atlantic coastal destinations in summer. Bernardo de Irigoyen 1370, 1st floor, in San Telmo (☎ 307-1956).

## Fares

The cost of domestic flights has risen dramatically in recent years. One alternative on some airlines is *banda negativa*, in which limited seats on a selected list of flights every month are available for discounts of about 40%. These are often but not always night flights and require advance purchase, but they are excellent bargains. Ask about other discount fares available through advance purchase, and to the cities of Córdoba and Mendoza.

## BUS

Buenos Aires' massive Estación Terminal de Omnibus is at Av Antártida Argentina and Ramos Mejía in Retiro, a short distance from Retiro train station. Its Centro de Informes y Reclamos (☎ 313-9594), Oficina 29 on the 2nd floor, provides general bus information and also monitors the taxis that serve the terminal; direct any complaint about taxi drivers to them.

Each of Retiro's hundred-plus bus companies has a desk resembling an airline ticket counter (some of them shared), from which it issues tickets to both national and international destinations. Discounted tickets are less prevalent than in the past, but student and university identification can still sometimes yield a reduction of 20% on any fare except special promotions.

Space prohibits more than the following representative sample of daily departures; for more detailed information, phone or visit the terminal. To the most popular destinations, departures are frequent and reservations are normally not necessary except during peak summer and winter holiday seasons, but purchasing your ticket a day ahead of time is still not a bad idea.

General Urquiza (☎ 313-2771) has nightly service to Montevideo (US$25, nine hours). La Internacional (☎ 313-3167) has regular buses to Asunción, Paraguay (21 hours), via the Gran Chaco towns of Formosa and Clorinda for US$56 regular, US$78 for more comfortable *servicio diferencial* or US$95 for *coche cama* sleepers. Nuestra Señora de la Asunción (☎ 313-2325) and Chevallier Paraguaya (☎ 313-2349) have comparable service and prices.

Pluma (☎ 313-3839) goes to Brazilian destinations, including Foz do Iguaçu (US$60, 19 hours), Porto Alegre (US$71, 21 hours), Florianópolis (US$85, 26 hours), Camboriú (US$90, 27 hours), Curitiba (US$95, 35 hours), São Paulo (US$101, 42 hours) and Rio de Janeiro (US$117, 48 hours). Rápido Yguazú (☎ 313-4139) also serves Brazilian routes.

Several companies cross the Andes to Santiago, Chile (US$60, 21 hours): TAC (☎ 313-2627), Chevallier (☎ 313-3288), and Fénix Pullman Norte (☎ 313-0134), the latter with connections to the Peruvian border at Arica. El Rápido Internacional (☎ 315-0804), Expreso Ormeño (☎ 313-2259) and Tepsa (☎ 27-6591) all have direct connections to Lima (US$160, 80 hours).

# TRAIN

There are no international rail services to or from Argentina.

Private operators have recently assumed control of the profitable freight service on the erstwhile state-owned railways, but they have shown no interest in providing passenger service except on the commuter lines described above. The provinces of Buenos Aires, Río Negro, Chubut, Tucumán and La Pampa continue to provide reduced long-distance passenger service.

The Mitre line operates from Estación Retiro, the Roca line from Estación Constitución, and the Sarmiento line from Estación Once de Setiembre (popularly known as 'Once'). Administered by the provinces of Buenos Aires and Río Negro, the Ferrocarril Roca (☎ 304-0035) serves the Atlantic beach resort of Mar del Plata, other destinations in Buenos Aires province, and northern Patagonia as far as Bariloche, in Río Negro province. Operated by the province of Tucumán, the Ferrocarril Mitre (☎ 312-6596) goes to Rosario, Santiago del Estero and Tucumán. The Ferrocarril Sarmiento (☎ 861-0041), though primarily a commuter line, still links the capital to Santa Rosa, in La Pampa province.

Classes of service range from the rigid bench seats of *turista* (tourist or 2nd class) to comfortable *coche cama* or *dormitorio* sleeper compartments. During holiday periods such as Christmas and around Independence Day (July 9), it is very important to buy tickets as far in advance as possible because train fares are still lower than bus fares on comparable routes.

# CAR & MOTORCYCLE

Although Argentina is self-sufficient in oil, the price of *nafta* (petrol) has risen to world levels at about US$0.80 per liter, although *gas-oil* (diesel fuel) is only about one-third of that. Unleaded fuel is widely available in provincial capitals and along main paved routes in the central part of the country, but it can still be difficult to find off the beaten track. The situation is improving as more vehicles using unleaded come on the market. In some areas, notably Buenos Aires province, tolls on recently privatized highways are very high – as much as US$4 per 100 km.

Although motorcycles have become fashionable among some Argentines, they are expensive and the author has never seen any place that rents them in Argentina. Motorcycle helmets are now obligatory.

## Documents & Insurance

Formally, Argentina requires an International or Inter-American Driving Permit to supplement your national or state driver's license. In practice, police rarely examine these documents closely and generally ignore the latter. Drivers must carry their title document (*tarjeta verde* or 'green card'; for foreign vehicles, customs permission is the acceptable substitute), triangular emergency reflectors (*valizas*), and one-kilo fire extinguishers. Headrests are also required for the driver and each passenger.

Liability insurance is obligatory, and police may ask to see proof of insurance at checkpoints. Fortunately, unlike many services in Argentina, it is reasonably priced; a four-month policy with US$1 million in coverage costs as little as US$90 (paid in cash) and is also valid, with slightly reduced coverage, in the neighboring countries of Chile, Bolivia, Paraguay, Brazil and Uruguay. Among reputable insurers are Seguros Belgrano, Seguros Rivadavia, and the Automóvil Club Argentino (ACA).

## Road Rules & Hazards

Anyone considering driving in Argentina should know that many Argentine drivers are reckless, aggressive and even willfully dangerous, ignoring speed limits, road signs and even traffic signals. Traffic accidents are the main cause of death for Argentines between the ages of five and 35.

Tailgating is a serious hazard – it is not unusual to see half a dozen cars a meter or less apart, waiting for their chance to overtake a truck which itself may be exceeding the speed limit. During the Pampas harvest season, pay particular attention to slow-moving farm machinery which, though not a hazard in its own right, brings out the worst in impatient Argentine motorists. Night driving is inadvisable, in some regions because of animals on the road but more often because of drivers who seem to believe they can see in the dark and, consequently, disdain headlights.

Argentine police contribute almost nothing toward traffic safety. In fact you will rarely see police patrolling the highways, where high-speed, head-on crashes are common, but you will meet them at major intersections and roadside checkpoints where they conduct meticulous document and equipment checks. If one of these policemen asks to check your turn signals (which almost no Argentine bothers to use), brake lights or handbrake, it may well be a warning of corruption in progress. Equipment violations carry fines up to US$200 but are most commonly pretexts for graft – if you are uncertain about your rights, state in a very matter-of-fact manner your intention to contact your embassy or consulate. Offer a *coima* (bribe) only if you are confident that it is 'appropriate' and unavoidable.

## Automóvil Club Argentino

If you drive in Argentina, especially in your own car, it may be worthwhile to join the Automóvil Club Argentino (ACA), which has offices, service stations and garages throughout the country, offering free road service and towing in and around major cities. ACA also recognizes members of overseas affiliates, such as the American Automobile Association (AAA), as equivalent to its own members and grants them the same privileges, including discounts on maps, accommodations, camping, tours and other services. Membership costs about US$30 per month, which is more expensive than most of its overseas counterparts.

ACA's head office (☎ 802-6061) is at Av del Libertador 1850 in the barrio of Palermo.

# BICYCLE

Bicycling is an interesting, inexpensive alternative for getting to Argentina. Racing bicycles are suitable for some paved roads, but these are often narrow; a *todo terreno* (mountain bike) would be safer and more convenient, allowing you to use the unpaved shoulder and the very extensive network of graveled roads throughout the country. Bicycling is an increasingly popular recreational activity among Argentines, and Argentine bicycles are improving in quality, but are still not equal to their counterparts in Europe or North America.

There two major drawbacks to cycling in Argentina. One is the wind, which can slow your progress to a crawl. Argentine motorists, with total disregard of anyone but themselves, are the other. On many of the country's straight, narrow, two-lane highways, they can be a real hazard to bicyclists.

WAYNE BERNHARDSON

Sculpture by Yoel Novoa, Centro Cultural San Martín

# HITCHHIKING

Along with Chile, Argentina is probably the best country to *hacer dedo* in all of South America. The major drawback is that Argentine vehicles are often stuffed with families and children, but truckers will frequently take backpackers. At *servicentros* at the outskirts of large Argentine cities, where they gas up their vehicles, it is often worthwhile soliciting a ride. Hitchhiking is never entirely safe and we don't recommend it. Travellers who do decide to hitch should understand the risks involved. When possible go in pairs, or let someone know what your plans are.

# BOAT

Buenos Aires has regular ferry and hydrofoil *(aliscafo)* service to Colonia, Uruguay, with bus combinations to Montevideo, as well as directly to Montevideo. These sail from Dársena Norte, near downtown at Madero and Viamonte, or from Dársena Sur, Av Pedro de Mendoza 20 in La Boca. There is now a US$10 departure tax from these terminals. For more information on these services, see the Montevideo and Colonia sections in the Excursions chapter.

Cacciola (☎ 749-0329), at Lavalle 520 in the riverside suburb of Tigre, goes daily to Carmelo, Uruguay, at 8 am and 3:30 pm for US$11; children pay US$7.50. Movilán/Deltanave (☎ 749-4119) also goes to Carmelo, at 8:30 am and 3:30 pm. Línea Nueva Palmira (☎ 749-0537) goes to Nueva Palmira, Uruguay, daily at 7 am except Mondays, when it leaves at 4:30 am.

# TRAVEL AGENTS

ASATEJ (☎ 311-6953, fax 311-6840), Argentina's non-profit student travel agency, is on the 3rd floor, Oficina 319-B, at Florida 835 in Retiro; it's the Argentine affiliate of STA Travel. Open weekdays from 11 am to 7 pm, it has the cheapest airfares available (the US$159 roundtrip to Santiago, Chile, is only slightly more than the equivalent bus fare). The agency also publishes a brochure of discount offers at hotels, restaurants and other businesses throughout the country for holders of international student cards.

Another youth- and student-oriented travel agency is the Asociación Argentina de Albergues de la Juventud (☎/fax 476-1001), 2nd floor, Oficina 6, Talcahuano 214, 1013 Buenos Aires. It issues hostel memberships and international student cards, and has a message board for travelers (mostly young Argentines) seeking companions for extended trips.

American Express (☎ 312-0900, fax 315-1866), Arenales 707 north of Plaza San Martín, will cash its own travelers' checks without additional commission, and offers many other services. Reader-recommended Swan Turismo (☎ 311-3537 or fax 311-3537), Viamonte 464 in the microcentro, will help renegotiate air passes and make connections with LADE or other airlines for which timetables are not easily available outside the country.

# WARNING

The information in this chapter is particularly vulnerable to change: prices for international travel are volatile, routes are introduced and cancelled, schedules change, special deals come and go, and rules and visa requirements are amended. Airlines and governments seem to take a perverse pleasure in making price structures and regulations as complicated as possible. You should check directly with the airline or a travel agent to make sure you understand how a fare (and ticket you may buy) works. In addition, the travel industry is highly competitive and there are many lurks and perks.

The upshot of this is that you should get opinions, quotes and advice from a s many airlines and travel agents as possible before you part with your hard-earned cash. The details given in the chapter should be regarded as pointers and are not a substitute for your own careful, up-to-date research.

# Getting Around

## TO/FROM THE AIRPORT

Buenos Aires has two airports. Nearly all domestic flights and some to neighboring countries leave from Aeroparque Jorge Newbery (☎ 771-2071), on the Costanera Av Rafael Obligado, only a few kilometers north of downtown in Palermo. Aeropuerto Internacional Ministro Pistarini (commonly known as 'Ezeiza', ☎ 480-0235), the international airport, is about 35 km south of downtown.

The cheapest alternatives to Aeroparque Jorge Newbery are city buses No 37C ('Ciudad Universitaria') from Plaza Italia in Palermo; No 45 northbound from Constitución, Plaza San Martín or Retiro, as well as intermediate points; and No 160B from Av Las Heras or Plaza Italia (US$0.50).

To Ezeiza, the cheapest alternative is the No 86 bus (US$1; be sure it says 'Ezeiza', since not all No 86s go to the end-of-the-line airport), which starts in La Boca and comes up Av de Mayo past the Plaza del Congreso. The more comfortable 'Servicio Diferencial', which costs about US$5, guarantees a seat. Theoretically neither allows very bulky luggage; normal backpacks and suitcases are OK, but for a judicious tip you should be able to take almost anything. Because of heavy traffic, figure at least 1½ hours to Ezeiza.

Manuel Tienda León (☎ 314-3636, 314-2577), Av Santa Fe 790 in Retiro, runs a comfortable and efficient service to Ezeiza (US$14 one-way, about 45 minutes depending on traffic) in buses and minibuses, depending on demand, and also offers hotel pickup. Regular services start at 4 and 5 am, continuing half-hourly until 11 pm. Hours for return services are 6:30 am to 9:30 pm. Manuel Tienda León service to Aeroparque starts at 7:10 am, then continues half-hourly to 10:10 pm. Return service starts at 7:50 am and stops at 10:50 pm.

Taxis to Ezeiza cost about US$30, plus a US$2 surcharge for using the *autopista* (freeway), but they may end up being cheaper than Manuel Tienda León if you have a group of three or four – try to negotiate with the driver. The Ministerio de Economía y Obras y Servicios Públicos issues a list of authorized taxi fares from Ezeiza. Taxis to Aeroparque cost about US$6 from downtown.

# BUS

Buenos Aires has a large and complex bus system serving the entire Capital Federal and Gran Buenos Aires. One of the best guides is the *Guia Peuser*, which details nearly 200 different routes and includes a foldout map. It's for sale at nearly all kiosks and bookstores. Another excellent guide is the *Capital Federal y Gran Buenos Aires* (Ediciones Lumi, Buenos Aires, 1994, commonly known as the 'Guía Lumi'), which comes in a slightly larger but very convenient wire-binder format. However, not all No 60 buses, for example, go all the way to Tigre, nor do all No 86 buses go to Ezeiza – check the sign in the window for their ultimate destinations.

Many porteños have memorized the system and can instantly tell you which bus to take and where to get off for a particular destination.

Unlike the Subte, fares depend on distance – when you board, tell the driver where you're going and he will charge you accordingly. Most buses now have automatic ticket machines, which also make small change. Drivers are usually polite enough to give warning of your stop. If not, or if you find yourself standing at the back of a crowded bus, ask other passengers for help. Anyone taller than Napoleon or Carlos Menem will have to bend over to see out the windows.

Like other porteño motorists, bus drivers are fast and ruthless, and accidents are not unusual. Hang on tight!

WAYNE BERNHARDSON

# TRAIN

Despite reductions in long-distance train service, local rail lines continue to serve most of Gran Buenos Aires. From Retiro, Ferrovías (the former Belgrano Norte line, ☎ 314-1444) goes to the city's northern suburbs, as does TMS Transporte Metropolitano General San Martín (☎ 772-5013). From Constitución, Transportes Metropolitanos General Roca (TMR, ☎ 304-0021) reaches the southern suburbs as far as the city of La Plata. Metrovías (ex-Ferrocarril Urquiza, ☎ 553-9214) runs the northwestern lines from Estación Federico Lacroze, at the terminus of Línea B of the Subte, while the Ferrocarril Sarmiento (☎ 861-0041) serves outlying southwestern districts from Estación Once (Subte Plaza Miserere Línea A). The Urquiza and Belgrano lines also run some tourist excursions in Buenos Aires province.

# UNDERGROUND

On Buenos Aires' oldest Subte line, starting at Plaza de Mayo, the tarnished elegance of the tiled stations and the worn vintage woodwork of the cars offer a distant reminder of the city's 'Belle Epoque'. South America's oldest underground railway is still quick and efficient, but it serves only a relatively small part of a city that has sprawled to be many times larger than when the system opened in 1913. Several of the stations, most notably Línea D between Catedral and Palermo, have impressive murals.

A private operator, Metrovías (☎ 553-9214 for complaints and comments between 10 am and 6 pm weekdays) has recently assumed operation of the system and promises improvements in cleanliness, security and emergency assistance. One of the first visible signs of progress is the introduction of comfortable new Japanese cars on Línea B, which runs under Av Corrientes. The company also intends to restore the magnificent tile artwork in many older stations. Note, however, that the doors on the vintage cars of Línea A do not always close automatically.

The Subte consists of five lines, each identified alphabetically (Líneas A, B, C, D and E). Four of these run from downtown to the capital's western and northern outskirts, while the other (Línea C) connects the two major train stations of Retiro and Constitución.

**Línea A** runs from Plaza de Mayo, under Av Rivadavia, to Primera Junta.
**Línea B** runs from LN Alem, under Av Corrientes, to Federico Lacroze, the station for the Ferrocarril Urquiza.

**Línea C** runs between the major train stations of Retiro and Constitución, with transfer stations for all other lines.

**Línea D** runs from Catedral, on the Plaza de Mayo, with a recent extension past Palermo to Ministro Carranza, at the junction of Av Cabildo and Av Dorrego.

**Línea E** runs from Bolívar, on the Av de Mayo, to Plaza de los Virreyes.

Fichas for the Subte cost about US$0.45. To save time and hassle, buy a pocketful, since lines get very backed up during rush hour and even at other times. Trains operate from 5.30 am to 1.30 am and are frequent on weekdays, but weekend waiting time can be considerable; Sunday closing time is much earlier. Backpacks and suitcases are permitted, which allows for convenient connections between Constitución and Retiro stations in particular.

At a few stations, like Alberdi, you can only go in one direction – in this case toward Primera Junta rather than Plaza de Mayo, so you may have to backtrack to reach your ultimate destination. At many stations, platforms are on opposite sides of the station, so make sure of your direction *before* passing through the turnstiles, or you may have to backtrack many stops to reach your destination – unless you prefer to leave and pay an additional fare.

# CAR & MOTORCYCLE

A car is not very useful because congestion is heavy, parking is difficult and expensive, and public transportation is abundant. No sane person would recommend driving in Buenos Aires but, for a price, all the standard rental agencies will let you take your chances. Rates tend to be a bit cheaper here than elsewhere in the country.

To rent a car, you must have a valid driver's license and be at least 21 years of age; some agencies may not rent to anyone younger than 25. It may also be necessary to present a credit card such as MasterCard or Visa.

Even at minor agencies, charges are now very high. The cheapest and smallest vehicles go for about US$27 per day plus US$0.27 per km (customers can sometimes negotiate a lower rate by paying in cash rather than by credit card). Insurance and gasoline are extra. Although unlimited mileage deals do exist, they usually only apply to weekly or longer periods and are very expensive. It's worth trying to make a reservation with one of the major international agencies in your home country, which can sometimes guarantee lower rates.

| AI | MT de Alvear 678 | ☎ 312-9475 |
| Alamo | Florida 375, 2nd floor | ☎ 325-7000 |
| Budget | Santa Fe 869 | ☎ 311-9870 |
| Dollar | Viamonte 611, 11th floor | ☎ 322-8409 |
| Hertz | Ricardo Rojas 451 | ☎ 312-1317 |
| Localiza | Paraguay 1122 | ☎ 375-1611 |

Motorists should be aware that the area bounded by Av Leandro Alem, Av Córdoba, Av de Mayo and Av 9 de Julio is off-limits to private motor vehicles, except for buses, taxis and delivery vans, weekdays between 7 am and 7 pm. Fines are stiff.

## TAXI & REMISE

Buenos Aires' numerous, reasonably priced taxis are conspicuous due to their black-and-yellow paint jobs. They are reasonably priced, and all are now digitally metered. It costs about US$1 to drop the flag and another US$0.10 per 100 meters. Drivers are generally polite and honest, but there are exceptions; be sure the meter is set at zero. If you're carrying a large amount of luggage, there may be a small charge in addition to the metered amount. Drivers do not expect a big tip, but it's customary to let them keep small change.

Remises are radio taxis without meters that generally offer fixed fares within a given zone and are an increasingly popular form of transportation that is slightly cheaper than ordinary taxis. Unlike taxis, they may not cruise the city in search of fares.

When it rains, demand is high and taxis can be hard to find, so you may have to wait out the storm in a confitería.

## WALKING

Its lack of hills helps make Buenos Aires a good walker's city; in the congested downtown, foot traffic often moves faster than vehicles. The most pleasant areas to explore on foot are San Telmo, La Boca, Recoleta and Barrio Norte, and the parks of Palermo and Belgrano. Walking can be exhausting, however, in the summer heat.

## BOAT

Rowboats (US$0.50) carry those passengers who don't care to walk across the high bridge over the Riachuelo, from La Boca to the industrial suburb of Avellaneda, in Buenos Aires province.

# ORGANIZED TOURS

Many agencies offer half-day and full-day city tours, but unless your time is very limited try to get around on your own. The Dirección General de Turismo (☎ 371-1496, 476-3612), in the Centro Cultural San Martín at Sarmiento 1551, offers free and very worthwhile (though often crowded) guided tours (in Spanish only) of city barrios on Saturdays and Sundays at 5 pm in summer, 3 pm the rest of the year. Phone for information or drop by to pick up a monthly list of their theme-oriented offerings, which meet at a given point to explore areas such as San Telmo, Palermo's parks and lakes, and Parque Lezama.

Buenos Aires Tur (☎ 371-2304), Lavalle 1444, Oficina 16, in Corrientes, offers city tours (US$14) by bus that visit locations in Palermo, Recoleta, the microcentro, San Telmo and La Boca. These take place daily at 9:30 am and 2:30 pm, Sundays at 2 pm only. Other tours include afternoon visits to Tigre and the Delta (US$29; with lunch included US$60) and a gaucho fiesta in the province of Buenos Aires (US$60). Buenos Aires Visión (☎ 394-2986), Esmeralda 356, 8th floor, in the microcentro has similar itineraries and also arranges excursions to La Plata.

# Things to See & Do

Most porteños 'belong' to a barrio where they have spent almost all their lives. The majority of the capital's 47 barrios are of relatively little interest to tourists, but a handful of them contain most of the capital's key attractions. This guide is organized around these barrios, which are defined in the Orientation section in the Facts for the Visitor chapter. Visitors would do well to familiarize themselves with the core barrios for orientation purposes.

Note that most museums charge about US$1 admission, but they are usually free of charge on Wednesdays or Thursdays. Many close in January and February, when most porteños take their holidays in Mar del Plata.

## AVENIDA DE MAYO & THE MICROCENTRO

Juan de Garay refounded Buenos Aires in 1580, about 1½ kilometers north of Pedro de Mendoza's presumed encampment near Parque Lezama in San Telmo. In accordance with Spanish law, he laid out the large Plaza del Fuerte (Fortress Plaza), later called the Plaza del Mercado (Market Plaza). The name was changed to Plaza de la Victoria after the victory over British invaders in 1806 and 1807. It acquired its present name of **Plaza de Mayo** after the month in which the Revolution of 1810 occurred.

WAYNE BERNHARDSON

Las Madres maintaining their vigil on the Plaza de Mayo

Major colonial buildings at this site included the **cabildo**, now much reduced and altered from the original construction between 1725 and 1765, and the church, built on a plot now occupied by the **Catedral Metropolitana**. Within the cathedral is the tomb of the repatriated San Martín, who died in France. In the center of the plaza is the **Pirámide de Mayo**, a small obelisk covering an earlier monument, around which the Madres de la Plaza de Mayo still march every Thursday afternoon in their unrelenting campaign for a full accounting of Dirty War atrocities.

At the east end of the plaza, the **Casa Rosada** (Presidential Palace), begun during the presidency of Domingo F Sarmiento, occupies a site where colonial riverbank fortifications once stood. Today it stands more than a kilometer inland as a result of land filling.

### Torcuato de Alvear

For better or worse, no other single person has left a greater imprint on Buenos Aires than its first mayor, Torcuato de Alvear, appointed to the post by President Julio Argentino Roca in 1882. Son of General Carlos de Alvear (a colleague of San Martín), the single-minded Torcuato immediately set out to transform the city from the cozy Gran Aldea to the 'Paris of the South', a world capital to showcase Argentina's international aspirations.

Even those who agreed with Alvear's goals sometimes questioned his methods. Convinced that Buenos Aires' architecture and public spaces should embody greatness, the Francophile mayor sought to replace the congested colonial streets of one-story houses and narrow sidewalks with wide boulevards linking grandiose buildings on expansive plazas. In implementing his plans, he literally allowed nothing to stand in his way: According to one story, when the telephone company was slow to move its lines in the admittedly unsightly Recova Vieja, an arcade crossing the present-day Plaza de Mayo, he personally cut the wires to speed up the demolition work.

The rejuvenated Plaza de Mayo was a triumph, as was the Av de Mayo (begun in 1889 but not completed until 1894, four years after Alvear's death). Not everyone thought highly of his taste, however – one of the signatures of his administration was a series of immense concrete grottos, most since demolished, in public parks throughout the city. He also drew criticism for favoring increasingly affluent northern barrios such as Recoleta and Palermo, while neglecting poorer areas such as San Telmo.

Alvear's egotism did have limits. When a municipal commission suggested renaming Recoleta's much improved Blvd Bella Vista after him, Torcuato at least had the modesty to insist that present-day Av Alvear be named after his father. ■

WAYNE BERNHARDSON

The Casa Rosada has been the center of power
for numerous Argentine presidents.

From the balcony of the Casa Rosada, Juan Perón, General Leopoldo Galtieri, Raúl Alfonsín and other Argentine politicians have convened throngs of impassioned Argentines when they believed a show of public support necessary.

Towering above the Casa Rosada, just south of Parque Colón, military engineers inspired by the Beaux Arts central post office (see below) built the army headquarters at the **Edificio Libertador**, the real locus of Argentine political power for many decades. In 1955, naval aircraft strafed the Casa Rosada and other downtown buildings in the so-called Revolución Libertadora that toppled Perón, while as recently as 1990 dissident junior officers of the so-called *carapintada* movement attempted to seize control of army headquarters and overthrow President Menem.

South of the Plaza de Mayo, bounded by Calles Alsina, Bolívar, Perú and Moreno, the **Manzana de las Luces** (Block of Enlightenment) includes the Jesuit **Iglesia San Ignacio** (1712), a late Baroque-style building that is the city's oldest colonial church. At the corner of Alsina and Defensa, the **Farmacia de la Estrella** is a functioning homeopathic pharmacy with gorgeous woodwork and elaborate turn-of-the-century ceiling murals, depicting health-oriented themes. Upstairs is the **Museo de la Ciudad** (see below).

On the north side of the plaza, the headquarters of the **Banco de la Nación** (1939), at Rivadavia and 25 de Mayo, was the work of famed architect Alejandro Bustillo. Most other public buildings in this area were constructed in the late 19th century, when the Av de Mayo first connected the Casa Rosada with the **Plaza del Congreso** and the **Palacio del Congreso**, obliterating most of the historic and dignified cabildo in the process. British diplomat James Bryce found these developments symbols of progress:

One great thoroughfare, the Av de Mayo, traverses the centre of the city from the large plaza in which the government buildings stand to the still larger and very handsome plaza which is adorned by the palace of the legislature. Fortunately it is wide, and being well planted with trees it is altogether a noble street, statelier than Piccadilly in London, or Unter den Linden in Berlin, or Pennsylvania Avenue in Washington . . . .

The streets are well kept; everything is fresh and bright. The most striking new buildings besides those of the new Legislative Chambers, with their tall and handsome dome, are the Opera-house, the interior of which equals any in Europe, and the Jockey Club, whose scale and elaborate appointments surpass even the club-houses of New York.

Bryce might have been surprised by modern Buenos Aires' faded elegance and failure to keep pace with European and North American capitals, but visitors to the area can still glimpse remnants of the city's 'Belle Epoque', even though the focus of downtown activities has moved north along streets like Florida and Lavalle, and Avs Corrientes, Córdoba and Santa Fe.

In the early part of the century Florida, then closed to motor vehicles between noon and 1:30 pm, was the capital's most fashionable shopping street – a status since lost to Av Santa Fe despite a recent renaissance achieved through the renovation of buildings such as the extraordinary **Galerías Pacífico** near Florida and Av Córdoba. Military privilege has at least guaranteed the pristine maintenance of landmarks like the Beaux Arts **Centro Naval**, across Av Córdoba from the Galerías Pacífico on the border of Retiro.

Today both Florida and perpendicular Lavalle are *peatonals* (pedestrian malls), while demolition of older buildings has created the broad avenues of Corrientes (the main theater district), Córdoba and Santa Fe. Among the most distinguished buildings on Florida, the **Banco de Boston** at the intersection with Diagonal Roque Sáenz Peña features a stone entryway carved in the USA and shipped to Buenos Aires to be mounted on the front of the building. A short distance away, at Roque Sáenz Peña 543, the **Edificio Menéndez-Behety** (1926) was the Buenos Aires headquarters of a Patagonian wool empire that transcended the boundaries of Argentina and Chile.

WAYNE BERNHARDSON

Banco de Boston

At the foot of Corrientes, the massive **Correo Central** (main post office, 1928) entered from Sarmiento, fills an entire block bounded also by Av LN Alem and Bouchard. It took 20 years to complete this impressive and beautifully maintained Beaux Arts structure, originally modeled on the main post office in New York City. The mansard (two-tier) roof was a later addition.

Even broader than Corrientes, Av 9 de Julio is a pedestrian's worst nightmare (fortunately, there's a tunnel underneath it). At the intersection with Av Corrientes, the famous **Obelisco** soars above the Plaza de la República. Dedicated in 1936 on the 400th anniversary of the first Spanish settlement on the Río de la Plata, the Obelisco is as much an icon of Buenos Aires as the Eiffel Tower is to Paris or the Washington Monument to Washington, DC.

Three blocks north of the Obelisco, on the west side of Av 9 de Julio, the **Teatro Colón** is Buenos Aires' major architectural and cultural landmark. It actually fronts on Libertad, opposite Plaza Lavalle; for more details, see the Corrientes & Congreso section below.

## Museo del Cabildo

Modern construction has twice truncated the mid-18th century cabildo, but there remains a representative sample of the *recova* (colonnade) that once ran entirely across the Plaza de Mayo. The two-story building itself is more intriguing than the scanty exhibits, which include mementos of the early 19th-century British invasions, some modern paintings in colonial- and early independence-era styles, and religious art from missions of the Jesuits and other orders. Look for a small group of fascinating early photographs of the plaza. The attractive interior patio has a modest confitería.

At Bolívar 65, the museum (☎ 343-1782) is open Thursday to Sunday 2 to 6 pm. Admission costs US$1.

## Catedral Metropolitana

Also on the Plaza de Mayo, built on the site of the original colonial church and not finished until 1827, the cathedral is an important religious landmark but an even more important national historical site, containing the tomb of José de San Martín, Argentina's most revered hero. In the chaos following independence, San Martín chose exile in France, never returning alive to Argentina even though, in 1829, a boat on which he traveled reached the shores of Buenos Aires on its way to Montevideo. Note the bas reliefs on the triangular facade above the neoclassical columns.

# Casa Rosada

Off limits during the military dictatorship of 1976 – 1983, the presidential palace is no longer a place to avoid – visitors can even approach and photograph the grenadiers who guard the main entrance. On the east side of the building, between it and Parque Colón, excavations have unearthed remains of the old fort and customs buildings that were buried during construction of new port facilities in the 1890s.

The basement Museo de la Casa de Gobierno (☎ 476-9841), entered at Hipólito Yrigoyen 219, exhibits the personal effects of Argentine presidents. Hours are Thursday and Friday only from noon to 6 pm.

# Manzana de las Luces

In colonial times, this was Buenos Aires' center of learning and, to some degree, it still symbolizes high culture in the capital. The first to occupy the block were the Jesuits; on the north side of the Manzana, fronting on Alsina, remain two of the five original buildings of the Jesuit **Procuraduría**. These date from 1730 and are currently undergoing a restoration that includes its defensive tunnels discovered in 1912. After independence, this site was occupied by the Universidad de Buenos Aires, the entrance for which is at Perú 222 (note the designation 'Universidad' on the facade, which extended across the entire block until remodeling in 1894).

Fronting on Bolívar, the **Iglesia San Ignacio**, with its rococo interior, appeared only in 1712; after the demolition of 1904, there remains only a single original cloister. It shares a wall with the **Colegio Nacional de Buenos Aires**, where generations of the Argentine elite have sent their children to receive secondary schooling and indoctrination.

Slow-paced tours conducted by the Instituto de Investigaciones Históricas de la Manzana de las Luces Doctor Jorge E Garrido (☎ 342-6973), Perú 272, provide the only regular public access to the block's interior, where there is a small theater-in-the-round reconstruction of Buenos Aires' first legislature, the neoclassical Sala de Representantes. Tours in Spanish only take place at 6 pm Friday, Saturday and Sunday, and cost US$2.

# Museo de la Ciudad

The ground floor of this turn-of-the-century building at the corner of Defensa and Alsina is home to the

Farmacia de la Estrella, while the former upstairs residence, reached by a spiral staircase, has both permanent and temporary exhibitions on porteño life and history, as well as a research library. Some exhibits can be very innovative, like a recent 'Doors of Buenos Aires' presentation focusing on everyday artistry as seen in commonplace objects such as knockers, handles, knobs and stained glass. Unfortunately, the staff can be surly, and the air is often thick with tobacco smoke.

Upstairs at Alsina 412, the Museo de la Ciudad (☎ 331-9855) is open weekdays from 11 am to 7 pm, weekends from 3 to 7 pm. Admission costs US$1 but is free on Wednesdays.

## Archivo y Museo Histórico del Banco de la Provincia de Buenos Aires Doctor Arturo Jauretche

Making sense of Argentina's chaotic economic history is no easy task, but this well-organized museum offers a superb introduction to the subject since viceregal times. It includes outstanding displays on the country's early economic regions, the financing of political independence and establishment of public credit (including the controversial Baring Brothers loans of the early 19th century), numismatics, and paper money and counterfeiting.

In the heart of the financial district at Sarmiento 362, the museum (☎ 331-1775, 331-7943) is open weekdays 10 am to 6 pm, Sundays 2 to 6 pm. Admission is free, and guided tours are available by appointment.

## Museo Mitre

Bartolomé Mitre was a soldier, journalist and Argentina's first legitimate president under the Constitution of 1853, although his term ran from 1862 – 1968 and he spent much of his term leading the country's armies against Paraguay. After leaving office, he founded the influential daily *La Nación*, still a porteño institution.

At San Martín 366, the Museo Mitre (☎ 394-7659) is a sprawling colonial edifice (plus additions) in which Mitre resided with his family – a good reflection of 19th-century upper-class life. A side exit led directly to the newspaper's offices. Take a glance at the library, which holds more than 80,000 volumes. Hours are Tuesday to Friday 1 to 6 pm, Sunday 2 to 6 pm. Admission is US$1.

# Reserva Ecológica Costanera Sur

During the years of the Proceso, military governments limited access to the Buenos Aires waterfront, filling the area across from the port with sediment dredged from the Río de la Plata and debris from the demolitions associated with the construction of the city's freeways and broad avenues. The result was a 350-hectare low-lying space protected by dikes, which was spontaneously colonized by trees, grasses, birds and rodents. In 1986, the municipal Concejo Deliberante declared the area an ecological reserve that, despite its lack of services, has become a popular site for weekend outings. It has also become a cruising area for the capital's homosexuals.

Reached by bus No 2 from Av Belgrano, the reserve (☎ 315-1320) is at Av TA Rodríguez 1550 (see the Capital Federal map). It's open daily from 7 am to 8 pm in summer, from 7 am to 6 pm the rest of the year. Guided visits (☎ 343-3778), including some by moonlight, can be arranged at Defensa 245 in San Telmo.

# Galerías Pacífico

Covering an entire city block bounded by Florida, Av Córdoba, San Martín and Viamonte, this impressive Parisian-style building has finally fulfilled the commercial purpose that its designers envisioned when they built it in 1889, with the proposed name of the Bon Marché. The worldwide economic crisis of the 1890s necessitated the sale of part of the unfinished building, subdivided into quarters by two large perpendicular passageways, to the Ferrocarril del Pacífico for its administrative offices; the railroad subsequently acquired the rest of the building, which became state property after nationalization of the railroads under Perón.

WAYNE BERNHARDSON

Galerías Pacífico caters to avid shoppers.

In 1945, the completion of vaulted ceilings above those passageways and a central cupola at their junction made space for a dozen panels, covering 450 sq

meters, by muralists Antonio Berni, Juan Carlos Cas-
tagnino, Manuel Colmeiro, Lino Spilimbergo (a close
friend of the famous Mexican muralist Davíd Alfaro
Siqueiros) and Demetrio Urruchúa. All were adherents of the Nuevo Realismo (New Realism) school,
heirs of an earlier social-activist tendency in Argentine
art. For years, the building went semi-abandoned, but
a joint Argentine-Mexican team later repaired and
restored the murals, which became a focal point of
the building's renovation as an upscale shopping
center in 1992.

## Other Downtown Museums

Visitors interested in colonial religious art, most notably
wood carvings, should visit the **Capilla San Roque** at
the Basílica San Francisco, a mid-18th century church,
remodeled several times. At Alsina 340, it's open only
on the 16th of every month.

The **Museo de la Policia Federal** (☎ 394-6857), in the
heart of the financial district at San Martín 353, 7th floor,
is open Tuesday to Friday, 2 to 6 pm. Children younger
than age 15 are not permitted.

# CORRIENTES & CONGRESO

West of Av 9 de Julio, the city's major landmark and
pride is the **Teatro Colón** at Libertad 621, one of the
world's finest performing arts venues and the Southern Hemisphere's largest theater until the construction of the Sydney Opera House. Half a block south,
fronting on Plaza Lavalle, note the colorful portals of
the **Conventillo de las Artes**, an artists' space at Libertad 543, only three doors away from the austere neoclassical **Escuela Presidente Roca** (1902). On the plaza
itself is a gaggle of used bookstalls frequented by
passing pedestrians and lunchtime browsers from
the French-style **Palacio de Justicia** (1904), popularly
known as the Tribunales, the federal law courts at
Talcahuano 550.

At the north end of Plaza Lavalle, at the corner of
Av Córdoba, Jewish symbols adorn the facade of the
**Templo de la Congregación Israelita**, Argentina's
largest synagogue. Concrete sidewalk planters, constructed after recent attacks against Jewish targets, provide security from potential car bombs, while a police
canine patrol stands guard across the street. Across Av
Córdoba, the lavishly ornamented **Teatro Cervantes**
(1921) is another landmark theater, built with private

funds but acquired by the state after it went broke in 1926. Its facade was designed as a replica of Spain's Universidad de Alcalá de Henares. The building underwent remodeling after a fire in 1961; it now houses the **Museo Nacional del Teatro** (National Theater Museum) and offers mime-led tours.

Av Corrientes' major landmark, the **Teatro General San Martín**, is the city's only major cultural construction of the post WWII era. Its utilitarian exterior camouflages pleasing interior spaces, including three theaters, a cinema and several galleries and exhibition spaces. Its 8th-floor **Museo de Artes Plásticas Eduardo Sívori**, a branch of the main site at the Centro Cultural Ciudad de Buenos Aires, is open noon to 8 pm daily except Monday; admission costs US$1 but is free Wednesdays. The **Museo de Arte Moderno** has a small facility on the 9th floor, which keeps identical hours. (The main site of the Museo de Arte Moderno is in San Telmo – see below.) The **Centro Cultural General San Martín** is a later addition, with entry from the Sarmiento side of the building.

Swedish architect Karl Nystromer designed the eclectic **Palacio de las Aguas Corrientes** (city waterworks, 1894), a classic of porteño architecture at Av Córdoba and Riobamba. Within the varnished brick building, topped by French-style mansard roofs, ground floor offices surround massive water tanks. The steady leak on the Riobamba side is a palpable symbol of the capital's decaying infrastructure.

Except for the **Palacio del Congreso** itself at the west end of Av de Mayo, opposite the Plaza del Congreso, the immediate Congreso area has fewer imposing landmarks than one might expect, but there are still occasional surprises like the rococo **Confitería del Molino** at Avs Rivadavia and Callao. Probably the greatest landmark, second only to the Teatro Colón as a classical performing arts center, is the **Teatro Avenida** at Av de Mayo 1212; nearly gutted by fire in 1979, it reopened in 1994 with a performance by Spanish tenor Plácido Domingo.

As you pass the **Mercado del Congreso**, Moreno 1749, glance upwards for a view of the *guardapolvos* (literally, 'dust guards') on the upper floors; instead of gargoyles or the like often found on neo-European porteño architecture, these mini-sculptures are cattle, swine and grapes. A bit out of the way, at Sarmiento 2573, is the obscure **Museo del Cine Pablo D Hicken**, the city's film museum.

# Teatro Colón

Ever since it opened in 1908 with a presentation of *Aida*, this world-class facility for opera, ballet and classical music has impressed visitors. Even through times of economic hardship, the elaborate Colón remains a high national priority, in part because it's the only facility of its kind in the entire country. Presidential command performances

WAYNE BERNHARDSON

take place on the winter patriotic holidays of May 25 and July 9, but no events take place in the summer months of January and February.

Within the lobby is a small but popular museum with exhibits of costumes, instruments and photographs of performers and performances. Very worthwhile guided tours, which cost US$5 and take place hourly between 9 am and 4 pm weekdays, and 9 am and noon Saturdays, are available in Spanish, English, German, French, Portuguese and even Danish, but only Spanish and English tours are always available. On these tours, visitors see the theater all the way from the basement workshops (which employ over 400 skilled carpenters, sculptors, wigmakers, costume designers and other *técnicos*), to the rehearsal rooms and the stage and seating areas. Note especially the *maquetas*, scale models used by the sculptors to help prepare the massive stage sets (the enormous pillars, statues and other props consist of painted lightweight Styrofoam). There are no tours in January.

Occupying an entire block bounded by Libertad, Tucumán, Viamonte and Cerrito (Av 9 de Julio), the imposing seven-story Colón (☎ 382-6632) seats 2500 spectators and has standing room for another thousand. The main entrance is on Libertad, opposite Plaza Lavalle, but tours enter from the Viamonte side.

# Museo Nacional del Teatro

Exhibits at this agreeably low-key museum trace the history of Argentine theater from its colonial beginnings, stressing the 19th-century contributions of the Podestá family, Italian immigrants who popularized the gauchesque drama *Juan Moreira*. Collection items include a gaucho suit worn by Gardel during his Hollywood film *El Día Que Me Quieras* and the *bandoneón* belonging to Paquita Bernardo, the first Argentine musician to play the accordion-like instrument, who died of tuberculosis in 1925 at the age of 25. There is also a photo gallery of famous Argentine stage actors.

Part of the Teatro Cervantes at Av Córdoba 1199, corner of Libertad, the museum (☎ 815-8883, ext 195) is open weekdays, noon to 7 pm. Admission is free.

## Palacio del Congreso

Costing more than twice its original budget, the Congreso set a precedent for contemporary Argentine public works projects. Modeled on Washington, DC's Capitol Building and completed in 1906, it faces the Plaza del Congreso, where the **Monumento a los Dos Congresos** honors the Congresses of 1810 in Buenos Aires and 1816 in Tucumán that led to Argentine independence. The monument's enormous granite steps symbolize the high Andes, while the fountain at its base represents the Atlantic Ocean, but the hordes of pigeons that stain the monument and foul its waters are poor surrogates for the Andean condor. In the waning days of the military dictatorship, graffiti blanketed the monument, but regular sand-blasting has since kept it relatively clean.

A block south of the Congreso at Alsina 1835, the **Biblioteca del Congreso** (☎ 371-3643) is the legislature's research library. It's also open to the public 24 hours a day.

WAYNE BERNHARDSON

Palacio del Congreso

# Museo del Cine Pablo D Hicken

The best exhibits at this mostly drab film museum are
in its Sala María Luisa Bemberg, containing sets and
scenery from the late director's well-known films *Camila*,
*Yo, La Peor de Todas*, and *Miss Mary* (the latter in English,
starring Julie Christie). Also interesting are models like
that of the *Merrimac*, on which Domingo F Sarmiento
sailed from the USA back to Argentina and learned
en route that he had been elected president in absentia.
There is also a good selection of historical photographs
from what has been one of Latin America's most important film industries. The museum (☎ 952-4528) is open
weekdays 9 am to 4 pm. Admission costs US$1, but is
free Wednesdays.

# SAN TELMO

South of Plaza de Mayo, still untransformed by the ram-
pant gentrification of areas like Recoleta and Palermo,
San Telmo is an artist's quarter where bohemians find
large spaces at low rents, but it's also the site of high-
density slum housing in *conventillos* (tenements) once
built as single-family housing for the capital's elite.

Changes are in the offing, though, as the Municipalidad's Programa Prosur invests nearly US$1 million in
sprucing up the area bounded by Defensa, Av San Juan,
Paseo Colón and Av Independencia. Improvements
have included widening sidewalks for cafés and street
fairs, planting trees, installing traditional street lamps
and cobbling the roadways. The idea is to encourage
tourist activities beyond the usual Sunday visit to Plaza
Dorrego or nighttime excursion to the barrio's tango
bars, but there's always the chance it will produce a
sanitized Santelmoland that costs the barrio its unique
colonial atmosphere.

San Telmo is famous for the rugged street fighting
that took place when British troops, at war with Spain,
invaded the city in 1806 and occupied it until the following year, when covert porteño resistance became open
counterattack. As British forces advanced up narrow
Calle Defensa, the impromptu militia, supported by
women and slaves pouring cauldrons of boiling oil and
water from the rooftops and firing cannons from the
balconies of the house at **Defensa 372**, routed the British back to their ships. Victory gave porteños confidence
in their ability to stand apart from Spain, even though
independence had to wait another decade.

The 18th-century **Iglesia y Convento de Santo
Domingo**, at Defensa and Av Belgrano, prominently
marks the approach to the barrio. At the corner of
Defensa and México, the stuccoed former **Casa de la**

**Moneda** (National Mint, 1877) now belongs to the army's Instituto de Estudios Históricos del Ejército. At the opposite corner of the block, behind an English-style brick facade at Balcarce 677, the mint's former **Anexo Casa de la Moneda** (1911) houses the Archivo del Ejército, the army's historical archive.

Only a block south, where a rushing arroyo once impeded transport in colonial times, the cobbled **Pasaje San Lorenzo**, between Defensa and Balcarce, hosts a Sunday art fair; the **Pasaje Giuffra**, two blocks south, also covered a former watercourse. Look for the so-called **Casa Mínima** at San Lorenzo 380, an example of the narrow-lot architectural style known as *casa chorizo* (sausage house). Barely two meters wide, the lot was reportedly a manumission gift from colonial slave owners to their former chattels. At Bolívar and Independencia is a noteworthy Carnaval-oriented **mural**.

To the east, on Paseo Colón, the oval Plazoleta Olazábal features Rogelio Yrurtia's masterful sculpture *Canto al Trabajo* (moved here from its original site on Plaza Dorrego). Across the plaza, the neoclassic **Facultad de Ingeniería** of the Universidad de Buenos Aires, originally built for the Fundación Eva Perón, is a oddball landmark once described by Gerald Durrell as 'a cross between the Parthenon and the Reichstag'. Two blocks south, at Carlos Calvo 257, a different sort of architectural oddity is the brick **Dansk Kirke**, a neo-Gothic Lutheran church dating from 1930. Two blocks west of the Dansk Kirke, at the corner of Carlos Calvo and Bolívar, the **Mercado San Telmo** (1897) is still a functioning fruit and vegetable market for barrio shoppers; the interior is far more spacious than the modest corner entrance would suggest.

At Defensa and Humberto Primo, **Plaza Dorrego** hosts the famous Sunday flea market, the Feria de San Telmo; on alternate Saturday nights in summer, the free city-sponsored 'Tango y Baile' showcases musicians and dancers, and gives porteños of all ages and classes a chance to strut their steps. Half a block east, at Humberto Primo 340, is the mid-18th century **Iglesia Nuestra Señora de Belén**, part of which contains the **Museo Penitenciario Nacional**, once a convent and later a women's prison.

Farther south, at Defensa and Brasil, the trees and shrubbery of **Parque Lezama** are suffering from years of municipal neglect. The presumptive site of Pedro de Mendoza's original foundation of the city, the park is appropriately home to the **Museo Histórico Nacional**. Across from the park, at Av Brasil 315, is the striking turn-of-the-century **Iglesia Apostólica Ortodoxa Rusa** (Russian Orthodox Church).

After a yellow-fever epidemic hit the once-fashionable area in the late 19th century, the porteño elite evacuated to higher ground west and north of the present-day microcentro. As immigrants began to pour into the city, many older houses became conventillos housing European families in cramped, divided quarters with inadequate sanitary facilities. One such conventillo was the **Pasaje de la Defensa**, now recycled as a shopping gallery, at Defensa 1179; originally built for the Ezeiza family in 1880, the two-story, three-patio edifice once housed 32 families.

Despite the neighborhood's historic colorful buildings, cramped conditions still exist – look for crumbling older houses with laundry hanging from the balconies. A good example is the sprawling building at the corner of Humberto Primo and Balcarce; another former conventillo, recently redeveloped as artists' workshops, is the **Galería del Viejo Hotel**, Balcarce 1053.

Visitors interested in the modern San Telmo should look for the informal giveaway newsletter *De Aquí Para Allá*, distributed throughout the barrio. Oriented toward community service, it offers an idea of the barrio as a place to live and labor rather than as a tourist ghetto.

## Museo Nacional del Grabado

This historic landmark displays a collection of mostly contemporary woodcuts and engravings in the restored early 19th-century Casa de la Defensa, which may retain some elements of the original structure despite an ill-advised remodeling for a restaurant in the 1970s.

At Defensa 372, the museum (☎ 345-5300) is open weekdays 2 to 6 pm, Sundays 1 to 6 pm. Admission costs US$2.

## Iglesia y Convento de Santo Domingo

This mid-18th century Dominican church (also known as the Iglesia de Nuestra Señora del Rosario) at the corner of Defensa and Belgrano has a long and colorful history. Still showing the scars of shrapnel launched against British troops who holed up here during the invasion of 1806, its **Museo de la Basílica del Rosario** displays the flags captured from the invaders. Secularized during the presidency of Bernardino Rivadavia, the building became a natural history museum, its original single tower serving as an astronomical observatory, until Rosas restored it to the Dominican order. It was gutted by fire during the 1955 Revolución Libertadora against Perón.

Hours are from 9 am to 1 pm and from 4:30 to 8:30 pm

WAYNE BERNHARDSON

British troops lived in the Iglesia y Convento de Santo
Domingo during the invasions of 1806 to 1807.

daily; guided tours take place at 3 pm Sundays. Alongside it, the **Instituto Nacional Belgraniano** lionizes
Argentina's second-greatest hero, Manuel Belgrano,
who is buried in a granite mausoleum.

# Museo Penitenciario Nacional

Containing a handful of worthwhile but poorly organized exhibits, the Iglesia Nuestra Señora de Belén at
Humberto Primo 378 was a Jesuit school until the
order's expulsion in 1767, when the Bethlemite order
took it over. After secularization in the early 1820s, it
became a men's and then a women's prison until 1978.
The best items on display are a photograph of the
famous Anarchist Simón Radowitzky's release from
Ushuaia, and a wooden desk carved by inmates at
Ushuaia for president Roberto M Ortiz. The museum
(☎ 361-5802) is open Tuesday to Friday, 10 am to noon
and 2 to 7 pm, and Sunday 10 am to noon and 1 to 5 pm.
Admission costs US$1.

# Museo Histórico Nacional

Appropriately located in Parque Lezama, this historical museum offers a panorama of the Argentine experience from its shaky beginnings to independence to the present. Its Sala de la Conquista displays paintings depicting the Spanish domination of wealthy, civilized Peru and Columbus' triumphant return to Spain, which contrast sharply with paintings of the Mendoza expedition's struggle on the shores of the Río de la Plata. There is also a map of Juan de Garay's second founding of the city, four decades later.

In the Sala de la Independencia and other rooms are portraits of major figures of the independence and republican periods, such as Simón Bolívar, his ally and rival San Martín both in his youth and in disillusioned old age, and Rosas and his bitter but eloquent enemy Sarmiento, the latter with his perpetual scowl. There are also portrayals of the British invasions of 1806 and 1807, and of late 19th-century porteño life.

At Defensa 1600, the Museo Histórico (☎ 307-1182) is theoretically open Wednesday through Sunday, 2 to 6 pm, but is frequently closed for repairs. To get there, take bus No 86 from Plaza Congreso.

# Helft Collection

Stressing modern Argentine painters and sculptors such as Guillermo Kuitca, Alberto Heredia and Libero Badii, but also including works by foreign artists as diverse as Marcel Duchamps, Man Ray and Yoko Ono, the very unconventional private collection of modern Argentine art belonging to Jorge Helft occupies a San Telmo house redesigned to display its contents under optimum conditions. Arranged by appointment only, guided tours (☎ 307-9175) are available in Spanish, English, French, German, Italian and Hungarian.

# Other San Telmo Museums

The **Museo del Traje** (Museum of Dress & Uniforms, ☎ 343-8427), Chile 832, displays civilian and military clothing from colonial times to the present.

The main site of the **Museo de Arte Moderno** (☎ 374-9426) is at Av San Juan 350 between Defensa and Balcarce, open weekdays 10 am to 8 pm, weekends noon to 8 pm. Admission costs US$1, but is free of charge Wednesdays. The museum closes the entire month of January.

# LA BOCA

Literally Buenos Aires' most colorful barrio, La Boca was settled and built up by Italian immigrants along the **Riachuelo**, a sinuous waterway lined with meatpacking plants and warehouses that separates the capital proper from the industrial suburb of Avellaneda in Buenos Aires province. Much of La Boca's color springs from the brightly painted houses and corrugated metal roofs of the **Caminito**, a popular pedestrian walk and former rail terminus that takes its name from a popular tango. The rest comes from petroleum and industrial wastes that tint the waters of the Riachuelo, where rusting hulks and dredges lie offshore and rowers strain to ferry passengers who prefer not to walk across the high girder bridge to Avellaneda.

It would probably be easier to refine the oleaginous Riachuelo (where malarial mosquitos once bred) into diesel fuel than to clean it up – indeed, it has even been suggested that mining its sediments for their accumulated mercury, chrome and other heavy metals might be a profitable enterprise. María Julia Alsogaray, President Menem's environment secretary, has pledged to swim in the Riachuelo at the completion of a highly publicized cleanup campaign, but by then she may well be hobbling in old age and the polluted watercourse solid enough to support her. When rains are heavy and tides are high, elevated sidewalks – a meter or more above street level – keep pedestrians dry as the waters rise. When floods submerge much of the surrounding area, people get around by rowboat.

Areas like La Boca were once places where immigrants could find a foothold in the country, but conditions were less than idyllic. British diplomat Bryce described them as

a waste of scattered shanties . . . dirty and squalid, with corrugated iron roofs, their wooden boards gaping like rents in tattered clothes. These are inhabited by the newest and poorest of immigrants from southern Italy and southern Spain, a large and not very desirable element among whom anarchism is rife.

In fact, French Basques preceded the Italians as the first settlers of La Boca. Today the area is still a flourishing working-class neighborhood, but it also sustains an artists' colony, the legacy of the late local painter Benito Quinquela Martín. The symbol of the community's solidarity is the Boca Juniors soccer team, the former club of disgraced superstar Diego Maradona. The team plays

Murals depicting life in La Boca line the walls of La Bombonera soccer stadium. (Photos by Wayne Bernhardson)

at the **Estadio Doctor Camilo Cichero**, more popularly
known by its nickname *La Bombonera*, at the corner of
Brandsen and Del Valle Iberlucea; along the Brandsen
side of the stadium, look for the murals of barrio life. For
a sense of the importance of the meat-packing industry
in the barrio, walk one block south to view the **Mercado
y Frigorífico Benincasa-Mazzello**, on Suárez between
Moussy and Del Valle Iberlucea.

Visitors arriving from San Telmo on the bus will note
the **Casa de Almirante Brown** in the 400 block of its
namesake avenue; this is a replica of the country house
of the Irish founder of the Argentine navy. A more
authentic landmark is the **Puente Nicolás Avellaneda**
on Pedro de Mendoza, a bridge across the Riachuelo

that links La Boca to the
industrial suburb of Avellaneda before the bridge's
completion in 1940, floods
had washed away several
others. Within the bridge
building is a scale model of
the construction. When its
escalators are not working,
most pedestrians prefer to

WAYNE BERNHARDSON

avoid climbing eight flights of stairs, opting instead to
pay US$0.50 to be rowed across the Riachuelo. Check
out the bas-relief sculptures at Pedro de Mendoza 1629
above the presently closed restaurant La Barca.

Tourists also come to La Boca to savor the atmosphere of **Calle Necochea**, a street lined with pizzerías
and garish cantinas. Many of the places formerly
housed brothels when the tango was not the respectable,
middle-class folk phenomenon it is today. To its east,
bounded by Ministro Brin, Suárez, Caboto and Olavarría, **Plaza Solís** is another hub of barrio activity. In
some ways this is a rough neighborhood, and some
indications of change are for the worse – graffiti that
was once confined to bare walls now mars the murals.

The No 86 bus from Congreso is the easiest route to
La Boca, although Nos 20, 25, 29, 33, 46, 53, 64 and 97
also stop in the vicinity of the Caminito.

## Museo de Bellas Artes de La Boca

Once the home and studio of Benito Quinquela Martín,
La Boca's fine-arts museum exhibits his works and
those of other early 20th-century Argentine artists (on
whom there is almost no accompanying information).
In keeping with the museum's waterfront/maritime
theme, one of its most entertaining features is an exhibition of painted bowsprits, but the most interesting
feature is Quinquela Martín's studio, which is the only
area with adequate natural light for viewing his oils of
barrio life. There are outdoor sculptures on the rooftop terrace.

At Pedro de Mendoza 1835, the museum (☎ 301-1080)
is open Tuesday to Saturday from 8 am to 6 pm. Admission is free. The street level is also home to the Escuela
Pedro de Mendoza, an elementary school.

## Museo de Cera

Wax-figure reconstructions of historical figures and dio-
ramas of scenes in Argentine history are the specialty
of this rather tacky private institution. Among the

historical personages depicted are Juan de Solís, Pedro de Mendoza, Juan de Garay, Juan Manuel de Rosas, Guillermo Brown and Carlos Gardel, but indigenous leaders such as Calfucurá, Catriel and Namuncurá are also immortalized.

In an interesting building at Del Valle Iberlucea 1261, the museum (☎ 301-1497) is open Wednesday though Friday from 10 am to 6 pm, weekends 10 am to 7 pm. Admission costs US$2.50.

## RETIRO

At the north end of the microcentro, beyond Av Córdoba, the barrio of Retiro derives its name from its erstwhile status as a monks' retreat on the city's outskirts during early colonial times. French landscape architect Charles Thays designed the densely forested **Plaza Libertador General San Martín**, once the site of a slave market and later of a bullring, which now features the obligatory equestrian statue of the Liberator. Surrounding the plaza are several landmark public buildings. The **Palacio San Martín**, an Art Nouveau mansion, was originally built for the elite Anchorena family and later acquired by the state for its Ministerio de Relaciones Exteriores y Culto (Foreign Ministry). The **Círculo Militar**, the largest private residence in Argentina (12,000 sq meters) was built for *La Prensa* founder Jose C Paz. On an odd triangular site at the corner of Florida and Santa Fe, **Parques Nacionales** occupies a neo-Gothic house built for the Haedo family at the turn of the 19th century.

Now military property, the Círculo Militar also houses the **Museo de Armas** (Weapons Museum, ☎ 312-9774) at Maipú 1030 at the corner of Av Santa Fe. It's open Wednesday, Thursday and Friday 3 to 7 pm. More interesting and worthwhile are the several modern art galleries in the vicinity; for more information on these, see the Shopping chapter. Retiro's major museum is the **Museo Municipal de Arte Hispanoamericano Isaac Fernández Blanco** on Suipacha between Arroyo and Av del Libertador.

Across Av del Libertador from Plaza San Martín stands the famous **Torre de los Ingleses**, donated by the city's British community in 1916. This Big Ben clone testifies to the truth in the common aphorism that 'an Argentine is an Italian who speaks Spanish, wishes he were English, and behaves as if he were French'. Ironically, since the 1982 Falklands War, the plaza in which the tower stands has been renamed the **Plaza Fuerza Aérea Argentina** (Air Force Plaza).

Opposite the plaza is the **Estación Retiro**, built in 1915 when the British controlled the country's railroad. While much of Retiro is a chic, upper-class area, that part beyond the **Estación Terminal de Omnibus** (1982) has long been a shantytown. It only recently has begun to enjoy basic municipal services like paved streets, a safe tap-water supply and regular electricity.

## Museo Municipal de Arte Hispanoamericano Isaac Fernández Blanco

Dating from 1921, this generally appealing museum (☎ 393-6318) is typical of a neocolonial style that developed as a reaction against French influences in turn-of-the-century Argentine architecture. Its exceptional collection of colonial art includes silverwork from Alto Perú (present-day Bolivia), oil paintings with religious themes, Jesuit statuary, costumes and antiques. Unfortunately, the museum makes little effort to interpret its collections and place them in any historical context.

Also known as the Palacio Noel, after the designing architect, the building and its collections suffered damage, since repaired, in the bombing of the nearby Israeli embassy in 1992. At Suipacha 1422, the museum's attractively landscaped, densely forested grounds are an attractive sanctuary from the bustling microcentro. Hours are from 2 to 7 pm daily, closed Monday, but it shuts down completely in January and February. Admission costs US$2 but is free on Thursdays.

# RECOLETA & BARRIO NORTE

Among the areas to which the upper-class porteños of San Telmo relocated after the yellow fever epidemic of the 1870s, Recoleta is today one of Buenos Aires' most fashionable districts. It takes its name from a Franciscan convent (1716), but it is best known for the **Cementerio de la Recoleta** (Recoleta Cemetery, 1822), an astonishing necropolis where, in death as in life, generations of the Argentine elite repose in ornate splendor. Barrio Norte, not really a formal barrio, is a largely residential western extension of Recoleta often grouped with Retiro, but the vernacular boundaries among all these areas and Palermo are often indistinct.

Alongside the cemetery, the **Iglesia de Nuestra Señora de Pilar**, a baroque-style colonial church consecrated in 1732, is a national historical monument. Within easy walking distance are the important **Centro**

## Life & Death in Recoleta & Chacarita

Death is the great equalizer, except in Buenos Aires. When the arteries harden after decades of dining at Au Bec Fin and finishing up with coffee and dessert at La Biela or Café de la Paix, the wealthy and powerful of Buenos Aires move ceremoniously across the street to Recoleta Cemetery, joining their forefathers in a place they have visited religiously all their lives. Perhaps no other place says more about Argentina and Argentine society.

According to Argentine novelist Tomás Eloy Martínez, Argentines are 'cadaver cultists' who honor their most revered national figures not on the date of their birth but of their death. Nowhere is this obsession with mortality and corruption more evident than at Recoleta Cemetery, where generations of the elite repose in the grandeur of ostentatious mausoleums. It is a common saying and only a slight exaggeration that 'it is cheaper to live extravagantly all your life than to be buried in Recoleta'. Traditionally, money alone is not enough: You must have a surname like Anchorena, Alvear, Aramburu, Avellaneda, Mitre, Martínez de Hoz or Sarmiento. The remains of Evita Perón, secured in a subterranean vault, are an exception that irritates the presumptive aristocracy.

One reason for this is that the dead often play a peculiar, and more than just symbolic, role in Argentine politics. Evita rests in Recoleta only after her embalmed body completed an odyssey during which it was moved from South America to an obscure cemetery in Milan to her exiled husband's house in Madrid, finally returning to Buenos Aires. (Embalming is uncommon in Argentina.) The man responsible for her 'kidnapping' was General Pedro Aramburu, a bitter political enemy of the Peróns.

Aramburu himself was held for 'ransom' by the left-wing Peronist Montoneros *after* his assassination in 1970. Only when the military government of General Alejandro Lanusse ensured Evita's return to Perón in Madrid did Aramburu's body reappear to be entombed in Recoleta, now only a few short 'blocks' from Evita. Juan Perón himself lies across town, in the much less exclusive graveyard of Chacarita, which opened in the 1870s to accommodate the countless yellow-fever victims of San Telmo and La Boca.

Although more democratic in conception, Chacarita has many tombs that match the finest in Recoleta. One of the most visited belongs to Carlos Gardel, the famous tango singer. Plaques from around the world cover the base of his life-size statue, many thanking him for favors granted. Like Evita, Juan Perón and others, Gardel is a near-saint toward whom countless Argentines feel a quasi-religious devotion. The steady procession of pilgrims exposes the pervasiveness of spiritualism in a country that prides itself on European sophistication.

WAYNE BERNHARDSON

Recoleta Cemetery

One of the best places to witness this phenomenon is the Chacarita tomb of Madre María Salomé, a disciple of the famous healer Pancho Sierra. Every day, but especially on the second day of each month (she died on October 2, 1928), adherents of her cult leave floral tributes – white carnations are the favorite – and lay their hands on her sepulcher in spellbound supplication. The anniversary of Gardel's death on June 26, 1935, is another major occasion, as pilgrims jam the cemetary's streets.

Organized tours regularly visit Recoleta Cemetery, open daily from 7 am to 6 pm on Calle Junín across from Plaza Alvear, but most visitors wander about on their own. To locate Evita's grave, ask directions to the relatively modest tomb of the 'Familia Duarte' (her maiden name). Outside the walls of the cemetery, the gourmet corridor of Calles RM Ortiz and Junín, along with the presence of a string of albergues transitorios (hotels that rent by the hour) on Calle Azcuénaga, raises interesting questions about the connections between food, sex and death in Argentina.

To visit Chacarita, which attracts fewer visitors than Recoleta, take Línea B of the Subte to the end of the line at Federico Lacroze, from which it is a short walk (see the Capital Federal map). Look for the tomb of 'Tomás Perón', but do not miss those of Gardel, Madre María, poet Alfonsina Storni, aviator Jorge Newbery, tango musician Aníbal 'Pichuco' Troilo and comedian Luis Sandrini. Hours are identical to Recoleta's. ∎

WAYNE BERNHARDSON

WAYNE BERNHARDSON

DAVE HOUSER

**Cultural Ciudad de Buenos Aires**, the **Museo Nacional de Bellas Artes** (Fine Arts Museum), and the **Centro Municipal de Exposiciones**, which hosts book fairs and other cultural events.

Recoleta's many attractive public gardens and open spaces include **Plaza Alvear**, **Plaza Francia** (where the capital's largest crafts fair takes place on Sundays) and other parks stretching into Palermo and Belgrano. One of the barrio's most characteristic and entertaining sights is the *pasaperros* – professional dog walkers who often stroll with a dozen or more animals on leash.

Among the monumental buildings is the neo-Gothic **Facultad de Ingeniería** (Engineering School) at the corner of Av Las Heras and Azcuénaga. The work of Uruguayan architect Arturo Prins, the never-completed building intended as the Facultad de Derecho (Law School) lacks the pointed ogival (vaulted) towers characteristic of the style.

---

### Walking the Dog

Buenos Aires supports a legion of *pasaperros* – professional dog walkers sometimes seen with a dozen or more canines on leash. Employed by busy or sedentary apartment-dwellers, who either can't or won't take the time to exercise their animals properly, pasaperros can spend 20 hours or more a week strolling through areas like Recoleta, Parque Lezama and even downtown with a variety of animals ranging from scruffy mongrels to expensive purebreds. On their frequent outings, they often develop a better rapport with the animals than do the owners, and the capital's leashed packs are a remarkably orderly and often entertaining sight. ∎

---

# Centro Cultural Ciudad de Buenos Aires

Part of the original Franciscan convent at Junín 1930, the renovated cultural center (also known as the Centro Cultural Recoleta) houses a variety of facilities, including museums, galleries, exhibition halls and a cinema. The **Museo Eduardo Sívori**, an unimpressive museum of Argentine art in the Centro Cultural, is open Tuesday to Friday from 3 to 8 pm, weekends from 10 am to 8 pm. Sívori was an Italo-Argentine painter who studied in Europe. While his works from that period reflect European subjects, later works returned to Argentine themes, mainly associated with rural life on the Pampas.

Within the same building, the **Museo Participativo de Ciencias** is a hands-on science museum. The **Microcine** offers films most days, and there are frequent free films outdoors in summer. Recent additions to the building include the **Plaza del Pilar**, a colonnade facing Av del Libertador and sporting a variety of restaurants for different tastes and budgets, and the upscale Buenos Aires Design shopping center.

## Museo Nacional de Bellas Artes

Dating from 1933, the former pump house for the city waterworks was designed by architect Julio Dormala and later modified by Alejandro Bustillo. Visitors who have seen the filthy Riachuelo in La Boca may be shocked at the blue, unpolluted waters in 'realist' painter Pío Collivadino's 1961 depiction of the waterway, but the country's most important art museum contains many other works of national and international significance, including many on porteño themes by Benito Quinquela Martín and other Argentine artists of the 19th and 20th centuries. Occasional sculptures and wood carvings add some variety, but the museum fails to reflect the vitality of the most contemporary porteño and Argentine art.

European masters on display include Renoir, Rodin, Monet, Toulouse-Lautrec and Van Gogh. At Av del Libertador 1473, just north of the cemetery, the museum (☎ 803-0802) is open daily except Monday 12:30 to 7:30 pm; Saturdays it opens at 9:30 am. Admission is free.

## Salas Nacionales de Cultura

Only a few minutes' walk from the Centro Cultural Recoleta, this museum (☎ 804-1163), housed in the Palais de Glace at Posadas 1725, offers rotating cultural, artistic and historical exhibitions, as well as the occasional commercial event necessitated by financial considerations. Once a skating rink, the unusual circular building is open weekdays from 1 to 8 pm, weekends from 3 to 8 pm.

# PALERMO

Ironically, Juan Manuel de Rosas' most positive legacy is the wide open spaces of Palermo, straddling Av de Libertador northwest of Recoleta. Once the dictator's private retreat, the area became public parkland after his fall from power. One measure of the dictator's disgrace is that the man who overthrew him, Entre Ríos caudillo and former ally Justo José de Urquiza, sits here astride his mount in a mammoth equestrian monument on the corner of Sarmiento and Figueroa Alcorta; the surrounding Parque 3 de Febrero bears the date of Rosas' defeat at the battle of Caseros, Entre Ríos. Domingo F Sarmiento, another contemporary who detested Rosas, was president of the country when development resumed.

When British diplomat James Bryce visited Buenos Aires after the turn of the century, he marveled at the opulence of the porteño elite who frequented the area and perhaps envisioned the capital's late 20th-century traffic congestion:

On fine afternoons, there is a wonderful turnout of carriages drawn by handsome horses, and still more of costly motor cars, in the principal avenues of the Park; they press so thick that vehicles are often jammed together for fifteen or twenty minutes, unable to move on. Nowhere in the world does one get a stronger impression of exuberant wealth and extravagance. The Park itself, called Palermo, lies on the edge of the city towards the river, and is approached by a well-designed and well-planted avenue.

Now a major recreational resource for all porteños, Palermo contains the city's **Jardín Botánico Carlos Thays** (the botanical gardens, infested with feral cats) at the intersection of Av Las Heras and Santa Fe. Nearby the **Jardín Zoológico** (zoo), recently a focus of controversy over its lease to a political crony of the Peronist mayor of Buenos Aires, fronts on Av Sarmiento. The **Rosedal** (rose garden) is on Av Presidente Montt, the **Planetario** at Avs Sarmiento and Figueroa Alcorta. The **Campo de Polo** (polo grounds) at Avs del Libertador and Dorrego is across the street from the **Hipódromo** (racetrack). As you might guess, some of these uses were not really intended for the masses, but the porteño elite no longer have the park to themselves. Visitors from all over the city now stroll its shady lanes, paddle canoes and pedal *biciscafos* (pedal boats) on its artificial lakes.

The area of Palermo closest to Recoleta, known as Barrio Parque or Palermo Chico, is home to many foreign diplomatic missions; the boundaries between the two barrios are less distinct on the ground than they are on catastral maps. The part of Palermo fronting on Av Córdoba, between Avs Pueyrredón and Coronel Díaz and bounded on the north by Calle Mansilla, is known as Palermo Viejo, while the section between Mansilla and Av Santa Fe is Alto Palermo. Much of Adolfo Bioy Casares' novel *Diary of the War of the Pig* takes place in an area delineated by between Av del Libertador, Av Santa Fe, Parque Las Heras and the Jardín Zoológico.

Things to See & Do

WAYNE BERNHARDSON

DAVE HOUSER

PHILIP COBLENTZ

Top: Parque 3 de Febrero
Middle: Pick-up soccer in Palermo
Bottom: Statuary in the Rosedal gardens

# Jardín Zoológico

Admission to the much improved Jardín Zoológico, entered on Av Sarmiento from either Av Las Heras or Av del Libertador, costs US$4 for adults, US$1 for children, plus small additional charges for the *granja infanta* (children's zoo), *calesita* (merry-go-round), *trencito* (train) and *laberinto* (maze). A *pasaporte* for all of these costs US$6 for adults, but they're free for kids.

# Jardín Japonés

Created in 1979, on the centenary of the arrival of Argentina's first Japanese immigrants, the Jardín Japonés (Japanese Garden) is one of the capital's best-kept public spaces. Because of the lack of suitable rock of any kind near Buenos Aires, the granite for the landscaping came from the rivers of Córdoba province.

Part of Parque 3 de Febrero, at Av Casares and Adolfo Berro just north of Plaza Alemania, the garden (☎ 804-4922) is open from 10 am to 7 pm daily, closed Mondays. Admission costs US$2 for adults, US$1 for children; it's free for retired people on Tuesdays and Wednesdays.

# Museo de Motivos Argentinos José Hernández

Whether intentionally or not, no other Buenos Aires museum so effectively exposes Argentina's ambivalence toward its national icon, the gaucho. Brimming with the gaucho accoutrements that typify the country's folk culture, it showcases items such as exquisite silverwork (credited to individual artisans rather than anonymous) from Bernardo de Irigoyen and vicuña ponchos from Catamarca. It also displays historical photographs of elite families like the Martínez de Hoz in their tailored gaucho drag – the Argentine equivalent of George Bush posing as a Texas buckaroo.

Other notable materials include precolonial basketry and pottery, Mapuche Indian crafts, and an excellent life-size recreation of a *pulpería*, a rural shop or 'company store' on a cattle or sheep *estancia*. Though the museum takes its name from the author of the gaucho epic poem *Martín Fierro*, its only display on Hernández himself consists of a sample of translations into such improbable languages as Chinese, Ukrainian and Slovak. In fact, the museum (☎ 802-9967) should really be called Museo Carlos Daws after the Anglo-Argentine who donated most of its artifacts. It's open weekdays from 8 am to 7 pm and weekends from 3 to 7 pm, at Av del Libertador 2373. Admission costs US$1, but it's free on Wednesdays. It's closed the entire month of February.

# Museo del Instituto Nacional Sanmartiniano

In Barrio Parque, occupying the small Plaza Grand Bourg at the junction of Aguado, Elizalde and Castilla, this temple of undiscriminating hero worship is a 1:75 scale replica of San Martín's home-in-exile at Boulogne-Sur-Mer, France. It's open weekdays from 9 am to noon and 2 to 5 pm, weekends 2 to 5 pm only.

## Palacio Errázuriz

The **Museo Nacional de Arte Decorativo** (National Museum of Decorative Arts, ☎ 802-6606) and the **Museo de Arte Oriental** (Museum of Oriental Art, ☎ 801-5988) share the Palacio Errázuriz, a stunning Beaux Arts building at Av Libertador 1902. Both are open weekdays from 3 to 7 pm.

## Biblioteca Nacional

After two decades of construction problems and delays, the national library moved from San Telmo to this modernistic facility in 1992, but the plaster is already cracking on some of the landscaped outdoor terraces. Prominent Argentine and Latin American literary figures such as Ernesto Sábato frequently offer lectures at the library. Open weekdays from 10 am to 9 pm, the library (☎ 806-4729) at Agüero 2510 overlooks Av del Libertador, offering panoramic views of the capital.

# LA COSTANERA

North of downtown (on the Palermo map), the Av Costanera R Obligado, popularly known as 'La Costanera', is a riverside strip of restaurants and discos with occasional green spaces providing the main riverside access for the inhabitants of Buenos Aires. Its major architectural landmark, the vaguely Tudor-style **Club de Pescadores** (Fishermen's Club), dates from 1937 and sits at the end of a 150-meter pier. Beyond Aeroparque Jorge Newbery, the municipal airport, the road loops around the **Balneario Parque Norte**, where many porteños take a break from the busy downtown area and dine at numerous moderately priced parrillas on weekends.

WAYNE BERNHARDSON

Barrio Belgrano

# BELGRANO

Bustling Av Cabildo, the heartbeat of Belgrano, is an overwhelming jumble of noise and neon reminiscent of the Las Vegas Strip except for its lack of casinos. As it is, it's one huge consumer feeding frenzy with little to commend it except its numerous cinemas. Fortunately, less than a block on the either side of Cabildo, Belgrano becomes a neighborly barrio of museums, plazas, parks and a decent range of restaurants, some of them fairly expensive. The barrio can be pretty dead on Sundays.

Only a block east of Av Cabildo, **Plaza General Manuel Belgrano** is the site of one of the capital's major outdoor markets, which is best from late afternoon on. Facing the plaza are two important museums. The

**Museo Histórico Sarmiento** (once the site of the Congreso and executive offices) honors President Domingo F Sarmiento), and the **Museo de Arte Español Enrique Larreta** displays the art collection of former resident novelist Enrique Larreta. Weekly guided tours of Belgrano, conducted by art historians under the auspices of this museum, take place Saturdays at 4 pm, weather permitting, and follow a variety of itineraries. Make reservations at the museum (see below) or at the Café de la Redonda across the street; these tours, which end with tea at the café, cost US$6.

Nearby the Museo de Arte stands the Italianate **Iglesia de la Inmaculada Concepción**, a church popularly known as 'La Redonda' because of its impressive dome. The **Museo Casa de Yrurtia**, a few blocks northwest of Juramento at O'Higgins 2390, once belonged to sculptor Rogelio Yrurtia.

WAYNE BERNHARDSON

Iglesia de la Inmaculada Concepción (La Redonda)

Three blocks east of Plaza Belgrano, French landscape architect Charles Thays took advantage of the contours of **Barrancas de Belgrano** to create an attractive, wooded public space on one of the few natural hillocks in the city. Retirees spend the afternoon at the chess tables beneath its *ombú* (umbra tree), while children skate around the bandshell. The nearby **Museo Libero Badii**, at 11 de Setiembre 1990, displays the unconventional work of one of Argentina's foremost modern sculptors.

Across Juramento from the Barrancas, Belgrano's incipient **Chinatown** fills about half the 2100 block of Arribeños, with a couple other business in the 2200 block. At its current rate of growth, it will take a long time to acquire a definable identity, but the single modest Chinese restaurant asserts its authenticity by not offering a Spanish-language menu. There are scattered Chinese businesses on nearby streets.

## Museo Histórico Sarmiento

Lagging only slightly behind the Instituto Sanmartiniano in its commitment to hero worship, this aging museum contains memorabilia of Domingo F Sarmiento, one of Argentina's most famous diplomats, statesmen and educators. Despite his provincial origins and the look of perpetual indignation on his face, the classically educated Sarmiento was an eloquent writer who analyzed 19th-century Argentina from a cosmopolitan, clearly Eurocentric point of view, most notably in his masterpiece polemic *Facundo, or Civilization and Barbarism* (widely available in English).

The building itself was briefly the site of the Congreso Nacional during the presidency of Nicolás Avellaneda, when both chambers voted to federalize the city of Buenos Aires, inciting a brief civil war with the powerful province of Buenos Aires. Though deteriorating, the house is presumably due for restoration work.

At Cuba 2079, opposite Plaza Belgrano, the museum (☎ 783-7555) is open from 3 to 7 pm Tuesday to Friday and Sunday. Admission is US$1, with informative guided tours at 4 pm on Sunday for no additional charge. From Congreso or Av Callao, take bus No 60, disembarking at Cuba and Juramento.

## Museo de Arte Español Enrique Larreta

Hispanophile novelist Enrique Larreta (1875 – 1961) resided in this elegant colonial-style house, opposite Plaza Belgrano, which now displays his private art collection to the public. The house itself is a study in spaciousness – if this were a conventillo, two families would probably live in the marble-columned bathroom alone. The collections are derivative despite the inclusion of interesting items such as 19th-century Spanish fans with painted scenes and landscapes. Photography is permitted only without flash.

Centered around a massive ginkgo tree, the gardens are magnificent but very formal in their organization. Open-air theater performances take place here in summer; enter from the Vuelta de Obligado side of the building. At Juramento 2291, the museum (☎ 784-4040) is open Monday, Tuesday, Wednesday and Friday 9 am to 1 pm and 3 to 7:45 pm, weekends only 3 to 7:45 pm. Admission is US$2. It is usually closed the entire month of January.

## Museo Casa de Yrurtia

Reclusive Rogelio Yrurtia (1879 – 1950), probably the country's greatest sculptor, is best known for his sculpture *Canto al Trabajo* on Plazoleta Olazábal in San Telmo. Yrurtia designed his Mudéjar-style residence with the expectation that it would house a museum. Cluttered with Yrurtia's work, which focuses on human torsos, and works by his wife, painter Lía Correa Morales, the house has a small but attractive garden the centerpiece of which is the larger-than-life-size *Boxers* (titled in English), first exhibited at the St Louis World's Fair. Yrurtia seems to have been ambivalent about fig leaves; only about half his figures have them. Among the non-Yrurtia items, the painting *Rue Cortot, Paris* is the only Picasso in the country.

At O'Higgins 2390, the museum (☎ 781-0385) is open Wednesday to Sunday from 3 to 7 pm. Admission costs US$1. Informative guided tours take place at 4:30 pm Saturday afternoons for no extra charge; guides can be a bit pedantic toward visitors whom they suspect know little Spanish.

## Museo Libero Badii

Jurist Valentín Alsina built this 19th-century Italian-Renaissance house on the Barrancas de Belgrano. It now displays the unconventional sculptures of one of Argentina's foremost modern artists. The private collection is open to the public at 11 de Setiembre 1990, but the Fundación Banco de Crédito Argentino (☎ 784-8650), which owns it, keeps irregular hours and usually locks the building – try standing around looking lost at the entry. Admission is free.

# ACTIVITIES

Visitors accustomed to easy access to public facilities for sports and exercise may find the congested downtown area frustrating, but health clubs and gyms are increasingly common in the microcentro and inner barrios. The extensive greenery of Recoleta and Palermo provides good areas for jogging, cycling and the like; rental bicycles are available at the Velódromo (bicycle track) at Av Belisario Roldan in Palermo's Parque 3 de Febrero.

Major upscale hotels have swimming pools open to their guests, but most other pools are open to members only and require a substantial membership fee and monthly dues. It's possible to swim in the artificial lake at the Balneario Parque Norte, but porteños generally go there just to hang out or eat at the numerous parrillas. Most people find the sediment-laden waters of the Río de la Plata unappealing for swimming, but some do take advantage of the relatively unpolluted channels of the Paraná delta, reached by launch from the suburb of Tigre, for an occasional dip despite the usually muddy approaches. Only those landowners wealthy enough to import sand have usable beaches, and then only briefly until the next heavy rain.

Buenos Aires' most convenient golf course is the Golf Club Lagos de Palermo (☎ 772-7261), at Av Valentin Alsina and Olleros on the border between Palermo and Belgrano. The three lighted clay courts at the Canchas de Tenis Bakerloo are at La Pampa 1235 in Belgrano, while the Buenos Aires Lawn Tennis Club (☎ 772-0983) is at Olleros 1510.

# LANGUAGE COURSES

Buenos Aires offers many opportunities for Spanish language instruction. Consult the Sunday classified section of the *Buenos Aires Herald*, which offers several columns' worth of possibilities, including individual tutoring and even opportunities for teaching English. The *Herald* also publishes an occasional education supplement that details a variety of learning alternatives, primarily but not exclusively oriented toward Spanish-speakers wishing to learn English.

Before signing up for a course, read the description carefully, note all fees and try to determine whether it suits your particular needs. Remember that small groups or individual tutoring offer the best opportunities for improving language skills, but the latter is usually considerably more expensive.

The Instituto de Lengua Española para Extranjeros (ILEE, ☎ 375-0730, fax 864-4942), Oficina C, 7th floor, Lavalle 1619, in Corrientes, has conversation-based courses at basic, intermediate and advanced levels. Private classes cost US$17 per hour, while group lessons (no more than four students) are US$12 an hour; specialized instruction in areas such as Latin American literature and commercial Spanish costs US$30 per hour. The institute can also help arrange accommodations in a private home for around US$400 to US$500 per month single, US$600 per month double.

Another alternative is the Instituto Nacional de Enseñanza Superior en Lenguas Vivas (☎ 393-7351), Carlos Pellegrini 1455 in the barrio of Retiro, where monthlong intensive courses, with four hours of instruction daily at a basic, intermediate or advanced level, cost $450. Three-month courses, with four hours of instruction weekly, cost US$50 per month.

In Congreso, Tradfax (☎ 382-8741), Montevideo 205, 6th floor, offers three-hour daily classes in general Spanish for US$180 per week; commercial Spanish classes cost about US$30 more per week, while individual classes cost US$18 per hour. The organization also arranges lodging in nearby hotels from US$210 per week single, US$245 per week double.

The Universidad de Buenos Aires (UBA, ☎ 343-1196, fax 343-2733), 25 de Mayo 221 in the microcentro, offers good instruction at its Laboratorio de Idiomas de la Facultad but only for a few hours weekly; this is suitable if you're staying for an extended period in the city, but it's not very efficient if your visit will be relatively brief.

# Places to Stay

Buenos Aires offers a wide range of accommodations, from youth hostels and down-in-the-mouth hospedajes to simple but very fine family-oriented hotels to five-star luxury lodgings of jet-set stature. Given the service sector's elevated price levels, there are few outstanding values, but affordable, acceptable accommodations are still available.

Budget accommodations tend to be well beyond their prime, though not necessarily bad, while many mid-range hotels are either showing their age or have undergone shoddy remodeling (this is even true of some top-end accommodations). There are, however, some good values in all categories, and a number of places still offer discounts up to 15% for payment in cash.

In ascending order of desirability, the main areas for budget accommodations are Constitución near the southern train station (abundant), San Telmo (limited), the microcentro (limited), and Av de Mayo and the Congreso/Corrientes area (abundant), but all these areas have both very good and very bad places. San Telmo is the most interesting and picturesque zone, followed by Congreso for its convenient access to the nightlife of Corrientes and Santa Fe. Both the microcentro and Congreso have decent mid-range accommodations as well. Many budget hotels double as *albergues transitorios*, short-term accommodations utilized by young couples in search of privacy.

In areas such as Retiro, Recoleta and Barrio Norte, top-end accommodations are the rule rather than the exception; budget travelers will find few alternatives, though some mid-range places exist. The microcentro and Congreso also have additional top-end hotels. Accommodations of all kinds are very limited in La Boca, Palermo and Belgrano, which are largely residential.

Travelers should note that tourist offices are usually reluctant to recommend budget accommodations or even to admit that they exist. This is partly because some of the cheapest accommodations can be pretty squalid, but mostly because the staff have the idea that foreign visitors should stay in *hoteles de categoria*, the best available (and usually very expensive) lodging. Often, with gentle persistence, travelers can extract information on more economic alternatives.

Hotel checkout times vary, but they are often as early as 10 am and rarely later than noon. While most places are flexible within reason, some will charge guests who overstay their limit for an extra day; travelers should verify each hotel's policy and to give advance notice if they need extra time. Most places are happy to provide temporary luggage storage for travelers with late afternoon or evening flights or bus trips.

Be aware that most hotels tack on very high additional charges for phone calls that guests place from their rooms.

# PLACES TO STAY – BOTTOM END

## The Microcentro & Monserrat

Central and friendly *Hotel Maipú* (☎ 322-5142), in an attractive building at Maipú 735, has simple but pleasant rooms, some with balconies, for $19/24 with shared bath, $25 double with private bath. *Hotel O'Rei* (☎ 393-7186), Lavalle 733 just a block from Florida, is still the best located budget hotel, but rooms fronting directly onto the Lavalle peatonal can be noisy. Several readers have griped about grumpy management, but others seem to find it just fine. Singles/doubles with shared bath cost US$19/25 double, but laundry facilities are no longer available.

Just off Av de Mayo at Tacuarí 80, *Gran Hotel España* (☎ 343-5541) is less magnificent than its name would suggest, but it does have very clean and reasonably spacious singles/doubles, all with private bath, for US$25/36.

## Corrientes & Congreso

Just beyond the microcentro, west of Av 9 de Julio, the theater district surrounding Av Corrientes and the area in and around the Congreso Nacional offer abundant inexpensive lodging of decent quality. Technically these fall into the barrios of San Nicolás, Monserrat and Balvanera, but they are more commonly referred to by their geographical designation.

The owner's son speaks some English at *Hotel Bahía* (☎ 382-1780), Av Corrientes 1212, where rates are US$20 double; they may give a 10% discount with student card. *Hotel Roma* (☎ 381-4921), Av de Mayo 1413, gets no better than a tepid endorsement. Its rooms go for $22/30 a single/double.

*Hotel Sportsman* (☎ 381-8021), in a pleasant older building in decent repair at Rivadavia 1425, is popular despite its indifferent staff. Rooms go for US$15/24 with shared bath, US$28/35 with private bath; the former is the better value. Under the same management is the slightly better *Hotel Europa* (☎ 381-9629), Bartolomé Mitre 1294, where doubles with private bath cost US$35.

At ramshackle but passable *Hotel Plaza* (☎ 371-9747), Rivadavia 1689, tiny singles with shared bath cost US$18 and only slightly more with private bath (don't confuse it with the exclusive Marriott Plaza Hotel in Retiro). *Hotel Central* (☎ 326-8785), Alsina 1693, has rooms with private bath for US$18/25. Some rooms are small at *Hotel Cevallos* (☎ 372-7636), Virrey Cevallos 261, but it's congenial, clean and well maintained for US$20/30.

*Hotel Callao* (☎ 476-3534), in an interesting building at Av Callao 292, has singles with shared bath for around US$16, and rooms with private bath for US$27/38. Greatly improved *Gran Hotel Oriental* (☎ 951-6427), Bartolomé Mitre 1840, offers rooms with shared bath for US$16/18 and others with private bath for US$20/22. Still a decent value is friendly *Gran Hotel Sarmiento* (☎ 476-2764), on a quiet block at Sarmiento 1892, where simple but very tidy rooms (some a bit cramped) with private bath cost US$25/35.

A few blocks north of the Autopista 25 de Mayo at Carlos Calvo 1463, *Hotel Carlos I* (☎ 305-3700) offers doubles for around US$25. Two blocks south of the autopista and not far from Estación Constitución, *Hotel La Casita* (☎ 27-0250) at Constitución 1549 has doubles for around $20.

## San Telmo

**Hostel** In a rambling old building with considerable charm, the official *Albergue Juvenil* (☎ 394-9112) at Brasil 675 near Constitución station and easily reached by Subte, has 90 beds, a TV lounge and a pleasant outdoor patio, but it can be noisy when groups from the provinces visit the capital. Prices run about US$9 per person including breakfast but no kitchen privileges. It's helpful and friendly, but sometimes closes between noon and 6 pm; HI/AYH membership is obligatory.

**Hotels** In San Telmo, probably the cheapest acceptable place is amiable, well-maintained *Hotel Zavalia* (☎ 362-1990) at Juan de Garay 474 near Parque Lezama, where singles/doubles with shared bath cost only US$8/12. Its main drawback is that families with children can make it noisy at times. Close to colorful

Plaza Dorrego is dilapidated but passable *Hotel Carly* (☎ 361-7710), Humberto Primo 464, with rooms for US$12/14 a single/double with shared bath. The staff is lackadaisical, but for this price you can't expect too much.

*Hotel Victoria* (☎ 361-2135), Chacabuco 726, has very good singles/doubles for US$15/25 with private bath; some rooms are a little musty, but it has a pleasant patio. *Hotel Embajador* (☎ 362-6617), across the street at Chacabuco 747, has similar facilities. *Hotel Bolívar* (☎ 361-5105), Bolívar 886, is the barrio's budget favorite; several rooms have sunny balconies for US$17 single, US$22 double with private bath. Union-run *Hotel Oxford* (☎ 361-8581), Chacabuco 719, offers singles/doubles for US$24/41 including breakfast.

The area around Estación Constitución has a number of places charging around US$20 double (this area has many albergues transitorios, which rent rooms on an hourly basis). Possibilities include *Hotel Atlas* (☎ 27-9587) at Perú 1681, or the enigmatically named *Hotel Miramar* (☎ 304-9069) at Salta 1429. For slightly more money, try *Hotel Esquel* (☎ 304-5722) at Av Brasil 1319, or *Hotel Autopista* (☎ 305-1634) at Salta 1444. Other adequate places include *Hotel Central* (☎ 304-3783) at Av Brasil 1327 and *Hotel Brasil* (☎ 304-5441) at Av Brasil 1340.

## Recoleta & Barrio Norte

For reasonable accommodations in a lively university area, try *Hotel Rich* (☎ 961-7942), at Paraguay 2080 near the Facultad de Medicina of the Universidad de Buenos Aires. Rates are US$20/30 with private bath.

*Residencial Hotel Lion D'Or* (☎ 803-8992), Pacheco de Melo 2019, is very cheap by barrio standards for US$20 to US$25 single, US$40 double, but it's often full.

## Outer Barrios

Hostel membership is not obligatory at *Albergue Oroño* (☎ 581-6663, 581-9387), which charges US$7 per person, but it's considerably less central at Espinosa 1628 near Av San Martín, north of Parque Centenario. Take bus No 24 or No 166 from downtown.

In an older house near the Caballito branch of the Universidad de Buenos Aires (Subte Primera Junta or Emilio Mitre) on Calle Puan, Juan Carlos Dima (☎ 432-4898) offers accommodations in private rooms, kitchen facilities, cable TV and phone for about US$10 per night. Phone ahead.

# PLACES TO STAY – MIDDLE

## The Microcentro & Monserrat

Many of the abundant mid-range hotels around Av de Mayo, bordering San Telmo and Congreso, are worn – though usually not dirty – or cheaply remodeled. Correspondents offer mixed reviews of *Hotel Avenida* (☎ 331-4341), Av de Mayo 623 two blocks west of Plaza de Mayo, where singles/doubles cost US$35/45 with private bath; several consider its much improved bright, spacious and air-conditioned rooms a lesser value than other cheaper places – perhaps because the staff are less cheerful than the rooms. For about US$40/55, *Turista Hotel* (☎ 331-2281), in the same block at Av de Mayo 686, has some adherents but has also drawn negative comment.

Recent readers' choices include the so-so *Novel Hotel* (☎ 345-0504) at Av de Mayo 915 for US$30/45; *Gran Hotel Hispano* (☎ 342-4431) at Av de Mayo 861 for US$40/52 with breakfast; and the *Astoria Hotel* (☎ 334-9061) at Av de Mayo 916 for $50/60 with private bath.

Away from Av de Mayo, the rest of the microcentro has several decent mid-range options. At *Hotel Plaza Roma* (☎ 311-1679), Lavalle 110 near LN Alem, rooms with private bath and breakfast cost US$35/54. Once a leading budget hotel, well-maintained *Petit Hotel Goya* (☎ 322-9311) at Suipacha 748 is no longer cheap at US$40/50, but it's friendly, spotless, central, quiet and comfortable. *Gran Hotel Argentino* (☎ 345-3078, 345-3082), Pellegrini 37, is reasonable value for US$46/57. *King's Hotel* (☎ 322-8461), Av Corrientes 623, is competitively priced at US$46/55.

For US$50/60 with breakfast, about half the price of other four-star accommodations, *Hotel Regidor* (☎ 314-7917), Tucumán 451, is an excellent value, but it can be snooty toward casually dressed visitors. Rates start around US$60/70 at places such as the *Tucumán Palace Hotel* (☎ 311-2298), Tucumán 384, which has drawn some criticism for 'deferred maintenance'. The *Liberty Hotel* (☎ 325-0261), Av Corrientes 632, charges US$60/75, while *Hotel Regis* (☎ 393-5131), Lavalle 813, costs US$65/75.

## Corrientes & Congreso

Near the Plaza del Congreso, the shopworn *Hotel Mar del Plata* (☎ 476-0466), Rivadavia 1777, charges about US$28/35 with shared bath, US$33/45 with private bath and breakfast. At *Hotel Napoleón* (☎ 383-2031), Rivadavia 1364, clean but tackily remodeled rooms with private bath and TV are no great bargain for US$50/60 and upwards. Rates are comparable at *Hotel Lourdes* (☎ 951-7467), Av Callao 44.

Some travelers like the once-elegant *Hotel Reina* (☎ 381-2496) at Av de Mayo 1120 near Av 9 de Julio, where singles/doubles with shared bath cost US$20/30, but some singles have been created with improvised partitions and are very small. Rates with private bath are US$25/37. For US$25/32, *Hotel Palace Solís* (☎ 371-6266), Solís 352/56 three blocks south of Plaza del Congreso, draws only faint praise from travelers. Readers have given higher marks to *Hotel Marbella* (☎ 383-8566) at Av de Mayo 1261 for $30/40 a single/double.

Among the best values is the *Chile Hotel* (☎ 383-7877), an Art Nouveau landmark at Av de Mayo 1297, where rooms with private bath cost US$30/45. Although the street noise is considerable, corner rooms have huge balconies with choice views of the Congreso Nacional and the Casa Rosada. *Nuevo Hotel Mundial* (☎ 383-0011), Av de Mayo 1298 across from Chile Hotel, has standard singles/doubles for US$40/55 and special rooms for US$60/70; the rest of the hotel doesn't quite match the attractive lobby, but it has a restaurant, hairdresser, boutique and other services.

The *Cardton Hotel* (☎ 382-1697), an older mansion in good repair at Perón 1559, is another excellent value. Singles/doubles with cable TV start at US$30/40. Under the same management is the thoroughly remodeled and recommended but slightly more expensive *Hotel Americano* (☎ 382-4223), nearby at Rodríguez Peña 265.

*Hotel Molino* (☎ 374-8941), Av Callao 164, charges US$40/52 with air-conditioning, private bath and telephone, but some rooms are small and front on this very noisy street. Spotlessly clean *Hotel Parlamento* (☎ 371-3789), Rodríguez Peña 61, is friendly but a bit worn for US$50/60. For the same price but including breakfast, rooms at the *Normandie Hotel* (☎ 371-7001), Rodríguez Peña 320, are more threadbare than its attractive lobby would suggest. In the heart of the theater district, the *Columbia Palace Hotel* (☎ 326-1906), Av Corrientes 1533, charges US$50/65.

The three-star *Sarmiento Palace Hotel* (☎ 953-3404), Sarmiento 1953, with cable TV and 24-hour room service, is clean, friendly and fairly quiet for $60/66. In a quiet building on a noisy street, the very clean and recommended *Hotel Ayamitre* (☎ 953-1655), Ayacucho 106, has rooms with TV, phone, and air-conditioning, but it's not the equal of the Americano, especially for US$55/70.

Charming and friendly *Hotel Lyon* (☎ 476-0100), Riobamba 251, has spacious, well-maintained suites with private bath, cable TV, telephone and other conveniences for US$64/72. Even larger ones cost only a little more, making it a good value for a family or group.

## Retiro

Modest *Hotel Central Córdoba* (☎ 311-1175), San Martín 1021, is friendly, pleasant, quiet, very clean and also very central; some rooms are small, but one might more charitably call them cozy. Rates are US$32/42 with private bath. *Gran Hotel Orly* (☎ 312-5344), Paraguay 474, is a good mid-range value for US$43/49, as is comfortably old-fashioned *Hotel San Antonio* (☎ 312-5381), Paraguay 372, for US$40/50 with breakfast.

Nearby at Paraguay 450, the somewhat rundown *Hotel Waldorf* (☎ 312-2071) charges US$54/63, while *Hotel Diplomat*, San Martín 918, is a bit dearer for US$55/65. One correspondent praises the centrally located *Promenade Hotel* (☎ 312-5681), MT de Alvear 444, which charges about US$60/70 a single/double, but another found its attractive lobby a misleading approach to 'grubby, grimy and noisy' rooms above.

## Recoleta & Barrio Norte

Friendly but ramshackle *Hotel Versailles* (☎ 811-5214), Arenales 1364, has spacious rooms and an excellent Barrio Norte location, but it's worn and past its peak for US$30/40. For US$47/60, the *Ayacucho Palace* (☎ 806-0943), Ayacucho 1408, has rather good prices considering its location. Location is also the best feature at the cordial *Alfa Hotel* (☎ 812-3719), Riobamba 1064, where simple but well-kept, sunny rooms cost US$40/50 (US$45/55 for slightly better rooms).

*Residencial El Castillo* (☎ 813-2048), in an older building at MT de Alvear 1893, is comparably priced at US$50/60. The otherwise dignified *Guido Palace Hotel* (☎ 812-0341), Guido 1778, has an excellent location and an attractive 5th floor patio, but the walls are scuffed and luxuries few considering the price of US$60/70 a single/double.

## Palermo

Accommodations of any kind are relatively scarce in Palermo, compared to other barrios, but there are a few mid-range choices on and around Av Santa Fe, near the

Plaza Italia Subte station on Línea D. *Hotel Pacífico* (☎ 771-4071), Santa María de Oro 2554, is plain and a bit worn for US$38/43. Under the same ownership, *Hotel Panamé* (☎ 771-4041), Godoy Cruz 2774, is a decent value at US$38/46 with private bath and TV, though some downstairs rooms are a bit dark. For US$38/50, the remodeled *Palermo Hotel* (☎ 773-7951), Av Santa Fe 4599, is spotlessly clean but lacks personality and sits on a noisy corner; some interior rooms are a bit small.

## Belgrano

Since Belgrano is primarily a residential area, accommodations of any kind are few. The handful of moderately priced hotels include *Key's Hotel* (☎ 772-8371) at Zapata 315 for US$24/40 single/double; *Hotel de la Rue* (☎ 551-4884) at Ramón Freire 1765 for US$35/45; and *Hotel Majale* (☎ 544-2711) at Ciudad de la Paz 2942 for US$40/50.

## PLACES TO STAY – TOP END

Top-end hotels almost invariably quote prices in US dollars, but they do accept Argentine currency; all of them take credit cards.

WAYNE BERNHARDSON

The elegant Alvear Palace Hotel opened in 1928.

## The Microcentro & Monserrat

Owners of the convenient *Hotel Phoenix* (☎ 312-4845), an architectural gem at San Martín 780, have made substantial investments in an attempt to restore the splendor of the days when it hosted the Prince of Wales; its 60 rooms now sport modern conveniences without diminishing the appeal of the original antiques. Improvements have come at a price, though, and what was recently a midrange hotel now costs US$79/90 a single/double.

Some visitors consider the four-star *Hotel Italia Romanelli* (☎ 312-6361), Reconquista 647, greatly overrated for US$77/86, citing high telephone charges (almost universal in Argentina, however) and very overpriced drinks. *Hotel Nogaró* (☎ 331-0091), Diagonal Presidente Julio A Roca 562, is a bit tattered by four-star standards, but a 15% cash discount makes rooms starting at US$106/118 a little more palatable. Among its more appealing features is the good natural light in most rooms, not always common in the densely built downtown. *Hotel Carsson* (☎ 322-3551), Viamonte 650, is central, clean and pleasant, with competent English-speaking staff; singles/doubles cost US$100/120. Rooms fronting on Viamonte tend to be noisy, however.

*Gran Hotel Colón* (☎ 325-1917), Carlos Pellegrini 507, charges US$144/158 for comfortable rooms with verdant (thanks to large potted plants) balconies overlooking the Obelisco near one of the capital's most famous (and noisiest!) intersections, Av 9 de Julio and Av Corrientes. Rates at the very central *Hotel Continental* (☎ 326-3251), Diagonal Roque Sáenz Peña 725, are US$106/118.

Conveniently central at Tucumán 535, the venerable *Claridge Hotel* (☎ 322-7700) charges US$254 for very comfortable rooms with cable TV and other amenities. The microcentro's other five-star accommodations are at the *Hotel Libertador Kempinsky* (☎ 322-2095), Av Córdoba 664, which charges US$248 a double.

## Corrientes & Congreso

Congreso is more a mid-range than an upscale area, but the four-star *Castelar Hotel* (☎ 383-5000, fax 383-8388), in a magnificent building at Av de Mayo 1152, is one of the best top-end values for US$70/80 – only slightly dearer than some truly mediocre mid-range places. The always crowded *Savoy Hotel* (☎ 814-3592), Av Callao 181, has doubles for US$120/140. The more prestigious *Bauen Hotel* (☎ 804-1600), Av Callao 360 near Av Corrientes, also charges US$140 for a double, and facilities include restaurants, a nightclub and even a theater.

# Retiro

The clean, comfortable *Crillón Hotel* (☎ 312-8181), Av Santa Fe 796, charges US$130/140 for singles/doubles, with a good buffet breakfast included.

Opposite Plaza San Martín at Florida 1005, Marriott has recently taken over the elegant *Plaza Hotel* (☎ 311-5011), which has an interesting Dutch-style dining room; rates are US$270 double. Rates and services are comparable at the *Elevage Hotel* (☎ 313-2082), Maipú 960. Opposite the Plaza Fuerza Aérea, the modern *Sheraton Hotel* (☎ 311-6330) at San Martín 1225 is less central and convenient, and much less personable. Singles/doubles cost well upwards of US$300.

# Recoleta & Barrio Norte

Probably the best top-end value in Barrio Norte is the three-star *Wilton Palace Hotel* (☎ 811-1818), Av Callao 1162, recommended for cleanliness and good service. Rooms go for US$88/98 a single/double.

Few places match the Old World charm of *Hotel Plaza Francia* (☎ 804-9631), Eduardo Schiaffino 2189, where singles/doubles cost about US$135/180. If you plan to eat so much that walking back to the hotel might be an effort, consider the five-star *Etoile Hotel* (☎ 804-8603), RM Ortiz 1835, located right on Recoleta's restaurant row. Standard suites start at US$170 per night, plus the whopping 21% IVA, and reach US$350 per night plus IVA. The recently renovated *Hotel Presidente* (☎ 325-5985), Cerrito 846, costs US$208 single or double. The *Park Hyatt Buenos Aires* (☎ 326-1234), Cerrito 1433, charges US$235 plus IVA.

At the elegant *Alvear Palace Hotel* (☎ 804-4031), Av Alvear 1891, doubles can reach $260 or more; another US$30 gets you a suite (most of which have spas). Since opening in 1928, it has been one of few places to maintain its standards through all the country's hard times. It has a particularly noteworthy rooftop garden.

One of the area's newest luxury lodgings, frequented by visiting entertainers, is the *Caesar Park Hotel* (☎ 814-5157), a brick construction at Posadas 1232. Singles/doubles cost US$310/350.

# Palermo

The *Torre Cristóforo Colombo* (☎ 777-9633, fax 775-9911), Santa María de Oro 2747 between Juncal and Cerviño, is a new luxury highrise 'aparthotel' starting at US$90 for one-bedroom 'junior' suites with kitchenette and up to US$180 for a three-room suite with a large outdoor terrace. Rates do not include the 21% IVA.

# Places to Eat

Food in Buenos Aires ranges from cheap and simple to costly and sophisticated. In some places, decent fixed-price meals are available for US$5 or less, but side orders such as french fires and soft drinks can drive a-la-carte prices up rapidly. Chinese *tenedor libre* restaurants provide the most food for the least money – all you can eat for as little as US$4 – but quality varies considerably. Most also offer a wide variety of Argentine standards.

In run-of-the-mill restaurants, which are often very good, the standard fare is basic pasta like ravioli and gnocchi, short orders such as *milanesa* (breaded steak usually fried but sometimes baked), and the more economical cuts of beef. Count on fried potatoes, green salads and desserts as well. By spending just a little more, you can find the same sort of food with better-quality ingredients. More cosmopolitan meals are available at the capital's innumerable high-class restaurants, but these can be very costly indeed. One good place to catch up on the latest in *haute cuisine* is the Good Living section in the Sunday *Buenos Aires Herald*, where Dereck Foster also offers the latest on Argentine wines. Be aware, however, that by his criteria, 'inexpensive' meals can easily cost US$15.

Travelers on a very limited budget should try the *rotiserías* (delis), which sell dairy products, roast chicken, pies, turnovers and *fiambres* (processed meats). Such places often have restaurant-quality food for a fraction of the price.

In price, burger-oriented fast-food clones such as *Pumper Nic* are shockingly expensive compared to standard restaurants serving much better food; in quality, they fall just short of vomitivo. For fast food, try bus or train terminal cafeterias or the ordinary *comedor*, which usually has a limited menu often including simple but filling fixed-price meals. Comedores also often serve *minutas* (short orders) such as steak, eggs, milanesa, salad and chips.

*Confiterías* serve mostly sandwiches, including *lomito* (steak), *panchos* (hot dogs) and hamburgers. *Restaurantes* offer much larger menus (including pasta, parrillada and fish), professional waiters and often more elaborate decor. There is, though, a great difference between the most humble and the most extravagant.

Restaurant meals are generally relaxed affairs. Breakfasts are negligible, but other meals can last for hours. Lunch starts around midday, but dinner starts much later than in English-speaking countries. Almost nobody eats before 9 pm, and it is not unusual to dine after midnight even during the week.

If a snack or drink is in order, consider stopping in at a café. Everything from marriage proposals to business transactions to revolutions originate in Buenos Aires cafés, where many Argentines spend hours on end over a single cup of coffee, although simple food orders are also available. Cafés also serve beer, wine and hard liquor.

Bars are establishments where people go to drink alcohol. Gentrified bars may be called pubs (pronounced as in English). Additional cafés and bars appear in the Entertainment chapter.

## ON THE MENU

Ever since European livestock transformed the Pampas into enormous cattle ranches, the Argentine diet has relied on beef. When Charles Darwin rode across the province of Buenos Aires in the 1830s, he could not contain his astonishment at the gauchos' diet, which he himself followed of necessity:

I had now been several days without tasting any thing besides meat: I did not at all dislike this new regimen; but I felt as if it would only have agreed with me with hard exercise. I have heard that patients in England, when desired to confine themselves exclusively to an animal diet, even with the hope of life before their eyes, have scarce been able to endure it. Yet the Gaucho in the Pampas, for months together, touches nothing but beef . . . . It is, perhaps, from their meat regimen that the Gauchos, like other carnivorous animals, can abstain long from food. I was told that at Tandeel, some troops voluntarily pursued a party of Indians for three days, without eating or drinking.

After scientists discovered fossil remains of the world's largest meat-eating dinosaur in Patagonia, an Argentine on the Internet joked that 'it figures that the world's greatest carnivore would be an Argentine'. Many Argentines recognize that a diet so reliant on beef is unhealthy, but sedentary porteños continue to ingest it in large quantities at the capital's countless parrillas. As long as you don't make it a way of life, you can probably indulge yourself on the succulent grilled meat, often stretched on a vertical spit over red-hot coals in the picture windows of the city's most prestigious restaurants.

To Argentines, the Spanish word *carne* (meat) is synonymous with beef – lamb, venison and poultry all fall under other categories. The most popular form is the *parrillada*, a mixed grill of steak and other cuts that no visiting carnivore should miss. A traditional parrillada will include offal such as *chinchulines* (small intestines), *tripa gorda* (large intestine), *ubre* (udder), *riñones* (kidneys) and *morcilla* (blood sausage), but don't let that put you off unless you're a vegetarian.

Despite the obsession with beef, Argentina offers more ethnic and regional variety than most visitors expect. Everyone quickly recognizes the Italian influence in such pasta dishes as spaghetti, lasagna, cannelloni and ravioli. Less obvious is the tasty *ñoquis* (gnocchi in Italian), an inexpensive staple when the budget runs low at the end of the month. Ñoquis are a traditional restaurant special on the 29th of each month, but in times of economic crisis people may joke that 'this month we'll have ñoquis on the 15th'.

Some regions of Argentina have very distinctive dishes, which are also available in the capital. The Andean Northwest (Noroeste Andino) is notable for spicy dishes, more closely resembling the food of the central Andean highlands than the blander fare of the Pampas. From Mendoza north, it is common to find Middle Eastern food. Argentine seafood, while less varied than Chilean, deserves attention, even though Argentines are not big fish-eaters. Fresh-water fish are outstanding but relatively unusual in the capital.

Since the early 1980s, health food and vegetarian fare have acquired a niche in the diets of some Argentines, but outside Buenos Aires and a few other large cities, vegetarian restaurants are less common. International cuisine of a high quality is readily available, especially if money is no object.

Chinese restaurants are becoming common in the capital. One bilingual menu from a Chinese restaurant near Congreso advertised 'camarones a la plancha' (grilled shrimp) and creatively mistranslated it into English as 'ironed shrimp'. Despite this vivid image, most Asian food in Argentina is unremarkable Cantonese, but a recent boom in tenedor-libre restaurants, where all-you-can-eat meals still cost as little as US$4, has been a boon for budget travelers. Most also have salad bars with excellent ingredients, but they also tack on a US$1 surcharge if you don't order anything to drink; prices for mineral water, soft drinks and beer are usually not outrageous, compared to upscale restaurants, but these restaurants make their profit on beverages.

---

**Meatless Meals in Cattle Country**

Argentine cuisine is known for red-meat dishes, but vegetarians no longer have much trouble making do except, perhaps, in the most out of the way places. Since the 1980s, vegetarian restaurants have become commonplace in Buenos Aires, and nearly all of them have the additional appeal of being tobacco-free.

Even standard parrillas serve items acceptable to most vegetarians – such as green salads (often large enough for two people) and pasta dishes such as ravioli, cannelloni and *ñoquis* – but before ordering pasta, be certain it doesn't come with a meat sauce. If you have trouble being served a meatless dish, try pleading allergies and remember that meat *(carne)* is beef – chicken, pork and the like are considered in a different category, though sometimes referred to as *carne blanca* (white meat). Vegans will find far fewer menu options. ■

---

# Breakfast

Argentines eat little or no breakfast. Most common is coffee, tea or *yerba mate* with *tostadas* (toast), *manteca* (butter) and *mermelada* (jam). In cafés, *medialunas* (small croissants), either glazed sweet or *saladas* (plain), accompany your *café con leche* (coffee with milk). A midmorning breakfast may consist of coffee plus a *tostado*, a thin-crust toasted sandwich with ham and cheese, and a glass of fresh-squeezed orange juice.

# Lunch & Dinner

Argentines compensate for skimpy breakfasts with enormous lunches, starting about noon or 1 pm, and dinners, never earlier than 9 pm and often much later.

Beef, in a variety of cuts and styles, is the most common main course. Most Argentines prefer beef *cocido* (well done), but restaurants will prepare it *jugoso* (rare) or *a punto* (medium) on request. French fries (chips) and/or green salad usually accompany beef dishes.

An asado or parrillada (see above) is the standard, ideally prepared over charcoal or a wood fire and accompanied by *chimichurri*, a tasty marinade. Serious carnivores should not miss *bife de chorizo*, a thick, tender, juicy steak. *Bife de lomo* is short loin; *bife de costilla* or *chuleta* is T-bone; and *asado de tira* is a narrow strip of roast rib. *Vacío* is sirloin. *Matambre relleno* is stuffed and rolled flank steak, baked or eaten cold as an appetizer. Thinly sliced, this rotisería standby makes excellent sandwiches. *Bife a caballo* comes topped with two eggs and chips.

WAYNE BERNHARDSON

Enjoying a snack on Plaza Dorrego in San Telmo

*Carbonada* is a beef stew with rice, potatoes, sweet potatoes, maize, squash, chopped apples and peaches. *Puchero* is a slow-cooked casserole of beef, chicken, bacon, sausage, morcilla, maize, peppers, tomatoes, onions, cabbage, sweet potatoes and squash; the cook may add garbanzos or other beans. Rice cooked in the broth is a common accompaniment.

Milanesa is one of the cheapest and commonest short-order items on the menu. This author is tired of ordinary milanesa, but tastier and more elaborate versions are available – try *milanesa napolitana* with tomato sauce and mozzarella, and *milanesa maryland*, made with chicken and accompanied by fried bananas and creamed corn.

*Pollo* (chicken) is sometimes part of the standard parrillada, but it also comes separately with french fries or salad. The standard fish is *merluza* (hake), most commonly fried in batter and served with mashed potatoes. Spanish restaurants are a good bet for well-prepared seafood.

## Snacks

One of the world's finest snacks is the *empanada*, a tasty turnover filled with vegetables, hard-boiled egg, olives, beef, chicken, ham and cheese or other fillings. These are cheap and available almost everywhere – buy them by the dozen in a rotisería before a long bus or train trip. Empanadas *al horno* (baked) are lighter than empanadas *fritas* (fried).

Pizza, a common market and restaurant snack, is one of the cheapest items on the menu when purchased by the slice. In many pizzerías, it is cheaper to eat standing up at the counter than seated at a table. Toppings are standardized – not customized as in North America – but there are more options when buying an entire pizza rather than slices. For slices, be sure to try *fugazza*, a cheap and delicious cheeseless variety with sweet onions, or *fugazzeta*, which comes with mozzarella cheese. Many Argentines eat their pizza accompanied by *fainá*, a dense chickpea (garbanzo) dough baked and sliced in the same shape as pizza.

For Argentines at home or on the road, a common afternoon snack is *mate con facturas* (mate with sweet pastries). If you go to visit an Argentine family in the afternoon, stop by the bakery to bring some facturas along.

## Desserts

Fresh fruit is the most common *postre* in Argentine homes, where uncouth North Americans and Australians will find that cultured Argentines surgically peel all fruit (except grapes) with a table knife. In restaurants, *ensalada de fruta* (fruit salad), *flan* (egg custard) or *queso y dulce* (cheese with preserved fruit, sometimes known as *postre vigilante)* are frequent choices. The 'dulce' can consist of *batata* (sweet potato) or *membrillo* (quince). Flan is topped with *crema* (whipped cream) or *dulce de leche*, a sweet caramelized milk which is an Argentine specialty. *Almendrado*, vanilla ice cream rolled with almonds, is also common.

---

**Screamy Stuff**

Coming from the Italian tradition, Argentine *helado* (ice cream) is the continent's best and comparable to the best anywhere else in the world. Chains like *Massera*, located throughout the country, are not bad, but the best Argentine ice cream comes from smaller *heladerías*, which make their own in small batches on the premises or nearby – look for the words *elaboración propia* or *elaboración artesanal*. Such places often have dozens of flavors, from variations on conventional vanilla and chocolate to common and exotic fruits and unexpected mixtures. During winter, when Argentines rarely eat ice cream, the best heladerías often close.

Rarely will Argentine ice cream disappoint you, but only truly special shops are mentioned in the text. When restaurant desserts seem a bit expensive, a quarter kilo is a relatively economical alternative, especially when shared. ∎

---

# Drinks

Argentines consume a great variety of liquids, both non-alcoholic and alcoholic. The most Argentine among them is mate, a cultural bellwether described in a sidebar in the Facts about Buenos Aires chapter.

There are few drinking restrictions, although 18 is the legal age for alcohol consumption in public.

**Soft Drinks** Argentines drink prodigious amounts of soft drinks, from the ubiquitous Coca-Cola to 7-Up to the local tonic water, Paso de los Toros. Mineral water, both carbonated *(con gas)* and plain *(sin gas)* is widely available, but tap water is potable despite the city's aging infrastructure. If no carbonated mineral water is available, *soda*, which often comes in large siphon bottles, is usually the cheapest thirst-quencher.

**Fruit Juices & Licuados** *Jugos* are not so varied as in tropical South America. For fresh-squeezed orange juice, ask for *jugo de naranja exprimido* – otherwise you may get tinned juice (oranges are very cheap in Argentina but, transformed into fresh juice, miraculously increase their value tenfold). *Pomelo* (grapefruit), *limón* (lemon) and *ananá* (pineapple) are also common. *Jugo de manzana* (apple juice), a specialty of Patagonia's Río Negro Valley, is available everywhere.

*Licuados* are milk-blended fruit drinks, but on request they can be made with water. Common flavors are banana, *durazno* (peach) and *pera* (pear).

**Coffee, Tea & Hot Chocolate** Serious coffee drinkers will be delighted to find that coffee will always be espresso (accompanied by enough packets of sugar to fuel a Brazilian Volkswagen). *Café chico* is a thick, dark coffee served in a very small cup. *Cortado* is a small coffee with a touch of milk, usually served in a glass – for a larger portion ask for *cortado doble*. Similar but containing more milk, *café con leche* (latte) is served for breakfast – avoid the error of ordering it after lunch or dinner, when you should request a cortado.

Tea, produced domestically in the provinces of Corrientes and Misiones, is also a common drink. Usually it comes with lemon slices, but if you drink it with milk, do not order *té con leche*, which means a tea bag immersed in warm milk. Rather, ask the waiter for *un poquito de leche*.

Argentine chocolate can be delicious. For breakfast, try a *submarino*, a semisweet chocolate bar dissolved in steamed milk, but note that prices vary greatly. Ordinary *chocolate*, made with powdered cocoa, can be surprisingly good if submarinos are not available.

**Alcohol** Beer, wine, whiskey and gin should satisfy most visitors' alcoholic thirst, but don't overlook *ginebra bols* (which differs from gin) and *caña* (cane alcohol), which are national specialties.

Quilmes, brewed in the Buenos Aires suburb but available everywhere, is an excellent beer. Bieckert is another popular brand. In bars or cafés, ask for the excellent *chopp* (draft or lager).

Argentine wines receive less publicity abroad than Chilean ones, but *tintos* (reds) and *blancos* (whites) are both excellent and inexpensive (when prices on almost everything else skyrocket, wines miraculously remain reasonable, and a bottle of good wine may be cheaper than a liter of Coca-Cola). Especially at home, where jug wines are present at almost all meals, Argentines often mix their wine with soda water.

The major wine growing areas are near Mendoza, San Juan, La Rioja and Salta. Among the best known brands are Orfila, Suter, San Felipe, Santa Ana and Etchart. Try to avoid cheap, boxed wines such as Termidor.

# PLACES TO EAT – BUDGET

## The Microcentro & Monserrat

For a nutritious if unspectacular budget meal try the basement cafeteria at *Restaurant Islas Malvinas*, Reconquista 335. *La Lecherísima*, Av Corrientes 839, has a variety of large salads, sandwiches and pasta. *Cabaña Blanca*, Florida 243, is an antiseptically pleasant milk bar with good sandwiches, fruit salads and the like. For equally cheap or even cheaper fare, try the hole-in-the-wall *Restaurant San Francisco*, Defensa 177 near Plaza de Mayo.

Most 'Italian' food is actually hybrid Italo-Argentine, despite Argentina's abundance of Italian surnames. Exceptions to this rule tend to be pricey, but *La Casona del Nonno* (☎ 322-9352), Lavalle 827, has good US$4 lunch specials, and the dining areas include a separate, well-ventilated nonsmoking section upstairs. The popular pizzería *Los Inmortales* (☎ 322-5493) has a branch at Lavalle 746.

*El Palacio de la Papa Frita* is a good, popular and reasonable chain offering a standard Argentine menu. It has a branch at Lavalle 735 (☎ 393-5849) and another at Lavalle 954 (☎ 322-1559).

The Patio de Comidas on the lower level of the Galerías Pacífico, on the Florida peatonal between Viamonte and Córdoba, has a number of moderately priced fast-food versions of some very good restaurants for about US$5 to US$7 or so, including *Sensu* for Japanese dishes, *Romanaccio* for pizza and pasta, and *Freddo* for ice cream (no cheaper than Freddo's anywhere else, however). Since all have common seating, it's a good choice for diners unable to agree on a single place to eat.

Culture-bound fast-food junkies will find nine *McDonald's* in Buenos Aires, the most central of which are at Lavalle 964 and Florida 570. The indigenous *Pumper Nic*, a McDonald's clone, has many locations throughout the city, including Av Corrientes 774 and Suipacha 435.

## Corrientes & Congreso

For around US$3 or even less, the express cafetería at supermarket *Coto*, Viamonte 1571, offers a wide variety of surprisingly good meals despite zero atmosphere (or maybe lots of it from another point of view – the entire main floor is blissfully tobacco-free). Another budget choice is the *Supercoop* chain, Sarmiento 1431.

Traditionally, one of the capital's most popular and economical parrillas is *Pippo* (☎ 374-6365), at Paraná 356 with another entrance on Montevideo. Another popular traditional parrilla is *Chiquilín* (☎ 49-5163) at Sarmiento and Montevideo.

Misleadingly named *Lin Lin* (☎ 381-3188) at Libertad 467 is not Chinese, but it does offer a choice of three courses, plus drink, for lunch or dinner, for only US$6.50. The self-service, tenedor-libre *Ratatouille*, Sarmiento 1810, offers decent vegetarian fare for US$8.

Among the Chinese all-you-can-eats in the area are *La Fronda* at Paraná 342, *Han Kung* at Rodríguez Peña 384, and *Yong Bin Kwan* at Rivadavia 2030. For authentic Korean food in spartan surroundings, try *Casa de Corea* at Perón 2489.

Although it's a chain, *Bar La Robla* (☎ 811-4484) at Viamonte 1613 prepares excellent seafood and standard Argentine dishes that are far from monotonous, in a pleasant environment at moderate prices. Its US$3.50 lunch specials, including an appetizer and a small glass of clericó, are an excellent value. Service is superb, and there's a small but clearly designated and effectively segregated tobacco-free area. Another convenient branch (☎ 381-3435) is at Montevideo 194.

*Cervantes II* (☎ 372-8869), Perón 1883, has enormous servings of standard Argentine fare at reasonable prices, but is often so crowded that patrons may wish to take their food away instead of eating in; alternatively, go late for lunch or early for dinner. They enforce the non-smoking section only if someone complains, however. Mobbed at lunch, *El Toboso* (☎ 476-0519), Corrientes 1848, is a decent and moderately priced parrilla with other kinds of daily specials, but very expensive drinks (US$2.50 for mineral water) drive up the prices. The paté spread is a nice touch not found at other similar places. *El Palacio de la Papa Frita* (☎ 326-8063) has an outlet at Av Corrientes 1612.

For inexpensive Italian food, try the *Vecchio Unione* (☎ 372-7750), in the basement of the Sociedad Benevolenza di Italia at Perón 1372; its US$7 menú ejecutivo for lunch is a real bargain because they seem willing to substitute just about anything on the list. The US$6 lunch specials are a good value at *La Fonda de Montserrat* (☎ 372-6282), Virrey Cevallos 178, which has barrio atmosphere and quick, friendly and excellent service. The food is otherwise fairly routine Argentine fare.

The consistently best pizzería is the unsung *Güerrín*, Av Corrientes 1372, which sells very inexpensive individual slices of superb fugazza, fugazzeta and other specialities, plus excellent empanadas, cold lager beer to wash it all down, and many appealing desserts. It's cheaper to buy at the counter and eat standing up, but there is a much greater variety of toppings if you decide to be seated and served, or order an entire pizza to take out.

The traditionally excellent *Pizzería Serafín*, nearby at Av Corrientes 1328, is well worth a visit – their chicken empanadas are always good. In the same site at Av Callao 83 since 1936, *La Americana* (☎ 371-0202) also has very fine pizza and exceptional empanadas, but the best chicken empanadas (usually breast meat) are at *La Continental*, Av Callao 202 at Perón. At the original branch of

*Los Inmortales* (☎ 326-5303), at Av Corrientes 1369 beneath the huge billboard of Carlos Gardel, try their very reliable pizzas as you peruse the historic photographs of Gardel and his contemporaries on the walls.

*Buenos Aires Herald* restaurant critic Dereck Foster notes that non-Argentine Latin American restaurants tend to start with good intentions and varied menus, but often retreat to more conventional local offerings. One place that may not do so is *La Casa de Orihuela* (☎ 951-6930), Alsina 2163, which serves exceptionally well-prepared Peruvian and regional dishes. Its US$6 fixed-price lunch is one of the city's best values, well worth a detour from other parts of town. The decor is pleasing, the service cheerful and efficient. *Restaurant Status*, Virrey Cevallos 261, is only marginally Peruvian but perhaps worth a stop if you're in the area.

For ice cream lovers, Buenos Aires is paradise. My favorite, distinguished by the outline map of Italy above its unpretentious storefront, is *Heladería Cadore* at Av Corrientes and Rodríguez Peña. Chocoholics could overdose on their exquisite chocolate amargo (semisweet chocolate) or chocolate blanco (white chocolate), while the mousse de limón (lemon mousse) also merits special mention. Several locals recommend *Saverio*, which has branches on Corrientes and in Recoleta.

## San Telmo

On balance, San Telmo probably offers the best combination of high-quality, low-priced dining in the city, though some of the most expensive restaurants are also here. The no-frills *Último Tango*, Pasaje San Lorenzo 379, attracts a crowd of mostly middle-aged men with surprisingly good three-course fixed-price lunches from US$5 to US$7; enjoy your meal with background tango music. Another good, inexpensive choice is *Jerónimo* (☎ 300-2624), Estados Unidos 407, where most entrees cost between US$3 and US$5, and desserts are about US$1.50. *La Vieja Rotisería*, on Defensa between Carlos Calvo and Estados Unidos, also prepares good budget food, as does *Café Bar Alexa* at Defensa 435.

Surrounding Plaza Dorrego are several caférestaurants, including *Café Bar Dorrego* at the corner of Defensa and Humberto Primo, and *Café del Arbol* at Humberto Primo 422. All the places on the plaza will serve their patrons outdoors under the trees (except, of course, when vendors jam the plaza for the Sunday flea market).

It's stretching it a bit to call *Nicole de Marseille*

(☎ 362-2340), Defensa 714, a French restaurant or even Franco-Argentine, but its three-course weekday lunches with a wide choice of entrees and desserts are a good value for US$6. *Almafuerte* (☎ 342-1729), Defensa 598, offers a varied Spanish-Argentine menu with cheap lunch specials. *Wonderful*, Defensa 1154, is a US$6 Chinese tenedor libre; drinks cost an additional US$2.

Reader-endorsed *Las Marías II*, at Bolívar 964-966, is a pizzería with friendly and efficient staff. On the fringes of San Telmo in Constitución, spicy cuisine from the northwestern Andean province of Jujuy is the specialty at friendly *La Carretería*, Brasil 656, across from the official youth hostel.

The name *Las Leñas* usually suggests a parrilla, but it's the unlikely name of an ice creamery on Defensa between Carlos Calvo and Estados Unidos. At the corner of Defensa and Brasil, across from Parque Lezama, *Heladería Florencia* also serves the cold stuff.

## Recoleta & Barrio Norte

One of the cheapest eateries in Recoleta is the simple but decent *Clapper's Café* (☎ 803-3314), Junín 1793 near the corner of Guido, but the attractive *Café de los Angeles* (☎ 801-1844), Guido 1936, also has a variety of relatively inexpensive lunch specials (beware the costly drinks and desserts). *Henry J Bean's* (☎ 801-8477), a US import at Junín 1749, is also reasonably priced.

*El Sanjuanino* (☎ 804-2909), Posadas 1515 at Callao, serves spicier regional versions of typical Argentine dishes such as empanadas, locro and sweets, and it also delivers within the immediate area. The classic pizzería *Los Inmortales* has branches at Av Callao 1165 (☎ 813-7551) and Av Alvear 1234 (☎ 393-6124). Part of a respectable pizza and pasta chain, *Romanaccio* (☎ 811-4071), Av Callao 1021, has a well-arranged nonsmoking section. At the corner of Azcuénaga and Peña, *Kugenhaus* has a good selection of takeout food and continental pastries.

A step up from most Chinese all-you-can-eats is *Gran Fu Ia* (☎ 803-5522), Av Las Heras 2379; the US$8 price tag for lunch or dinner reflects its higher-quality fare, including items such as prawns not normally found in such places. It also prepares spicy a-la-carte dishes that most Argentines avoid.

For the capital's best selection of cheeses, visit *Sorbera Sola* (☎ 812-3462), MT de Alvear 1521, which carries both domestic and imported varieties well beyond the common mozzarella and parmesan.

For ice cream, try any of several branches of *Heladería Freddo*, the most convenient of which are at Ayacucho and Quintana, and at Junín and Guido. Despite recent expansion (Aerolíneas Argentinas now serves Freddo's ice cream on international flights), the company has maintained its traditional high quality.

## La Boca

For the most part, the food of La Boca is fairly ordinary but also rather inexpensive by current Argentine standards. The sidewalk seating and colorful decor at *La Barbería* (☎ 301-8770), Pedro de Mendoza 1965, make it a good place to stop for a cold beer or cider on tap, but the empanadas are a little expensive (though very good). *Puerto Viejo* is a decent parrilla, two blocks south at the corner of Pedro de Mendoza and Quinquela Martín.

WAYNE BERNHARDSON

WAYNE BERNHARDSON

Cantinas in La Boca

*El Viejo Puente de Mario* (☎ 301-2170), Almirante Brown 1499 at the corner of Pedro de Mendoza, is cheap for minutas but much more expensive for seafood. *La Orquesta*, Aráoz 701, has moderately priced pasta and salads in an attractive setting.

Across the street from Boca Juniors' 'Bombonera' stadium, *La Cancha* (☎ 362-2975), Brandsen 697, is a popular hangout for soccer fans. *El Samovar de Rasputín*, on Del Valle Iberlucea 1251 near Pedro de Mendoza, is cheap and very informal, as is *El Lunfa*, almost next door at Del Valle Iberlucea 1243, which has live music.

Like the other gaudy cantinas on its street, *Spadavecchia*, Necochea 1180, is more notable as a place to party than to eat, but the food is passable. It's only open for evenings, but other nearby eateries are also open for lunch: *Gennarino* at Necochea 1210, and *Tres Amigos* and *Il Piccolo Vapore*, on opposite corners of Necochea and Suárez.

*Helados Sorrento*, Olavarría 658, serves the barrio's best ice cream.

## Retiro

*Alimentari*, San Martín 899 at Paraguay, has outstanding medialunas for breakfast. *Yinyang* (☎ 311-7798) is a macrobiotic restaurant at Paraguay 858.

Inexpensive *Parrilla al Paso*, Paraguay 445, is a recent readers' recommendation. Reader endorsements for vegetarian restaurants include *Giardino*, with branches at Suipacha 429 and Lavalle 835; *Verde Esmeralda* at Esmeralda 370; and *Granix* at Florida 126 and Florida 461.

Travelers who won't be crossing the Andes will find passable Chilean seafood and other national dishes at *Los Chilenos*, Suipacha 1042. Of the Chinese tenedor-libre restaurants, try *Macau* at Suipacha 477 or *China Doll* at Suipacha 544.

## Palermo

*La Casona de Tía Teresa*, on the border between Recoleta and Palermo at Las Heras 2843, has a fixed-price Italian lunch for US$8. Porteño diners jam the nearby *Río Rhin Norte* (☎ 802-0197), Tagle 2521, for a wide variety of four-course lunch or dinner specials for US$7.

*La Querencia*, Lazo 3110, specializes in spicy Tucumán-style empanadas. The Palermo branch of the excellent but still economical chain *Bar La Robla* (☎ 71-2497; see the Corrientes & Congreso section above for more detail) is at Gascón 1701. *El Caballito Blanco*, at the corner of Las Heras and Billinghurst, is a reasonably priced pizzería.

Ice cream addicts will find the Palermo branch of *Freddo* at the corner of Av del Libertador and Teodoro García. *Toots*, at the corner of Godoy Cruz and Cerviño, also serves very fine ice cream.

## Belgrano

Belgrano's best cheap eats are at the cafeteria at the local branch of the supermarket *Coto*, on Av Cabildo between Maure and Gorostiaga. The menu is identical to that at the Viamonte branch near Av Corrientes (see the entry for Corrientes & Congreso above).

Spicy Jujuy cuisine is the rule at *La Chaya* (☎ 783-3955), a takeout restaurant at Ciudad de la Paz 2296. *Cloé* (☎ 784-8436), Cuba 2208 at Mendoza, is a popular neighborhood confitería with decent light meals. *Yinyang* (☎ 788-4368) is a macrobiotic restaurant at Echeverría 2444.

Reasonably priced Middle Eastern food attracts diners to *Al Shawarma de Aladino* (☎ 788-0328), Echeverría 2487, open for lunch and dinner daily except Sunday. It also offers vegetarian specials, takeout food, and live music and dance Thursday, Friday and Saturday nights. *Buffet Libre* (☎ 784-2900), Juramento 1650, has all-you-can-eat fare for US\$8.

Ice cream addicts will find the Belgrano branch of *Freddo* at the corner of Juramento and Arcos. *Furchi*, Av Cabildo 1506, serves Italian-style gelato.

## Outer Barrios

*Recopa 2* (☎ 433-0104), an ice-cream shop at Pedro Goyena 1401 in the Caballito neighborhood near the Facultad de Filosofía y Letras of the Universidad de Buenos Aires (Subte Primera Junta), serves an unearthly white chocolate with dark-chocolate-covered almonds.

# PLACES TO EAT – MIDDLE

## The Microcentro & Monserrat

If you visit only one parrilla in Buenos Aires, ignore the bogus rent-a-gauchos at *La Estancia* (☎ 326-0330), Lavalle 941, and focus on excellent food at moderate prices. Highly regarded, but pricier, microcentro parrillas include *La Rural* (☎ 322-2654) at Suipacha 453; *La Posta del Gaucho* (☎ 322-6784) at Carlos Pellegrini 625; *Los Troncos* (☎ 322-1295) at Suipacha 732; and *La Posada de 1820* at San Martín 606.

*Los Idolos*, a pizzería at Suipacha 436, is popular but its atmosphere and service are better than its food. A bit dearer than most Italian restaurants, but excellent and still reasonable by current standards, is *Broccolino* (☎ 322-7652), Esmeralda 776. *ABC* (☎ 322-3992), Lavalle 545, is a popular lunchtime choice for Middle European specialties like goulash. The microcentro's best Chinese restaurant, not a tenedor libre, is *Oriente* at Maipú 512.

## Corrientes & Congreso

Spanish restaurants are usually the best alternatives for seafood, which is otherwise not particularly prized by Argentines. In addition to its pleasant atmosphere, *Los Teatros* (☎ 374-4946), Talcahuano 360, has outstanding seafood, chicken and pasta dishes. It's named for its location in the theater district. *El Hispano* at Salta 20 and *Villarosa* at Hipólito Yrigoyen 1389 are both good choices for Spanish cuisine. For Basque food, try *Laurak Bat* (☎ 381-0642) at Av Belgrano 1174. *Chez Moi*, San Juan 1223 in Constitución, serves up French cuisine.

Congreso's most prestigious parrilla is *La Cabaña* (☎ 381-2373), Entre Ríos 436, but recent reports suggest declining service. Complaints that the Argentine legislature never accomplishes anything for lack of attendance may be true, at least when the *Quorum* (☎ 951-0855), directly behind the Congreso Nacional at Combate de los Pozos 61, offers a US$13 'menú legislativo'. The ornate, almost rococo interior at *Confitería del Molino* (☎ 952-6016), Av Callao 20 near the Congreso building, also merits a visit from anyone seeking turn-of-the-century ambience and exquisite sweets.

*La Casa China* (☎ 371-1352), Viamonte 1476, is a step above its tenedor-libre competitors for Asian food.

## San Telmo

Part of San Telmo's Casal de Catalunya cultural center at Chacabuco 863, *Hostal del Canigó* (☎ 304-5250, 300-5252) serves Catalonian specialties like pollo a la punxa (chicken with calamari) as well as other Spanish and Argentine dishes. Prices are not cheap (the fixed-price menú ejecutivo costs US$9), but portions are large and the dining room's woodwork and tilework lend it great atmosphere. Lunch comes with a complimentary glass of sherry. One block south, at Chacabuco 947, the *Federación de Sociedades Gallegos* also serves Spanish seafood, while *Taberna Baska* (☎ 383-0903) at Chile 980 serves Basque food.

In a restored colonial house at Defensa 1000 near Plaza Dorrego, *La Casa de Esteban de Luca* (☎ 361-1582) has very fine food at moderate prices. More upscale is *Antigua Casca de Cuchilleros* (☎ 362-3811) at Carlos Calvo 319. *El Virrey de San Telmo* (☎ 361-0331), Humberto Primo 499, offers an international menu.

For Swiss cuisine, try *La Petit*, Salta 2158 in Constitución. French cuisine is the focus at attractive *La Convención* (☎ 361-6201), Carlos Calvo 375. *La Scala de San Telmo* (☎ 362-1187), Pasaje Giuffra 371, serves a midrange to upscale international menu to the accompaniment of live classical music.

## Retiro

*Dora* (☎ 311-2891), Av LN Alem 1016, is popular in part for its massive portions; menu prices appear steep, but most dishes suffice for two people – the imposing half portion of bife de chorizo (US$9), for instance, weighs nearly half a kilo. LP correspondents have also praised its seafood and pasta, as well as 'incredible' desserts (which *are* expensive). Nearby *El Salmón* (☎ 313-1731), at Reconquista 968 near Paraguay, has a similar and slightly cheaper menu.

Two parrillas, *La Chacra* (☎ 322-1409) at Av Córdoba 941 and *Las Nazarenas* (☎ 312-5559) at Reconquista 1132, are among the capital's most prestigious. *La Mosca Blanca* (☎ 313-4890), Av Ramos Mejía 1430, has a good reputation and reasonable prices. *La Cantina China* (☎ 312-7391), Maipú 976, offers Chinese dishes more than a step above the usual tenedor libre.

*Filo* (☎ 311 0312), San Martín 975, is a lively pizza-and-pasta place where the menu changes frequently. It's not strictly vegetarian and prices are a bit upscale, but *Alicia* (☎ 393-6981), Av Santa Fe 959, is a natural foods restaurant with an excellent takeout bakery – try the tasty barley biscuits.

## Recoleta & Barrio Norte

Many new restaurants have opened in the Plaza del Pilar development, a food mall alongside the Centro Cultural Recoleta; the offical address is at Av Pueyrredón 2501, but it's more easily accessible from the Junín entrance to the center. Choices range from relatively cheap fast-food offerings to elaborate and sophisticated fare. One of the best values is *Munich del Pilar* (☎ 806-1111), where a US$9 weekday menú ejecutivo offers a choice of meat, chicken or pasta entrées and includes drinks. *Molière*, closest to the Centro Cultural, serves an excellent grilled salmon with appetizer and a large glass of house wine for US$15; service is well intentioned but erratic.

Several others in the complex are worth checking out: *Café Champs Elysée* (more a confitería), known for its tantalizing desserts; *Caruso*, a pricey trattoría; *Campo del Pilar*, a parrilla; *Café Rex* with its cinematic décor; *La Doma*, which has an expensive fixed-price menu; *Mumy's*, serving pricey hamburgers but also some reasonable combinations; *Romanaccio*, good for pizza and pasta; *Fishy Bar*, a fast-food option; and *Puerto Marisko*, offering expensive seafood.

One of Buenos Aires' most enduring vegetarian alternatives, *La Esquina de las Flores* (☎ 811-4729), Av Córdoba 1599, also has a health-food store; its daily fixed-price meals cost US$10 (US$6 for children), but there are less expensive a-la-carte choices as well. The Esquina is also something of a cultural center, offering lectures and workshops on food, diet, health and similar topics, and producing radio and TV programs.

One of Recoleta's better values is *Patio López* (☎ 807-0611), Vicente López 1955, where good lunches cost US$10, dinners US$12, with occasional bargain specials. By Recoleta standards *Bar Rodi* (☎ 801-5230), Vicente López 1900, is a good value for beef and pasta.

With seafood specials ranging from US$14 to US$17, *El Figón de Bonilla* (☎ 804-7771), Junín 1721, is reasonable by Recoleta's restaurant-row standards. *Café de las Flores*, at the corner of Posadas and Ayacucho, is a moderately priced place with an adequate smoke-free section.

At the corner of Schiaffino and Av del Libertador, in the highly regarded Hotel Plaza Francia, *Restaurant Schiaffino* costs around US$10 for lunch and US$15 for dinner. *La Rueda* (☎ 804-2226), Quintana 456, is a midrange parrilla charging around US$14 for lunch, US$18 for dinner.

For pizza, try informal *Pizza Banana* (☎ 812-6321), Ayacucho 1425 at Pacheco de Melo; *La Gomería* (☎ 803-6170) at Vicente López 2134; or *Pizza Cero* at Av Alvear and Schiaffino. *Restaurant Ruso* (☎ 805-7079), Azcuénaga 1562 in Barrio Norte, is a new restaurant specializing in Russian food at reasonable prices (at least by Barrio Norte standards). Also in Barrio Norte at Av Santa Fe 2321, attractive *Guadalest* (☎ 825-6425) serves fine pasta and imposing desserts – most of them large enough for two. It is also one of few places in town that takes the trouble to ask diners whether they prefer the nonsmoking section.

Renowned as a good value, the *Restaurant del Club Sirio* (☎ 806-5764), Pacheco de Melo 1902, serves a US$18 Middle Eastern tenedor libre Monday to Saturday evenings. *Watani* (☎ 806-0553), part of the Club Libanés at Junín 1460, also serves Middle Eastern food.

# Palermo

Attractive *Fiori y Canto* (☎ 963-3250), on the edge of Palermo Viejo at Av Córdoba 3547, offers a varied menu of pizza, pasta and parrilla, with particularly delicious homemade bread. *La Zí Teresa di Napoli*, Las Heras 2939, is a good Italian possibility, but *Pizza Cero* (☎ 803-3449), Cerviño 3701, has better decor than food.

*Mandato* (☎ 802-4258), Scalabrini Ortiz 3191, is a moderately priced neighborhood parrilla-and-pasta restaurant that may be the only place in town to go to talk baseball – owner Jorge Fuertes has coached the sport, watches it on international cable and still plays softball on occasion. After midnight Fridays and Saturdays it turns into a popular pub for neighborhood youth.

*La Cátedra* (☎ 774-9859), Cerviño 4699 (Subte Plaza Italia), serves an excellent three-course lunch, including a small bottle of wine and coffee, for US$12 weekdays; its US$7 salad bar is even more economical, but a-la-carte prices are notably higher. *María Luz* (☎ 774-3122), Sinclair 3236 near Av del Libertador, is an attractive neighborhood restaurant with reasonable prices – less than US$10 for appealing crepes. Near the polo grounds, *Lotus Neo Thai*, at Ortega y Gasset 1782, is the only eatery of its kind in the city.

# Belgrano

*El Ceibal* (☎ 784-2444), Av Cabildo 1421, traditionally one of the capital's better parrillas and pizzerías, recently relocated from Palermo; it has less atmosphere than before, but the service and food are still fine, and prices are moderate. On weekends they offer a dozen different menúes ejecutivos for US$8 or US$9 – try northwestern Argentine specialties such as locro, cazuela de humita and tamales tucumanos.

*Antiguo Belgrano*, at the corner of Cuba and Blanco Encalada, is an agreeable beer-and-pizza kind of place. *Tía Teresa de Belgrano*, Juramento 1775, serves moderately priced Italian specialties, while *Gabbiano*, Cuba 2272, is a more expensive Italian choice.

*L'Altro Cesare* (☎ 781-7365), Monroe 2248, is a very fine Italian restaurant with outstanding service and some innovative dishes – try the canelones con humita (maize) for US$8 and the very light chocolate mousse (US$5) for dessert. Most pasta dishes are quite reasonable, though some of the more unusual sauces cost extra, making it expensive for diners who are not selective. The small nonsmoking area is not really adequate.

*Munich Belgrano* (☎ 784-1989), Monroe 2444, is no

relation to its near-namesake in Recoleta but serves an Argentine-continental menu. *Casita Suiza* (☎ 781-9961), opposite Plaza Noruega at Mendoza 2587, prepares moderately priced Swiss dishes like fondues. Reservations are essential at *Mis Raíces* (☎ 786-6633), Arribeños 2148, which specializes in Jewish food.

North of Aeroparque, *Los Años Locos* (☎ 783-5126) is a popular parrilla on the Costanera Av Rafael Obligado at La Pampa. Technically, it's just beyond Belgrano, in the outer barrio of Núñez. Several similar restaurants dot the Costanera, which loops through the area here.

## Outer Barrios

Despite its out-of-the-way location in the barrio of Barracas, south of Constitución and San Telmo, *Buenos Aires Sur* (☎ 301-6758), Villarino 2359, is a very popular and highly recommended bar-restaurant among both locals and visitors. Bus No 12 goes there from Plaza Italia and Plaza del Congreso, while Nos 20 and 45 go there from Retiro and Plaza de Mayo.

# PLACES TO EAT – TOP END
## The Microcentro & Monserrat

*Cicerón*, Reconquista 647, is an upscale Italian restaurant in the Hotel Italia Romanelli. *El Pulpo* (☎ 311-0330), Tucumán 400, is widely considered the city's best seafood restaurant, with prices to match.

An open secret is the popular smorgasbord at the *Swedish Club* (☎ 334-1703), 5th floor, Tacuarí 143. Theoretically open to members only, it now takes place every Wednesday, but visitors can 'request' an invitation by phone. The US$26 price tag makes it a special occasion for most people.

## Corrientes & Congreso

*Yuki* (☎ 942-5853), Venezuela 2145, is an expensive but highly regarded Japanese restaurant.

## San Telmo

San Telmo lacks top-end accommodations, but upscale and even formal dining is another matter; jacket and tie are pretty much obligatory at places like *La Tasca de San Fermín*, on Carlos Calvo between Defensa and Balcarce, and *El Repecho de San Telmo* (☎ 362-5473), housed in a landmark late colonial builiding at Carlos Calvo 242.

# Retiro

Highly regarded *Dolli* (☎ 327-2134), Av del Libertador 312, serves a Mediterranean menu, with meals in the US$30-plus range. For French cuisine, try *Catalinas* (☎ 313-0182) at Reconquista 875. *A'Mamma Liberata* (☎ 393-0962), Maipú 974, serves Italian food.

# Recoleta & Barrio Norte

If price is no object, check out Recoleta's restaurant row on Junín and RM Ortiz, opposite the Cementerio de la Recoleta and the Centro Cultural. Fixed-price lunches or dinners are in the US$20 to US$30 range, but a-la-carte meals can be much dearer.

Among the local institutions are *Gato Dumas Cocinero* (☎ 806-5802) at Junín 1747; *Harper's* (☎ 801-7155) at Junín 1763; *Clark's* (☎ 801-9502) at Junín 1777; and *Hippopotamus* (☎ 804-8310) at Junín 1787, which offers a reader-endorsed US$18 menú ejecutivo. Also on the premises is a popular but very formal disco/nightclub.

*Lola* (☎ 804-3410), RM Ortiz 1809, features an expensive French menu; the desserts include a US$7 flan. *Cabaña Las Lilas* (☎ 804-9464), RM Ortiz 1813, is a parrilla, while *Sensu* (☎ 804-1214) at RM Ortiz 1815 serves Japanese food. *Don Juan* (☎ 804-5045) at RM Ortiz 1827 has a more international menu, while *La Tasca de Germán* (☎ 804-2943), RM Ortiz 1863, specializes in Spanish cuisine, and *Estilo Munich* (☎ 804-4469), RM Ortiz 1871, offers a continental menu.

Long acknowledged as one of Buenos Aires' best prestige restaurants, *Au Bec Fin* (☎ 801-6894), Vicente López 1825, has prices to match. *Robertino* (☎ 803-1460), Vicente López 2158, is upscale Italian, as is *Subito* (☎ 815-1725), at Posadas 1245 in the Patio Bullrich shopping center. Another Japanese choice is the expensive *Midori* (☎ 814-5151), in the Caesar Park Hotel at Posadas 1252.

A new addition to the list of continental restaurants is Barrio Norte's appealing *French Bistro* (☎ 806-9331), at French 2301 at the corner of Azcuénaga. Seafood lovers should check out *Cantabria* at Av Callao 1235.

# Palermo

On the fringes of Recoleta/Palermo Chico, *Le Trianon* (☎ 806-6058), Av del Libertador 1902, is an upscale French restaurant where weekday lunch specials cost around US$20. *Río Alba* (☎ 773-5748), Cerviño 4499, is an elegant, expensive parrilla in the heart of the barrio. *Llers* (☎ 773-9303), Demaría 4711 at Sinclair, is one of the capital's elite Argentine-style restaurants.

# Belgrano

The *2020 Restaurant* (☎ 783-6156), Arcos 1926, is an expensive Italian locale where fixed-price meals cost upwards of US$20. *Cien Años*, Amenábar 2075, serves French food.

*Chinatown*, Juramento 1656, around the corner from barrio's actual (and rather small) Chinatown, is generally regarded as the city's best Chinese restaurant. *Tomasso*, Av del Libertador 5932, is one of the city's landmark restaurants for pizza and pasta.

# Entertainment

Travelers should note that for many entertainment events, including movies, live theater and tango shows, *carteleras* along Av Corrientes sell a limited number of heavily discounted tickets; most tango shows aren't worth US$40, but for half that they're worth considering. Buy tickets as far in advance as possible, but if you want to see a show or movie on short notice, especially at midweek, just phone or drop by to see what's available. Discount tickets for the newest shows or most recently released hit films are rare.

Cartelera Vea Más (☎ 372-7285, 372-7314, ext 219), Local 19 in the Paseo La Plaza complex at Corrientes 1660, is open daily from 10 am to 11 pm. Although the street address is on Corrientes, this cubbyhole office is more easily accessible from Sarmiento, one block south. Three blocks east, Cartelera Baires (☎ 372-5058), at Local 25 in the Galería Teatro Lorange at Corrientes 1372, is open Monday through Thursday from 10 am to 10:30 pm, Friday and Saturday from 10 am to midnight, and Sunday from 2 to 10:30 pm. Yet another cartelera (☎ 821-6077) is at Vidt 1980 in Palermo, just off Av Santa Fe (Subte Estación Bulnes).

## CAFÉS & BARS

Café society is a major force in the life of Argentines in general and porteños in particular – they spend hours solving their own problems, the country's and the world's over a chessboard and a cheap cortado. Many of these places double as bars, serving alcohol as well as caffeine, but their atmosphere can range from bare bones to true luxury.

Av Corrientes is a favorite hangout for Argentine intellectuals. Famous for a bohemian atmosphere is the spartan *Café La Paz* (☎ 46-5542), Av Corrientes 1599. *Café Pernambuco*, Av Corrientes 1680, also has a good atmosphere for a cup of coffee or glass of wine.

*Viejos Tiempos*, Defensa 360, is a San Telmo bar with good ambience. *Bar del Museo*, opposite the Museo de la Ciudad at Alsina and Defensa just south of Plaza de Mayo, also draws a bohemian crowd.

Favorite microcentro hangouts include the *Young Men's Bar* (☎ 322-9543) at Av Córdoba 800 and the always-crowded *Florida Garden* (☎ 312-7902), Florida 899, which is popular among politicians, journalists and other influential people. Another possibility is the *Richmond* (☎ 322-1341), Florida 468.

Before or after dining, some of the porteño elite while away the hours on caffeine at *La Biela* (☎ 804-0432), Quintana 598 in Recoleta. The rest exercise their purebred dogs nearby, so watch your step when crossing the street to *Café de la Paix* (☎ 804-6820), Quintana 595. Another elegant place is the Alvear Palace Hotel's *Winter Garden* in Recoleta.

Some hybrid cafés double as bookstores, offering live music, poetry readings, occasional films and the like. The *Foro Gandhi* (☎ 374-7501), Av Corrientes 1551, is an arts-oriented coffee house offering live tango music and foreign film cycles at bargain prices. The very attractive *Clásica y Moderna* (☎ 812-8707), Callao 892 near Córdoba in Recoleta, is an intimate, sophisticated bookstore-café offering mid-range to upscale meals, with occasional live performances of folk, jazz and popular music; it also keeps the day's newspapers for patrons' convenience.

For more café listings, see the Places to Eat chapter.

# TANGO

Finding spontaneous tango is not easy, but you'll have the best luck at the Municipalidad's 'Tango y Baile' programs on San Telmo's *Plaza Dorrego*, where a wide cross-section of the porteño public dances to the sounds of live and recorded music. Free of charge, these performances take place semi-regularly on Saturday nights in summer, attracting tourists without pandering to them.

Plenty of clubs in San Telmo and La Boca portray Argentina's most famous cultural export for prices up to US$40 per show. From its publicity, *Casa Blanca* (☎ 331-4621), Balcarce 668 in San Telmo, appears to glory in hosting disgraced heads of state (such as Brazil's Fernando Collor de Mello and Mexico's Carlos Salinas de Gortari) and dropping the names of show-biz patrons (Omar Sharif, Oliver Stone and Eric Clapton). It does present some of the biggest names in tango, however; regular shows take place weekdays at 10 pm, Saturday at 9 and 11 pm.

Other San Telmo *tanguerías* include *El Viejo Almacén* (☎ 362-3602) at Balcarce and Independencia (note the mural on the wall across the street); the less formal *A Media Luz* (☎ 331-6146) at Chile 316; and the very lively *Los Dos Pianitos* (☎ 361-2188) at Pasaje Giuffra 305, which goes to all hours of the morning. *Bar Sur* (☎ 362-6086), Estados Unidos 299, is popular for both dining and dancing; there is no cover charge, but the US$20 drink minimum buys only around three beers.

The flagrantly touristic but nevertheless highly praised dinner show at *Tango Mío* (☎ 303-0568, 303-6970), Ituzaingó 1200 in Barracas south of San Telmo, costs US$55 and includes transport to and from your hotel, as well as wine and champagne.

DAVE HOUSER

WAYNE BERNHARDSON

DAVE HOUSER

Top left:   Gardel immortalized in tile
Top right:   Dancers at Plaza Dorrego
Bottom:   Many tango clubs, such as this one in San Telmo, offer classes before the real dancing begins.

More central tango spots include *Tanguería Corrientes Angosta* at Lavalle 750 in the microcentro and *Caño 14* at Talcahuano 975 in Barrio Norte. *La Casa de Carlos Gardel* (☎ 962-4264), at Jean Jaurés 735 (Subte Carlos Gardel or Pueyrredón) in the Abasto area of Balvanera, was in fact once Gardel's home. *Café Homero* (☎ 773-1979), a popular neighborhood tanguería at Cabrera 4946 in Palermo Viejo, has no cover charge but does enforce a US$20 minimum-consumption rule. Café Homero also has a downtown site (☎ 864-5126) in the Paseo La Plaza complex at Av Corrientes 1660.

Several places around town provide tango instruction; for general information, contact the *Academia Nacional del Tango* at Av de Mayo 831 in Monserrat, alongside Café Tortoni. The *Universidad de Buenos Aires*, in the microcentro at 25 de Mayo 217, teaches beginner lessons (US$7 for non-students) from 6:30 to 8 pm Fridays, and more advanced dancers take the floor from 8 to 10 pm. *El Dorado*, Hipólito Yrigoyen 947 in Monserrat, offers lessons at 8:30 pm Thursday and Friday, with full-fledged dancing starting at 10:30 pm. The *Teatro Suizo*, on Rodríguez Peña near Sarmiento, also has inexpensive tango lessons.

# CLASSICAL MUSIC

The *Teatro Colón* (☎ 382-0554), Libertad 621, is Buenos Aires' landmark classical music venue, having hosted figures as prominent as Enrico Caruso, Plácido Domingo, Luciano Pavarotti and Arturo Toscanini. The season for opera and classical music runs from March through November but really hits its stride in the winter months of June through August. The Orquesta Filarmónica de Buenos Aires, often featuring guest conductors from throughout Latin America, normally plays Monday evenings at 9 pm.

Other classical music venues include *Teatro Avenida* (☎ 381-0662) at Av de Mayo 1212 in Congreso, which specializes in ballet, and the *Teatro Coliseo* (☎ 313-5943) at MT del Alvear 1125 in Recoleta. Tickets for classical performances range from about US$20 to US$70, but some venues offer series discounts.

# THEATER

Av Corrientes, between Avs 9 de Julio and Callao, is the capital's Broadway or West End, but there are many dozens of venues throughout the city, where live theater enjoys widespread popularity – during the peak winter season, upwards of a hundred different scheduled events may take place. Tickets at the most prestigious theaters, like the Cervantes and the Avenida, can cost anywhere from US$20 up to US$100 for prime attractions, but check *carteleras* for bargain seats. The *Buenos Aires Herald* and other newspapers carry thorough listings of major productions, but some deserving theater companies receive relatively little attention from the mainstream media.

Major theater venues include *Teatro Nacional Cervantes* (☎ 476-4224) at Libertad 815 near Plaza Lavalle in Recoleta; *Teatro Avenida* (☎ 381-3193) at Av de Mayo 1212 near Plaza del Congreso; *Teatro Presidente Alvear* (☎ 374-6076) at Av Corrientes 1659; *Teatro Blanca Podestá* (☎ 382-9140) at Av Corrientes 1283; the uniquely designed *Teatro Complejo La Plaza* (☎ 326-8781) at Av Corrientes 1660; *Teatro Esmeralda* (☎ 322-3600) at Esmeralda 425 in the microcentro; and *Teatro del Sur* (☎ 383-5702) at Venezuela 1286 five blocks southeast of the Plaza del Congreso. One of the Municipalidad's most interesting free weekend tours stops at several of these venues; for more details, see 'Organized Tours' in the Getting Around chapter.

One of the best formal facilities is *Teatro General San Martín* (☎ 374-8611), Av Corrientes 1530, which has several auditoriums that sometimes host free events. Free theater presentations take place at many different sites, including *Teatro Margarita Xirgu* alongside the Casal de Catalunya (☎ 300-5252) at Chacabuco 863/875 in San Telmo (performances are in Spanish rather than Catalan). Less conventional companies to watch for, most of which have no regular venue but appear sporadically around town, include *Casita de la Selva* (☎ 672-5700) at La Selva 4022 in the outlying barrio of Vélez Sarsfield, Catalinas Sur, La Runfla, Diablo Mundo and Las Calandracas.

The *Teatro Fundación Banco Patricios* (☎ 372-5651) underwrites unconventional theater in its remodeled facilites at Av Callao 312 one block south of Av Corrientes. The intimate *Teatro El Vitral* (☎ 371-0948), Rodríguez Peña 344 also one block south of Corrientes, has three small venues seating about 40 people each. Another intimate theater venue/company is the *Equipo Teatro Payró* (☎ 312-5922), San Martín 766 in the microcentro. The Grupo Teatral Escena Subterránea performs works like *La Persecución* in the capital's subway stations. The very appealing *Merlyn Café* (☎ 786-3349), Cuba 2290 in Belgrano, is a jazz club that stages small-scale theater programs.

*Teatro de la Ribera* (☎ 302-8866), Pedro de Mendoza 1821 in La Boca, is a community-oriented theater company presently suffering financial difficulties; the building itself was a donation of artist and booster Benito Quinquela Martín, who almost singlehandedly put the barrio on the tourist map.

# CINEMAS

Buenos Aires is famous for its cinemas, which play first-run films from around the world, but there is also an audience for unconventional and classic films. The main cinema districts are along the Lavalle peatonal, west of Florida, and on Avs Corrientes and Santa Fe, all easy walking distance from downtown. The barrio of Belgrano also has a concentration of cinemas. Ticket prices have risen dramatically in recent years, but most cinemas offer half-price discounts on Wednesdays and sometimes for the first afternoon showing. Wednesday showings can be mobbed, so go early.

The *Sala Leopoldo Lugones* at the Teatro General San Martín, Av Corrientes 1530, regularly offers thematic foreign film cycles as well as reprises of outstanding commercial films. Unfortunately, since the bombings of the Israeli embassy and the AMIA Jewish cultural center, the *Cinemateca Hebraica*, Sarmiento 2255, has been closed as a cinema venue.

Since Spanish translations of English-language film titles are often very misleading, check the *Buenos Aires Herald* to be certain what's playing. Except for children's films and cartoon features, which are dubbed, foreign films almost always appear in the original language with Spanish subtitles.

# DANCE CLUBS

Recoleta and Palermo are the main areas for the capital's dance clubs, which tend to be exclusive and expensive – cover charges are often US$20 and upwards, and drinks are also pricey. One of the best values, with a young and unpretentious crowd, is *Gallery*, Azcuénaga 1771 in Barrio Norte/Recoleta. The cover charge is US$6, while large drinks cost about US$5 each.

*Hippopotamus* (☎ 802-0500), Junín 1787, is a Recoleta institution, as is *Afrika* (☎ 804-4031) at Av Alvear 1885 in the Alvear Palace Hotel. *Le Club*, Quintana 111, is on the boundary between Retiro and Recoleta, as is nearby *Shampoo* (☎ 813-4427), Quintana 362. *Morocco*, Hipólito Yrigoyen 851 in Monserrat, is a favorite haunt of Argentine and other Spanish-speaking pop stars.

Open until 6 am, the lively *Hanoi* (☎ 806-5312), at Av Casares and Sarmiento near Palermo's Parque 3 de

Febrero, has a US$15 cover charge and a high-priced restaurant. The well-established *Trump's* (☎ 801-9866), Bulnes 2772 in Palermo, is another dance club, as is *Metrópolis*, Av Santa Fe 4389.

Visitors to *New York City* (☎ 551-9341), Av Alvarez Thomas 1391 in the barrio of Villa Ortuzar, near the boundary with Chacarita and Colegiales, should know that this is a favored haunt of the alleged Dirty War torturer Alfredo Astiz.

Gay visitors will find several congenial bars and dance clubs in the Recoleta/Barrio Norte and Palermo areas, some of which welcome mixed groups. Among the possibilities are *Contramano* (men only, cover charge US$8 with one drink) at Rodríguez Peña 1082 in Retiro: *Area* at Junín 1081 in Barrio Norte; and *Experiment* (☎ 328-1019) at Carlos Pellegrini 1085. In Palermo, try *Nada* at Laprida 1523 (a no-cover pub with US$5 drinks); *Teleny* (US$10 cover with one drink) at Juncal 2479; *Bunker* (mixed cientele) at Anchorena 1170, and *The Line* at Av Santa Fe 3213.

## ROCK & BLUES

Buenos Aires has a thriving rock and blues scene; for the most up-to-date information, consult *Clarín's* Friday Suplemento Jóven, which also lists free events, and the weekend editions of *Página 12*.

*El Subsuelo* (☎ 476-2479), in the basement at the Pasaje de la Piedad alley just off Mitre 1571 in Congreso, is an 'intimate' (microscopically tiny) venue with good live music, including rock, blues and jazz. *La Comedia* (☎ 812-4228) is at Rodríguez Peña 1062, near the intersection of Avs Callao and Santa Fe.

*Hendrix*, San Lorenzo 354, is worth a trip to San Telmo, as is *La Trastienda* (☎ 342-7650) at Balcarce 460 and *Arpegios* at Cochabamba 415. *El Samovar de Rasputín* (☎ 302-3190), Iberlucea 1251 in La Boca, presents blues and rock bands on weekends.

## JAZZ

Founded in 1858, the famous *Café Tortoni* (☎ 342-4328), Av de Mayo 829 in Monserrat, has occupied its present site only since 1893. Oozing 19th-century atmosphere from the woodwork and billiard tables, it presents traditional jazz on weekends. La Porteña jazz band plays Thursdays at 8:30 pm, the Creole jazz band Fridays at 11:30 pm, and the Fénix jazz band Saturdays at 11:15 pm. Informal enough that patrons discard their peanut shells on the floor, *Bárbaro* (☎ 311-6856), Tres Sargentos 415 in Retiro, employs some of the same groups on other nights.

For contemporary jazz, try *Oliverio* (☎ 371-6877), just off Av Corrientes at Paraná 328, or the *Cotton Club de Buenos Aires* (☎ 325-1708) at Av Corrientes 636 in the microcentro. The very appealing *Merlyn Café* (☎ 786-3349), Cuba 2290 in Belgrano, showcases live jazz and serves reasonably priced meals.

# CULTURAL CENTERS

One of Buenos Aires' best cultural resources is the high-rise *Centro Cultural San Martín* (☎ 374-1251), with free or inexpensive galleries, live theater and lectures. Films show at its Sala Leopoldo Lugones. Most visitors enter from Av Corrientes, between Paraná and Montevideo, but the official address is Sarmiento 1551, where there is a shaded alcove with rotating exhibitions of outdoor sculptures and occasional free concerts on summer weekends. Visit the front desk for a monthly list of events, or check the board outside the Corrientes entrance.

At Junín 1930 in Recoleta, the *Centro Cultural Ciudad de Buenos Aires* (☎ 803-1041) also offers free or inexpensive events, such as art exhibitions and outdoor films on summer evenings. Similar facilities include the *Complejo Cultural Ricardo Rojas* (☎ 953-0390) at the Universidad de Buenos Aires, Av Corrientes 2038 in Corrientes, and the *Centro Cultural Sur*, on the border between Constitución and Barracas at Av Caseros 1750, which has live music, food, juices and the like.

The United States Information Agency's *Lincoln Center* (☎ 311-7148), Florida 935 in Retiro, has an excellent library that carries *The New York Times*, the *Washington Post* and English-language magazines. The center also has satellite TV transmissions from the States and often shows free, sometimes very unconventional, films. You need not be a US citizen to attend but must show identification before being admitted. Hours are Monday, Tuesday, Thursday and Friday from 10:30 am to 6:15 pm, and Wednesday from 5 to 9:30 pm. It's closed weekends and on US holidays.

Another source of information for North Americans is the *Instituto Cultural Argentino-Norteamericano* (☎ 322-3855, 322-4557), Maipú 672 in the microcentro. The *Instituto Goethe* (☎ 315-3327), 1st floor, Av Corrientes 319 also in the microcentro, offers German-language instruction, lectures, films and even concerts. The *Alianza Francesa* (☎ 322-0068) is at Av Córdoba 936.

# SPECTATOR SPORTS

Spectator sports in Buenos Aires are limited primarily to soccer, horse racing, polo and boxing, though tennis, rugby, cricket and Formula One automobile racing have their adherents (some visitors may conclude that most porteño drivers consider themselves Formula One competitors). Among the best known Argentine athletes and sports figures are soccer legend Diego Maradona, tennis stars Guillermo Vilas and Gabriela Sabatini, the late boxers Oscar Bonavena and Carlos Monzón, and ex-Formula One standout Carlos Reutemann, now a Peronist politician in the province of Santa Fe.

## Soccer

I have struggled to appreciate 90 minutes of apparently vigorous exercise that seems always to end in a scoreless tie, but the consensus is that Argentine soccer is world-class. The fans are no less rabid than in Europe – wear a hard hat if attending a match at Boca Juniors' 'Bombonera' stadium as violence does occasionally break out. *Barras bravas* are the Argentine equivalent of British 'football hooligans'.

Buenos Aires has the highest density of first-division soccer teams in the world – eight of the country's 20 are based in the capital, while another five are nearby in the suburbs of Gran Buenos Aires. For information on tickets and schedules, contact the clubs listed below; where two addresses and telephones appear, the first is club offices, while the second is the stadium, where tickets are normally purchased. *Entradas populares* (standing-room admissions) cost around US$10, while *plateas* (fixed seats) cost US$20 and upward, depending on their location and the significance of the match.

**Argentinos Juniors**
Punta Arenas 1271
☎ 551-6887
Boyacá 2152
☎ 582-8949

**Boca Juniors**
Brandsen 805
in San Telmo
☎ 362-2260

**Ferrocarril Oeste**
Cucha Cucha 350
☎ 431-9203
Martín de Gainza 244
☎ 432-3989

**Huracán**
Av Caseros 3159
☎ 91-6713

Av Almancio
Alcorta 2570
☎ 942-1965

**River Plate**
Av Presidente Figueroa
Alcorte 7597
☎ 788-1200

**San Lorenzo y Almagro**
Av Fernández de
la Cruz 2403
☎ 923-9212

Av Perito Moreno between
Av Fernández
de la Cruz and Varela
☎ 924-3455

**Unión Española**
Fernández 2100
☎ 613-0968

Santiago de
Compostela 3801
☎ 612-9648

**Vélez Sarsfield**
Av Juan B Justo 9200
☎ 641-5663

# Horse Racing

Buenos Aires' *Hipódromo Argentino* (☎ 774-6807), at the intersection of Av del Libertador and Av Dorrego in Palermo, is the site of horse races on Mondays, Fridays and Sundays. Admission costs upwards of US$10, and betting starts at US$2.

# Polo

The *Campo Argentino de Polo*, at the intersection of Av del Libertador and Av Dorrego in Palermo just across from the Hipódromo Argentino, is the site of the annual Campeonato Argentino Abierto Argentino de Polo (Argentine Open Polo Championship), which celebrated its centenary in 1993. Participation is not exactly for the masses, but most polo events are open to the public free of charge; for current information, contact the Asociación Argentina de Polo (☎ 331-4646), Hipólito Yrigoyen 636 in Monserrat, which keeps a schedule of activities throughout the country.

Shoppers interested in polo gear can visit La Martina (☎ 478-9366) at Paraguay 661 in Retiro or La Polera (☎ 806-0586) at Uriburu 1710 in Barrio Norte. La Martina also organizes full-day polo lessons, with afternoon matches, on the outskirts of the capital.

# Pato

Of gaucho origins, the polo-like game of *pato* takes its name from the original game ball, which was literally a duck encased in a leather bag (since replaced by a ball with handles). In what passes for an animal rights victory in Argentina, the live duck is no longer ripped to shreds. Likewise, the players no longer face death or dismemberment in what was a very violent sport.

For information on pato matches and tournaments, which usually take place at the polo grounds in Palermo, contact the Asociación Argentina de Pato (☎ 311-0222), Av Belgrano 530, 5th floor, in San Telmo.

# Boxing

The main venue for boxing matches is *Luna Park* (☎ 311-1990), an enclosed stadium at Bouchard 465, at the foot of Av Corrientes.

WAYNE BERNHARDSON

These boxers are pulling no punches at
Casa Museo Rogelio Yrutia.

# Shopping

Compulsive shoppers will adore Buenos Aires. The main shopping zones are downtown, along the Florida peatonal and the more fashionable and more expensive Av Santa Fe. Retiro (around Plaza San Martín) and Recoleta also offer plentiful options. Popular street markets take place in San Telmo, Recoleta and Belgrano. Buenos Aires' best buys are antiques, jewels, leather goods, shoes, and souvenirs such as mate paraphernalia.

It's worth reiterating that many places that accept credit cards add a 10% surcharge – ask before you pay.

## WHERE TO SHOP
### Galerías & Department Stores

Ritzy one-stop shopping centers, some of them recycled landmarks, have begun to take business away from the microcentro's traditional commercial center. The most appealing of these is the restored Galerías Pacífico (☎ 311-6323), occupying an entire block bounded by Florida, Córdoba, San Martín and Viamonte. It houses an outstanding selection of shops and restaurants on three levels. Visit the information booth near the street-level entrance on Florida for a copy of the monthly guide, which includes a diagram of shops and businesses and listings by specialty.

WAYNE BERNHARDSON

Elegant Patio Bullrich once housed bulls.

The famous Harrods at Florida 821 in Retiro, which once rivaled its London namesake, has become an ill-stocked, dark and depressing venue that looks as if it's about to hold a going-out-of-business sale.

The Patio Bullrich (☎ 815-3501) at Av del Libertador 750 is a 24,000-sq-meter building where livestock auctions were once held. It has undergone an elegant remodeling job but suffers from an oppressive atmosphere of heavy-handed security almost reminiscent of the Proceso era – the rich go about their business nonchalantly while everyone else trembles in fear of disappearing off the street. On the other hand, if you need Persian rugs, US$800 suits and the like, it's worth a visit. There's another entrance opposite the Caesar Park Hotel on Posadas, near the Retiro-Recoleta border.

Alto Palermo Shopping Center (☎ 821-6030), Av Coronel Díaz 2098 at Arenales (Subte Estación Bulnes), is a modern mall-type facility with nearly 200 shops. The airy Paseo Alcorta (☎ 801-8035), at Jerónimo Salguero 3172 in Palermo, covers 100,000 sq meters.

## Markets

One of the capital's most interesting shopping districts, San Telmo is known for its fascinating flea market, the Feria de San Telmo, which takes place both Saturday and Sunday from 10 am to about 5 pm on Plaza Dorrego (vendors prefer that customers refrain from touching items on display). Prices have risen considerably at the nearby gentrified antique shops, but there are good restaurants, and buskers and mimes often perform unannounced.

The Feria Artesanal Plaza General Manuel Belgrano, at Juramento and Cuba in Belgrano, takes place weekends and holidays from 10 am to 8 pm, but it gets better as the day goes on – not until 4 or 5 pm do legitimate craftsworkers finally outnumber kitsch peddlers.

Another popular artisans' market takes place on Sundays in Recoleta's Plaza Francia, just north of Av Pueyrredón.

## Art Galleries

Most of Buenos Aires' dozens of art galleries offer fairly conventional works, either European or consciously derivative of European traditions, but a handful of venues promote more locally based, innovative works. For an up-to-date listing of events and current exhibits, consult the monthly tabloid newsletter *Arte al Día* (☎ 805-7672), available at galleries and museums throughout the city.

In modern Argentine art, the consistently best gallery is Ruth Benzacar (☎ 313-8480), downstairs at Florida 1000 in Retiro, but other worthwhile places (all in Retiro) include Federico Klem (☎ 311-2527) downstairs at MT de Alvear 636, Rubbers (☎ 393-6010) at Suipacha 1175, and Vermeer (☎ 394-3462) across the street at Suipacha 1168. Under the railroad bridge in Palermo, Der Brücke (☎ 775-2175) at Av Libertador 3883 also displays interesting work.

At Del Valle Iberlucea 1271 in La Boca, La Vuelta de los Tachos is a small gallery where business depends on the barrio's reputation as an artists' colony.

# Bookstores

Buenos Aires' landmark bookseller El Ateneo (☎ 325-6801), Florida 340 in the microcentro, has a large selection of travel books in the basement, including Lonely Planet guides. In addition to its emphasis on Argentine history and literature, it also stocks foreign language books, which are unfortunately expensive. Librería ABC at Av Córdoba 685 in Retiro and Hachette (☎ 322-6947) at Av Córdoba 936 in the microcentro have similar stock. Atlántida (☎ 311-6323), in the Galerías Pacífico at Florida and Córdoba, also offers a good selection of current books. Fondo de Cultura Económica (☎ 322-0825), Suipacha 615 in the microcentro, is a major Spanish-language publisher that operates an expanding chain of bookstores offering general interest material in addition to its own history, economics and sociology titles.

For the most complete selection of guidebooks in town, including nearly every Lonely Planet title in print, visit the specialty shop Librerías Turísticas (☎ 963-2866, fax 962-5547) at Paraguay 2457, near Barrio Norte (Subte Pueyrredón). Its prices are also the most reasonable for foreign language guidebooks.

Av Corrientes, between Avs 9 de Julio and Callao, is a popular area to browse for books. Just west of Callao, Bookstore (☎ 374-8422), Corrientes 1872, provides a very attractive environment for readers and offers a good selection of new books in all categories, including children's books. It also functions as a gallery and cultural center. Despite its name, the English-language stock is very limited.

Visiting academics and curiosity seekers should explore the basement stacks at Platero (☎ 382-2215), Talcahuano 485 in Congreso, perhaps the capital's best bookstore. Its inventory includes a remarkable selection of new and out-of-print books about Argentina and Latin America. The staff is knowledgeable in almost every field of interest, and trustworthy and efficient in packaging and sending books overseas. Another good shop with similar stock is Aquilanti (☎ 952-4546), Rincón 79 in the Congreso area.

French speakers can find a wide selection of reading material at Oficina del Libro Francés, with locations at Esmeralda 861 in Retiro (☎ 311-0363) and Talcahuano 342, 2nd floor, in Corrientes (☎ 46-4747).

Several street markets have good selections of used books. Check out the Plaza Lavalle near Platero in Corrientes; Av Santa Fe outside the Palermo Subte station; and outside the Primera Junta Subte station (end of the line for Línea A).

DAVE HOUSER

WAYNE BERNHARDSON

Street fairs and bookstalls provide excellent
opportunities for people-watching.

# WHAT TO BUY

## Antiques & Collectibles

San Telmo is the main zone for antiques, though La Boca
also merits some exploration. In addition to Sunday's
outdoor Feria de San Telmo on Plaza Dorrego, Defensa
from Pasaje Giuffra south past Plaza Dorrego is lined
with antique shops, most of them excellent. Many are
within small galerías, including Galería Cecil on Pasaje
Giuffra, Galería French at Defensa 1070 opposite Plaza
Dorrego, and Galería de la Defensa at Defensa 1179,
half a block south of Plaza Dorrego.

Among the San Telmo shops worth a stop are Arte
Antica Antigüedades (☎ 362-0861) at Defensa 1133 and
Loreto Antigüedades (☎ 361-5071) in the Galería French.

Vía Caminito, Aráoz 774 in La Boca, is a low-key shop that specializes in local art and collectors' items such as sheet music and movie posters. Nearby Siglo XX Cambalache, Aráoz 802, is a good antique and second-hand store.

## Leather Goods & Shoes

Among the city's many leather shops, try Kerguelen (☎ 922-2907) at Santander 747 in the barrio of Parque Chacabuco (Subte Estación José María Moreno); Rossi y Carusso (☎ 811-5357) at Av Santa Fe 1601 in Recoleta; Chiche Farrace (☎ 383-6233) at Av de Mayo 963 and in the Galerías Pacífico; Carteras Italianas at MT de Alvear 720 in Retiro; Campanera Dalla Fontana at Reconquista 735, El Sol at Av Libertador 1096 in Recoleta; and Jota U Cuero at Tres Sargentos 439 in Retiro. Celina Leather (☎ 312-9207), Florida 971 in Retiro, gives 15% discounts to holders of student cards.

For shoes, you can look just about anywhere along Av Corrientes or Florida. For women's footwear, try Andrea Carrera at Maipú 943 in Retiro or Celine at Florida 793. For men's shoes, try Guante at Florida 271 or Delgado at Florida 360 both in the microcentro.

For an only-in-Buenos-Aires experience, visit the porteño outlet of Pierre Cardin (☎ 476-0560), which shares a building with the capital's chapter of the not-yet-defunct Communist Party, Av Callao 220 between Perón and Sarmiento.

WAYNE BERNHARDSON

Pierre Cardin and his oh-so-serious neighbors

## Crafts & Souvenirs

For typical souvenirs such as silverwork and mate paraphernalia, check out places like Artesanías Argentinas
(☎ 812-2650) at Montevideo 1386 in Barrio Norte;
Friend's at Av Santa Fe and Esmeralda in Retiro; Martín
Fierro at Santa Fe 908 in Retiro, or Iguarán (☎ 812-0531)
at Libertad 1260. Shops offering student discounts
include Rancho Grande (☎ 311-7603) at LN Alem 564 in
the microcentro and Patagonia at Av Córdoba 543.
Several provincial tourist offices, especially those along
Av Santa Fe and Av Callao, have small but worthwhile
selections of regional crafts.

## Videos

For sale or rental of video versions of Argentine films,
check Alquileres Lavalle (☎ 476-1118) at Lavalle 1199 or
Blakman Video No Convencional at Ayacucho 509,
both in Corrientes. Note that Argentine videos use the
European format and may be incompatible with North
American systems.

# Excursions

Just outside the Capital Federal, Buenos Aires province offers several interesting and worthwhile destinations: the riverside suburb of Tigre and the Paraná Delta (including the island of Martín García), the provincial capital of La Plata, the devotional center of Luján, and the province's gaucho capital, San Antonio de Areco.

Just as economic hardship forced the owners of Britain's stately homes to open their properties to the public, so hard times in the ranching sector have nudged owners of the Pampas' expansive estancias to open their gates and houses to tourists, both for day trips and extended stays. Provided the visitor understands their limitations, these are ideal for a weekend in the country, but some are very expensive.

Círculos Mágicos (☎ 813-0206, 815-2803), Uruguay 864, 3rd floor, arranges upscale visits and overnight trips to luxurious estancias where travelers can pursue activities such as riding, polo and tennis surrounded by the illusion of the bygone gaucho era. Another estancia tour operator is José de Santis (☎ 361-8335), Juan de Garay 431, 7° A.

Other excursions take travelers across the Río Paraná to the Uruguayan capital of Montevideo and the colonial gem of Colonia del Sacramento, commonly known simply as Colonia. Uruguay requires visas of all foreigners, except those from neighboring countries (who need only national identification cards) and nationals of Western Europe, Israel, Japan and the USA. All visitors need a tourist card; valid for 90 days, it is renewable for another 90.

Uruguay has recently imposed visa requirements on Canadians in response to Canadian government visa requirements for Uruguayans. These include a return ticket, a photograph, and a payment of US$30 to a Uruguayan consulate. Canadians may well question whether a day trip from Buenos Aires is worth the cost and hassle.

## TIGRE & THE DELTA DEL PARANÁ

Within commuting range of the capital, this riverside suburb is a popular weekend retreat and the best point of departure for exploring the Delta del Paraná and visiting historic Isla Martín García. One of Tigre's best

attractions is the **Puerto de Frutos**, where a big weekend crafts fair is held each weekend. Its restaurant serves up tasty dishes.

## Orientation

Tigre is at the confluence of the Río Luján and the Río Tigre, beyond which is the 2000-km maze of waterways that constitutes the delta. The delta's major channel is the Río Paraná de las Palmas.

## Places to Stay & Eat

Hotels are relatively few in the delta, but try *Hotel Laura* (☎ 749-3898) on Canal Honda off the Paraná de las Palmas for US$60 double with private bath weekdays, US$80 weekends. It also offers a US$15 delta excursion. *Hotel I'Marangatu* (☎ 749-7350), on the Río San Antonio, charges US$80 during the week, US$100 on weekends, while *La Manuelita* (☎ 749-0987), on the Río Carapachay, costs US$45 during the week, US$50 weekends. *Hotel Astor* is strictly an *albergue transitorio*.

WAYNE BERNHARDSON

WAYNE BERNHARDSON

WAYNE BERNHARDSON

The Delta del Paraná, just north of Buenos Aires, provides
welcome relief from the city's frenetic pace.

On the Río Tres Bocas, about 20 minutes from Tigre by launch, *La Riviera* (☎ 749-6177, 749-5960) is a popular restaurant offering good food and live music. It's frequented by gay clientele (but by no means exclusively). On weekends during Carnaval, the celebrants are at their most outrageous.

## Getting There & Away

Bus No 60 from Av Callao in Buenos Aires goes all the way to Tigre (US$1), but the Ferrocarril Mitre, leaving from Plataformas 1 or 2 from Estación Retiro, is probably quicker when traffic is heavy. It's also a bit cheaper (US$1.20 return).

## Getting Around

Interislena runs a series of *lanchas colectivas* from Tigre's Estación Fluvial to various destinations in the delta for $3 to $5 per person, depending on the distance. They will drop you off or pick you up at any riverside dock – just flag them down as you would a bus.

# ISLA MARTÍN GARCÍA

Navigating among the densely forested multiple channels of the Tigre and Paraná rivers, en route to historic Martín García, travelers can easily imagine what ideal sites these were for contraband activities during colonial times. Just off the Uruguayan littoral, directly south of the city of Carmelo, the island is most famous – or infamous – as a prison camp; four Argentine presidents have been held in custody here, and the Servicio Penitenciario de Buenos Aires province still uses it as a halfway house for prisoners near the end of their terms. At present, though, the island is more a combination of historical monument, tranquil nature reserve and recreational retreat from the bustle of the federal capital.

## History

In colonial times, Spain and Portugal contested possession of the island. Unlike the sedimentary islands of the flood-prone delta, 180-hectare Martín García rises 27 meters above sea level; this high ground made it suitable for a fortress to guard the approach to the Uruguay and Paraná rivers. Irish Admiral Guillermo Brown gave the United Provinces of the River Plate their first major naval victory here in 1814, when a commando raid dislodged royalist troops who escaped to Montevideo. Both England and France took advantage of Argentine conflicts with Brazil to occupy the island in the early 19th century.

For most of the 20th century, the Argentine navy has controlled the island. At the turn of the century, Nicaraguan poet Rubén Darío lived in what is now the natural history center while serving as Colombian consul in Buenos Aires. During WWI authorities briefly detained the crew of the German destroyer *Graf Spee*, sunk off Montevideo.

The Argentine military regularly confined political prisoners here, including Presidents Hipólito Yrigoyen (twice in the early 20th century), Marcelo T de Alvear (around the same time), Juan Domingo Perón (briefly in 1945) and Arturo Frondizi (1962 – 1963). Many speculate that the military dictatorship of 1976 – 1983 used the island as a detention center and that sealed subterranean tunnels may contain evidence of such activity.

## Things to See & Do

Martín García's main points of interest are its historic buildings. The **Oficina de Informes**, uphill from the muelle (passenger pier), is also the headquarters of the Servicio Penitenciario, which manages the island halfway-house prisoners. Other buildings of interest include the ruins of the former **Cuartel** (naval barracks), the **Panadería Rocio** (a bakery dating from 1913), the rococo **Cine-Teatro**, the **Museo de la Isla** and the **Casa de Ciencias Naturales**. At the northwestern end of the island, beyond a block of badly overgrown houses, the **Puerto Viejo** (old port) has fallen into disuse due to sediments that have clogged the anchorage. The **cemetery** contains the headstones of many conscripts who died in an epidemic in the early 20th century.

The densely forested northern part of the island offers quiet, pleasant walks if you don't mind fending off the mosquitos. South of the airstrip, the **Zona Intangible** is closed to casual hikers because of its botanical value and the hazard of fire.

Comedor El Solís (see below) has a swimming pool open to the public.

## Organized Tours

Guided tours depart from Cacciola's Terminal Internacional (☎ 749-0329) at Lavalle 520 in Tigre; tickets are also available at their downtown Buenos Aires office (☎ 322-0026) at Florida 520, 1st floor, Oficina 113. The enclosed catamaran leaves Tigre at 8 am, returning from

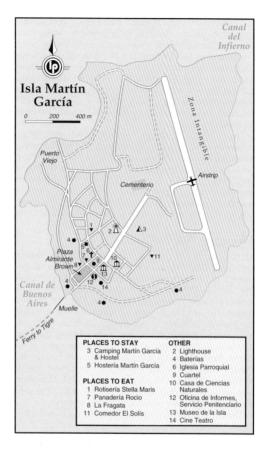

**Isla Martín García**

0    200    400 m

*Canal del Infierno*

*Zona Intangible*

*Puerto Viejo*

Airstrip

*Cementerio*

*Plaza Almirante Brown*

*Canal de Buenos Aires*

*Muelle*

*Ferry to Tigre*

**PLACES TO STAY**
3  Camping Martín García & Hostel
5  Hostería Martín García

**PLACES TO EAT**
1  Rotisería Stella Maris
7  Panadería Rocio
8  La Fragata
11  Comedor El Solís

**OTHER**
2  Lighthouse
4  Baterías
6  Iglesia Parroquial
9  Cuartel
10  Casa de Ciencias Naturales
12  Oficina de Informes, Servicio Penitenciario
13  Museo de la Isla
14  Cine Teatro

Martín García at 5 pm (be dockside at 4 pm, however). It costs US$28 return. For US$42, the tour includes lunch at the Cacciola's La Fragata restaurant, but there are cheaper and better meal alternatives.

On arrival at the island, Buenos Aires province collects a US$2 per person entrance fee to support the maintenance of its Reserva Natural y Cultural Isla Martín García. Passengers then split into two groups – those who opt for the full excursion receive a free aperitif, while the rest follow a very well-informed guide to the island's many well-preserved historic buildings. Very worthwhile if you understand Spanish, the 1½-hour tours leave plenty of time for exploring the island.

WAYNE BERNHARDSON

WAYNE BERNHARDSON

Above:   Detail of Cine Teatro
Below:   Former naval barracks

## Places to Stay & Eat

Pleasant, shady *Camping Martín García* (☎ 413-2682, 208-2883 for reservations, which are essential) costs US$3.50 per person; it also offers hostel accommodations for US$6.50 per person. The facility tends to be very crowded in summer and on weekends, so the best time for an overnight stay is probably on weekdays or just before or after the peak summer season.

Cacciola offers full-board overnight packages, including transportation, for US$105 per person at its *Hostería Martín García*; additional nights cost US$50 per person. Three-day, two-night packages with half-board cost US$109; each additional day is US$35.

*Comedor El Solís*, with a US$8 tenedor libre including tasty boga and dessert, is a much better value than the expensive lunch at Cacciola's *La Fragata*, which is included in the full excursion. Drinks at Solís are extra but not outrageous. *Rotisería Stella Maris* also has decent, simple meals and drinks, while the *Panadería Rocio* is renowned for its fruitcakes.

## Things to Buy

Artisanal goods available at shops on the island include mate gourds and wooden ships, along with the usual T-shirts and mugs manufactured elsewhere.

## Getting There & Away

Without your own boat, the only practical way to the island is a guided tour that departs from Tigre (see Organized Tours above). To get to Tigre from downtown Buenos Aires, take city bus No 60 from Av Callao (US$1). Leave early, since it takes around 1½ hours. Visitors camping on Martín García who do not wish to take the guided tour pay only US$23 return.

## LA PLATA

After the city of Buenos Aires became Argentina's federal capital, Governor Dardo Rocha founded La Plata in 1882 to give the province its own new capital. After detailed study, Rocha selected Pedro Benoit's elaborate plan, closely resembling that of Washington, DC, with major avenues and broad diagonals connecting the city's public buildings and numerous plazas. La Plata's grandiose public buildings reflect Benoit's intention to build an important administrative, commercial and cultural center, but the city does not overwhelm the human dimension.

La Plata, 56 km southeast of Buenos Aires via RP 14, is a town of about 210,000. Its basic design is a conventional grid, but the superposition of numerous diagonals forms a distinctive diamond pattern, connecting the plazas and permitting traffic to flow smoothly between them. While most public buildings are on or around Plaza Moreno, the commercial center is near Plaza San Martín.

## Information

The Entidad Municipal de Turismo (☎ 25-8334, 27-1535), Calle 47 No 740 between Calle 9 and Diagonal 74, is friendly and helpful but keeps limited hours (from 8 am to 2 pm weekdays only). It distributes a sketchy city map and a few brochures.

## Walking Tour

In the middle of **Plaza Moreno**, which occupies four sq blocks between Calles 12 and 14 and Avs 50 and 54, La Plata's **Piedra Fundacional** (Founding Stone) of 1882 marks the city's precise geographical center. Across from the plaza, on Calle 14 between Avs 51 and 53, visit the neo-Gothic **cathedral** (begun 1885, completed 1903); inspired by medieval antecedents in Cologne and Amiens, it has fine stained glass and polished granite floors. The building's museum is open daily from 8 am to noon and 2 to 7 pm.

On the opposite side of Plaza Moreno is the **Palacio Municipal** (1886), designed in German Renaissance style by Hannoverian architect Hubert Stiers; note on either side the modern towers housing most provincial government offices. Two blocks north, on Calle 10 between Avs 51 and 53, the unfinished **Teatro Argentino** replaces an earlier, much more distinguished building destroyed by fire.

Three blocks farther north, on Av 7 opposite Plaza San Martín, is the provincial **Palacio de la Legislatura**, also in German Renaissance style. To the west, on Calle 50 between Calle 6 and Av 7, the French Classic **Pasaje Dardo Rocha** is La Plata's major cultural center. Detour three blocks west, to Av 7 between 47 and 48, to view the original buildings of the **Rectorado de la Universidad Nacional** (1905, once a bank) before returning via Calle 6 to the Flemish Renaissance **Casa de Gobierno**, housing the provincial Governor and his retinue, on the north side of Plaza San Martín. If it's a hot day, stroll up Calle 54 to the landmark **Cervecería Modelo** for a cold lager beer.

WAYNE BERNHARDSON

Palacio de la Legislatura

# Paseo del Bosque

Plantations of eucalyptus, gingko, palm and subtropical hardwoods cover this 60-hectare park at the northeastern edge of town. Its facilities include the **Anfiteatro Martín Fierro**, an open-air facility that hosts summer drama festivals, the **Museo de Ciencias Naturales** (see below), the **Observatorio Astronómico** (open from 7 am to 1 pm weekdays), the symbolic United Nations of the **Jardín de la Paz** (Garden of Peace), a small **Jardín Zoológico** (a zoo open weekdays from 9 am to 9 pm, weekends from 10 am to 9 pm) along Av 52, and several university departments.

# Museo de Ciencias Naturales

When Buenos Aires became the federal capital, provincial authorities built this museum, in the spacious park known as Paseo del Bosque, to house the archaeological and anthropological collections of lifetime director Francisco P Moreno, the famous Patagonian explorer.

Finished in 1889, the building itself consists of an attractive oval with four stories and a mezzanine with showrooms, classrooms, workshops, laboratories, offices, libraries and storage. Its exterior mixes Corinthian columns, Ionic posterior walls and Hellenic windows, with Aztec and Inca embellishments. Since 1906, the university's school of natural sciences has functioned here.

The museum (☎ 39125, 21-9066) is open daily (except for January 1, May 1 and December 25) from noon to 6 pm weekdays and from 10 am to 6 pm weekends and holidays. Admission is US$2.

## La República de los Niños

Evita Perón sponsored this small-scale reproduction of a city for the education and enjoyment of children. It was completed shortly before her death in 1952. From the Plaza de la Amistad, a steam train circles this architectural hodgepodge of medieval European and Islamic styles, with motifs from Grimms' and Andersen's fairy tales. Like most public works projects of its era, it is showing its age, but is worth a visit if you have crabby kids to appease; otherwise it's sort of a bargain-basement Disneyland.

República de los Niños (☎ 84-0194) is on Camino General Belgrano Km 7 and Calle 501, north of La Plata in the suburb of Manuel Gonnet. From Av 7 in La Plata, take bus No 518 or 273; not all No 273 buses go all the way. Admission is US$3 per person, which includes the aquarium and *granja* (farm), but the train ride and doll museum require separate admission.

WAYNE BERNHARDSON

The strange mishmash of architectural styles found at La República de los Niños appeals to adults as well as children.

## Places to Stay

Since visitors to La Plata are often government officials on per diem, hotels price their rooms accordingly. One of few budget hotels, the friendly but run-down *Hospedaje Roca* (☎ 21-4916), Calle 47 No 309, has singles/doubles for US$15/20 with shared bath, US$18/30 with private bath. Try also *Hospedaje García*, Calle 2 No 525.

Moderately priced *Hotel Saint James* (☎ 21-8089), Calle 60 No 377, charges US$25/35 without breakfast. *Hotel Plaza* (☎ 21-0325), near the train station at Av 44 No 358, charges US$30/40 without breakfast but has a 3rd-floor budget double for US$30. Similar in price and standard is one-star *Hotel Roga* (☎ 21-9553), Calle 54 No 334, where clean, comfortable rooms with private bath cost US$41/55.

At the top end are three-star lodgings like *Hotel La Plata* (☎ 21-1365), which has a nice restaurant, at Av 51 No 783 near Plaza Moreno; rooms cost US$45/60. *Hotel Cristal* (☎ 21-1393), Av 1 No 620, charges US$47/62, while *Hotel San Marcos* (☎ 42385) at Calle 54 No 523 costs $50/67. Four-star *Hotel Corregidor* (☎ 25-6800), Calle 6 No 1026, offers many luxuries for US$82/95.

## Places to Eat

Among La Plata's traditional favorites are *Everton*, on Calle 14 between Calles 63 and 64, and *Club Matheu*, Calle 63 between Av 1 and Calle 2, both with limited but good menus at affordable prices. Pricier but very pleasant is the *Restaurant Club Hípico* in the Paseo del Bosque.

For a good parrillada, try *El Chaparral*, Av 60 and Calle 117, which has excellent mollejas (sweetbreads). On Plaza Paso, Avs 13 and 44, *El Quijote* occupies a commonplace building but has delicious food, particularly the ensalada de frutos de mar (seafood salad). Local lawyers recommend the *Colegio de Escribanos*, Av 13 between Calles 47 and 48.

*Pasta y Punto*, Calle 47 No 787, is a very fine, pleasantly decorated Italian restaurant that is a good value,

---

### Cervecería Modelo

The quintessential La Plata experience is drinking and eating at this 85-year-old tavern, known simply as *La Modelo*, at the corner of Calles 54 and 5. On a warm summer night, you can pass hours at their sidewalk tables, savoring excellent *cerveza tirada* (lager beer) and complimentary peanuts. For something more substantial, try lomito with chips. ■

though it's not really cheap; alongside it is *Todo Natural*, a good natural foods market. Another popular Italian place, at Calle 47 and Diagonal 74, is *La Trattoría*. *La Lechonera Platense*, on Diagonal 74 between 48 and 49, specializes in pork.

## Getting There & Away

**Bus** Río de la Plata (☎ 313-3580 in Buenos Aires) has buses every half hour from Estaciónes Once, Constitución and Retiro in Buenos Aires (US$2). The Terminal de Omnibus in La Plata (☎ 21-0992) is at Calles 4 and 42.

**Train** From Buenos Aires, Transportes Metroplitanasa General Roca (TMR, ☎ 304-0021) has hourly trains from Constitución (1½ hours, US$1). La Plata's turn-of-the-century Estación Ferrocarril General Roca (☎ 21-9377, 21-2575), at Av 1 and Calle 44, features an interesting Art Nouveau dome and wrought-iron awning, but deferred maintenance has left it less impressive than it once was.

## LUJÁN

According to legend, in 1630 the oxen pulling a wagon that contained a small statue of the Virgin en route from Brazil to a Portuguese farmer in Peru would not budge until the gauchos removed the statue. The devoted owner cleared the site and built a chapel where the Virgin had chosen to stay, about five km from present-day Luján.

La Virgen de Luján became Argentina's patron saint, but she now occupies the neo-Gothic basilica, one of the city's two main tourist attractions. The other is a colonial historical-museum complex. On the east bank of its namesake river, Luján is only 65 km west of Buenos Aires.

## Information

There's an Oficina de Informes Turísticos (☎ 20032) at the bus terminal, but the Dirección de Turismo (☎ 20453) at Edificio La Cúpula, at the west end of Lavalle, is more knowledgeable and better supplied with information and brochures.

## Basílica Nuestra Señora de Luján

Every year four million people from all over Argentina visit Luján to honor the Virgin for her intercession in

WAYNE BERNHARDSON

Ex-voto kiosk in Luján

affairs of peace, health, forgiveness and consolation. The terminus of their pilgrimages is this huge neo-Gothic basilica, where the 'Virgencita' (she is known by the affectionate diminutive) occupies a *camarín* (chamber) behind the main altar. Devotees have covered the stairs with plaques acknowledging her favors.

Every October, since the Dirty War, a massive Peregrinación de la Juventud (Youth Pilgrimage) originates in Buenos Aires' Once Station, 62 km away. In the days of the military dictatorship, when any mass demonstration was forbidden, this walk had tremendous symbolic importance, but since the restoration of democracy it has become more exclusively devotional. The other large gathering of believers takes place May 8, the Virgin's day.

Near the basilica, the **Museo Devocional** houses *ex-votos* (gifts) to the Virgin, including objects of silver, wood and wax, musical instruments and icons from all over the world. It's open Tuesday to Friday from 1 to 6 pm, weekends from 10 am to 6 pm.

## Complejo Museográfico Enrique Udaondo

Bounded by Calles Lezica y Torrezuri, Lavalle, San Martín and Parque Ameghino, this museum complex occupies three full hectares. It includes the 30 rooms of the **Museo Colonial e Histórico**, housed in colonial buildings like the **Cabildo** and the so-called **Casa del Virrey** (though no viceroy ever actually lived there). Exhibits cover the area's history from pre-Columbian

WAYNE BERNHARDSON

The cabildo (town hall)

times but stop abruptly in 1953. The **Museo de Transporte** has four showrooms, plus a patio with colonial wagons, a windmill and a horse-powered mill.

Museum hours are Wednesday from 12:30 to 4:30 pm, Thursday and Friday from 11:30 am to 4:30 pm, and weekends from 10:45 am to 6 pm. The combined library/archive is open weekdays from 9:30 am to 6 pm but closes in January.

## Places to Stay

**Camping** For about US$4 per person per day, *Camping 7* on RN 7 (Av Carlos Pellegrini) across the Río Luján is basic and less than perfectly maintained, but it's OK for a night. There is another more expensive campground along the river near the Dirección Municipal de Turismo at Edificio La Cúpula. Informally, pilgrims camp just about anywhere they feel like it.

**Hospedajes & Hotels** Several budget hotels cater to the pilgrims who come throughout the year. On the north side of the basilica is friendly *Hospedaje Carena* (☎ 21287), Calle Lavalle 114, offering singles/doubles at US$12/15 with private bath. Similar in price and standard is *Hotel Santa Rita* (☎ 20981), Torrezuri 857 at Lezica, where small, musty but clean rooms with private bath cost US$15/20. Opposite the bus terminal, *Hospedaje Royal* (☎ 21295), 9 de Julio 696, has small rooms at US$20/28.

Also nearby is the dark and worn but clean and friendly *Hotel Venecia*, Calle Almirante Brown 100, which has small rooms with private baths and fans, for

US$15/20. Rates are similar at *Hotel Victoria* (☎ 20582), Lavalle 136. South of the basilica is the once-elegant *Hotel de la Paz* (☎ 24034), 9 de Julio 1054. Although it's now worn around the edges, the owners are friendly and the rooms are acceptable at US$20/30.

The only two-star hotel, the *Real Hotel Luján* (☎ 20054), Av Nuestra Señora de Luján 816, is a good value at US$25/35, including private bath and telephone. For the most improbable hotel name in this major devotional center, I nominate *Hotel Eros* (☎ 21658), San Martín 129. Very clean, small rooms with no exterior windows cost US$25/35 with private bath.

## Places to Eat

There is a slew of cheap, fixed-menu restaurants near the basilica along Av Nuestra Señora de Luján, where very aggressive waiters nearly yank tourists off the sidewalk. Off the central plaza, quiet *Restaurant Don Diego*, Colón 964, has excellent but pricey Argentine food. *Restaurante Match Point*, San Martín 199, is cheaper but serves smaller portions; ACA members receive discounts.

Highly regarded, *L'Eau Vive* is a convent-run restaurant at the south end of town between Entre Ríos and Doctor Luppi at Constitución 2112.

## Getting There & Away

**Bus** Transporte Luján (Línea 52) leaves from Plaza Miserere (Estación Once) in Buenos Aires, while Transportes Atlántida (Línea 57) connects Luján with Palermo. Talsa leaves frequently from Once for US$3. Luján's Estación Terminal de Omnibus is at Av de Nuestra Señora del Rosario, four blocks north of the basilica.

**Train** The Ferrocarril Sarmiento still runs trains daily to and from Estación Once (Plaza Miserere Subte) in Buenos Aires.

# SAN ANTONIO DE ARECO

Dating from the early 18th-century construction of a chapel in honor of San Antonio de Padua, this serene village is the symbolic center of Argentina's vestigial gaucho culture and host to the country's biggest gaucho celebration, Día de la Tradición, in November. Nestled in the verdant pampas of northern Buenos Aires province, it was the setting for Ricardo Güiraldes' famous novel *Don Segundo Sombra* (1927). Güiraldes' nephew Adolfo played the role of Don Segundo in the 1969 film version, in which many locals served as extras.

Unlike nearly every other Argentine city, San Antonio's street life centers not around the plaza but on the main commercial street of Alsina, where there's a wealth of quality artisanal goods for sale – this is one of the best places in the country for typical souvenirs. On the south bank of the Río Areco, 113 km west of Buenos Aires, the town's an exceptionally popular weekend destination for porteños. June 13 is the Día del Santo Patrono (Patron Saint's Day).

## Information

Friendly but sometimes patronizing to foreigners, San Antonio's Dirección de Turismo (☎ 3165) is on Castex between Arellano and Zapiola. It's open from 7 am to 2 pm weekdays, from 10 am to 5 pm weekends (when it serves up to 800 visitors daily), and distributes a useful pocket-size guide, updated monthly, with a map and other useful information. It also distributes *Pregon Turismo*, a new tabloid-size publication that provides more detailed material on San Antonio's attractions.

## Things to See & Do

San Antonio's compact center lends itself well to walking. At the beginning of the 18th century, **Plaza Ruiz de Arellano** was the site of the corrals of the town's founding estanciero; in its center, the **Monumento a Vieytes** honors locally born Juan Hipólito Vieytes, a figure in the early independence movement. Around the plaza are several historic buildings, including the **Iglesia Parroquial** (Parish Church) and the **Casa de los Martínez** (site of the main house of the original Ruiz de Arellano estancia).

Conspicuously featured in the film version of *Don Segundo Sombra*, the **Puente Viejo** (1857) across the Río Areco follows the original cart road to northern Argentina; once a toll bridge, it's now a pedestrian bridge leading to the **Parque Criollo y Museo Gauchesco Ricardo Güiraldes**, San Antonio's major visitor attraction (see below).

Ricardo Güiraldes and Segundo Ramírez, the real-life role model for the character Don Segundo Sombra, both lie in the **Cementerio Municipal** at the south end of town, at the junction of RN 8 and Soldado Argentino.

## The Rise & Romance of the Gaucho

No one could have predicted the rise to respectability of that accidental icon, the Argentine gaucho. Dressed in baggy *bombacha*, the modern gaucho, with a leather *rastra* round his waist and a sharp *facón* in his belt, is the idealized version of a complex historical figure. Directly or indirectly, to most Argentines and foreigners, he is a latter-day version of the romantic characters portrayed in José Hernández' epic poem *Martín Fierro* and Ricardo Güiraldes' novel *Don Segundo Sombra*. Like his counterpart, the North American cowboy, he has received elaborate cinematic treatment. Ironically, only when he became a sanitized anachronism did he achieve celebrity.

MICHAEL PETTYPOOL

Without the rich pastures of the Pampas and the cattle and horses that multiplied on them, the gaucho could never have flourished. In a sense, he replaced the Pampas Indian; usually a mestizo, he hunted burgeoning herds of cattle just as the Querandí Indians did the guanaco and rhea. As long as cattle were many, people few, and beef, hides and tallow of limited commercial value, his subsistence and independence were assured. This achieved, he could amuse himself gambling and drinking in the saloon or *pulpería*. In the 19th century, observers like Domingo Sarmiento thought the gaucho indolent but grudgingly acknowledged that he led a good life:

> Country life, then, has developed all the physical but none of the intellectual powers of the gaucho. His moral character is of the quality to be expected from his habit of triumphing over the forces of nature; it is strong, haughty and energetic. Without instruction, and indeed without need of any, without means of support as without wants, he is happy in the midst of his poverty and privations, which are not such to one who never knew nor wished for greater pleasures than are his already.

Even as Sarmiento wrote, the gaucho's independent, self-sufficient way of life was in decline. Just as the gauchos had replaced the Pampas Indians, so large landowners squeezed out the gauchos. The primitive livestock economy gave way to *saladeros*, which made use of a wider variety of products – processed hides, tallow and salted or jerked beef.

For their saladeros, landowners needed labor; the gaucho, with his horseback skills, was a desirable if unwilling source of manpower, but landowners were not reluctant to use their influence to coerce him. Classifying the gaucho as a 'lawless' element, discriminatory laws soon required internal passports, and men without jobs could no longer travel freely over the Pampas. Punishment for 'vagrancy' was often military conscription. As sheep replaced cattle on the Pampas, land was fenced and marked, forcing the gaucho to the fringes or onto the estancias.

Unlike the frontier, the estancia was not a democracy, and the gaucho was no longer his own master, even though his livestock skills were still in seasonal demand. He became instead a hired hand for an institution the physical aspects of which bespoke hierarchy. As European immigrants came to occupy many saladero jobs, which often were detested by real gauchos, friction arose between gaucho 'natives' and Italian 'gringos'. Despite resistance, the day of the free-roaming gaucho was over by the late 19th century.

Ironically, about this time, Argentina discovered the gaucho's virtues in what has become known as *literatura gauchescha* ('gauchesque' literature, or literature *about* as opposed to *by* the usually illiterate gauchos). *Martín Fierro* romanticized the life of the independent gaucho at the point at which he was disappearing, much like the open-range cowboy of the American West.

Hernández deplored both opportunistic strongmen like Juan Manuel de Rosas, who claimed to speak for the gaucho, and 'civilizers' like Sarmiento, who had no scruples about discarding the people of the countryside. The gaucho's fierce independence, so often depicted as lawlessness, became admirable, and Hernández almost single-handedly rehabilitated the image of the gaucho as Argentines sought an identity in a country rapidly being transformed by immigration and economic modernization. Having fought alongside the gaucho, Hernández eloquently championed him in the public forums of his country and pleaded for his integration into the country's future, noting the positive gaucho values that even Sarmiento admitted: courtesy, independence and generosity. By the time the gaucho's fate was decided, urban Argentines had elevated him to a mythical status, incorporating these values into their own belief system. ■

MICHAEL PETTYPOOL

# Parque Criollo y Museo Gauchesco Ricardo Güiraldes

Inaugurated by the provincial government in 1938, a decade after Güiraldes' death, this elaborate museum is, on one level, a spurious Gaucholand of restored and/or fabricated buildings idealizing and fossilizing the history of the Pampas. On the other hand, its 90 hectares also provide an unalloyed introduction to the gaucho as a modern cultural phenomenon, allowing visitors to appreciate the degree to which his consciousness has infused contemporary Argentine society.

The centerpiece of the complex is the **Casa del Museo**, a 20th-century reproduction of an 18th-century casco, which includes a Sala de los Escritores on gaucho literature (including the desk and chair of Walter Owen, who translated the gauchesco classic *Martín Fierro* into English); a Sala Pieza de Estanciero with a wooden bed belonging to Juan Manuel de Rosas (perhaps the ultimate rural landowner); and a Sala del Gaucho with horsegear and various works of gauchesque art. Two rooms are dedicated to Güiraldes himself, another to his wife Adelina del Carril de Güiraldes, and yet another to his painter cousin Alberto.

More authentic, or at least more venerable, than the Casa del Museo is the **Pulpería La Blanqueada**, a mid-19th century building displaying a credible re-creation of a rural tavern. Alongside the pulpería are **La Tahona**, an 1848 flour mill brought here from the town of Mercedes, and the **Galpón y Cuarto de Sogas**, where the estancia might have stored its carriages. Nearby is **La Ermita de San Antonio**, a colonial-style chapel with some colonial artifacts.

North of the river on Camino Ricardo Güiraldes, reached via the Puente Viejo, the grounds and buildings of the Museo Gauchesco (☎ 2583) are open weekdays from 10 am to 3 pm except Tuesday (when it is closed), weekends and holidays from 10 am to 5 pm. Admission is US$2 for adults, US$1 for retired persons.

# Fiesta de la Tradición

Lasting a week in November, this 90-year-old festival celebrates San Antonio's gaucho past. By presidential decree, San Antonio is the 'sede provincial de la tradición' (provincial site of tradition). The actual Día de la Tradición is November 10, but celebrations are moved to the following Sunday for convenience. Attractions include lectures, artisanal exhibits, guided tours of historic sites, displays of gaucho horsemanship, folk

## Historic Estancias

Surrounding San Antonio de Areco are a number of estancias offering overnight accommodations in the range of US$125 per person, plus IVA, with full pension; activities like horseback riding and polo usually cost extra. Director María Luisa Bemberg shot part of her historical drama *Camila* at **Estancia La Bamba** (see the San Antonio tourist office for details on accommodations and tours).

For a day in the country, countless porteños choose **Estancia La Cinacina**, where US$30 buys an all-you-can-eat asado, entertainment in the form of folkloric music and dance, a tour of the estancia's museum, and horseback riding. **Estancia Cinacina** (☎ 2045), at Mitre 9 only six blocks from Plaza Ruiz de Arellano, is less crowded and more comfortable on weekdays. Its Buenos Aires representative is Empresa Que La Opera (☎ 342-1986, 342-2841), Mitre 734, 10° B; tours including transportation from the capital cost US$60.

Certainly the most historic of nearby estancias is the Güiraldes family's **Estancia La Porteña** (☎ 322-6023/5694 in Buenos Aires), which dates from 1850 and has a garden designed by the renowned French architect Charles Thays, responsible for major public parks including Buenos Aires' Jardín Botánico. **Estancia El Ombú** (☎ 92080; 793-2454 in Buenos Aires) belonged to General Pablo Ricchieri, who first inflicted universal military conscription on the country. ∎

dancing and the like. If you're visiting San Antonio at this time, make reservations far in advance for the limited accommodations.

## Places to Stay & Eat

San Antonio has decent but very limited accommodations; prices for lodging may rise on weekends, when reservations are advisable. Reservations are absolutely essential during the Fiesta de la Tradición in November.

The spacious, shady riverside *Camping Club Náutico* has clean toilets and hot showers, but is overpriced for US$10 per tent, plus US$5 per vehicle (the latter levied the first night only). The cheapest regular accommodations (by no means bad) are at conveniently located *Hotel San Carlos* (☎ 3106) at Zapiola and Castex. *Hotel Residencial* (☎ 2166), Segundo Sombra and Rivadavia, is very comparable and slightly more expensive.

*Residencial El Hornero* (☎ 2733), at Moreno and San Martín, charges US$25 per person, while *Hotel Fuaz* (☎ 2487) at Av Doctor Smith 488 costs US$52 double with breakfast. San Antonio's most attractive accommodations are at *Hostal de Areco* (☎ 4063), Zapiola 25, which charges US$30 per person with breakfast Sunday through Thursday, US$35 per person Friday and Saturday. Another good value is *La Posada del Ceibo* (☎ 4614) on Irigoyen between RN 8 and Av Smith, which charges US$20 per person Monday through Thursday or US$30 per person Friday through Sunday.

San Antonio is surprisingly short of places to eat. The only halfway appealing place downtown is *Pizzería Dell'Olmo* (☎ 2506), Alsina 365; *La Costa* (☎ 2481), a parrilla at Belgrano and Zerboni, has a decent tenedor libre for about US$10.

Far better is *Ramos Generales*, Bolívar 66, a very new restaurant convincingly decorated as a turn-of-the-century general store. It suffers a bit from self-conscious cuteness but has good homemade pasta and the like (hold the salt, though) at reasonable prices. They also offer excellent overnight accommodations for US$25/40 a single/double.

## Things to Buy

San Antonio's artisans are known throughout the country, with many of their apprentices practicing their trades in other cities and provinces. Mate paraphernalia, rastras (silver-studded belts) and facones (long-bladed knives), produced by skilled silversmiths, are among the most typical. Internationally known Raúl Horacio Draghi (☎ 4207), Guido 391, also works in leather; other top silversmiths include Miguel and Martín Rigacci, Av Quetgles 333, and Alvaro Ignacio Caldera (☎ 2599), Alsina 17.

For horse gear and gaucho clothing, check out Sogas Areco, Moreno 280. Cristina Giordano de Bincaz (☎ 2829), Sarmiento 112, sells weavings. El Boliche de Ramírez, on Güiraldes opposite the Museo Gauchesco, carries a bit of everything.

For artisanal chocolates, try La Olla de Cobre, Speroni 433. In addition to its restaurant, Ramos Generales, Bolívar 66, also produces homemade sweets, cheeses and salami. Dulces del Pago (☎ 4751), Zerboni 136 or Nogueira 125, makes a variety of fruit preserves.

## Getting There & Away

Frequent buses from Buenos Aires take 1½ hours (US$3.50). San Antonia's Terminal de Omnibus is at Av Doctor Smith and General Paz.

On Sundays, the tourist-oriented train *El Tren del Oeste* goes to San Antonio from Lacroze Station in Buenos Aires.

# COLONIA

Only an hour or two from Buenos Aires across the Río de la Plata, Colonia (full name Colonia del Sacramento) is one of the Southern Cone's unappreciated gems, attracting many thousands of Argentines but only a handful of the foreign tourists who visit the Argentine capital.

Founded in 1680 by the Portuguese Manoel Lobo, the town occupied a strategic position almost exactly opposite Buenos Aires across the Río de la Plata, but it was more important as a source of contraband, which undercut Spain's jealously defended mercantile trade monopoly. British goods made their way from Colonia into Buenos Aires and the interior through surreptitious

WAYNE BERNHARDSON

WAYNE BERNHARDSON

Many beautifully maintained *cachilas* can be seen in Colonia's streets.

exchange with the Portuguese in the Paraná Delta; for this reason, Spanish forces intermittently besieged Portugal's riverside outpost for decades.

Although the two powers agreed over the cession of Colonia to Spain around 1750, the agreement failed when Jesuit missionaries on the upper Paraná refused to comply with the proposed exchange of territory in their area. Spain finally captured the city in 1762 but failed to hold it until 1777, when authorities created the Viceroyalty of the River Plate. From this time, Colonia's commercial importance declined, as foreign goods could proceed directly to Buenos Aires.

The capital of its department, Colonia is a pleasant town of about 20,000. The streets of its historic colonial core are shaded by sycamores in the summer heat. In the course of the day, the town discloses its many aspects as sunlight strikes whitewashed colonial buildings and the river; the latter, living up to its name, is silvery in the morning but turns brownish by midday.

## Information

The municipal Oficina de Información Turística (☎ 2182) is at General Flores 499. While not especially well informed, the staff has numerous brochures difficult to obtain elsewhere. Hours are weekdays from 7 am to 8 pm, weekends from 10 am to 7 pm. The Ministerio de Turismo (☎ 4897) maintains a ferry port branch that is more efficient and helpful.

Arriving at the port from Buenos Aires, you can change money at Cambio Libertad or Banco República, which pays slightly lower rates and charges US$1 commission for traveler's checks. Downtown, try Cambio Colonia at General Flores and Alberto Méndez or Cambio Viaggio at General Flores 350.

## Walking Tour

Also known as La Colonia Portuguesa (the Portuguese Colony), Colonia's Barrio Histórico begins at the **Puerta de Campo**, the restored entrance to the old city on Calle Manoel Lobo, which dates from the governorship of Vasconcellos in 1745. A thick fortified wall runs south along the Paseo de San Miguel to the river. A short distance west is the **Plaza Mayor 25 de Mayo**, off of which leads the narrow, cobbled **Calle de los Suspiros** (Street of Whispers), lined with tile-and-stucco colonial houses. Just beyond this street, the **Museo Portugués** has good exhibits on the Portuguese period, including Lusitanian and colonial dress. Colonia's museums are generally open from 11:30 am to 6 pm.

At the southwest corner of the Plaza Mayor are the **Casa de Lavalleja**, once the residence of General Lavalleja, and the ruins of the 17th-century **Convento de San Francisco** and the 19th-century **faro** (lighthouse). Open from 10:30 am to noon Thursday, the faro provides an excellent view of the old town. At the west end of Plaza Mayor, on Calle del Comercio, is the **Museo Municipal**; next door is the so-called **Casa del Virrey**, the Viceroy's House, although there was never a viceroy in Colonia. At the northwest corner of the plaza, on Calle de las Misiones de los Tapes, the **Archivo Regional** contains a small museum and bookshop.

At the west end of Misiones de los Tapes is the **Museo de los Azulejos** (Museum of Tiles), a 17th-century house with a sampling of colonial tilework (the museum was closed at last report). From there, the riverfront **Paseo de San Gabriel** leads to Calle del Colegio, where a right to Calle del Comercio leads to the **Capilla Jesuítica**, the ruined Jesuit chapel. Going east along Av General Flores and then turning south on Calle Vasconcellos, you reach the landmark **Iglesia Matriz** on the Plaza de Armas, also known as Plaza Manoel Lobo.

Across General Flores, at España and San José, the **Museo Español** has exhibitions of replica pottery, clothing, and maps of the colonial period; it's closed Tuesday and Wednesday. At the north end of the street is the **Puerto Viejo**, the old port. One block east, at Calle del Virrey Cevallos and Rivadavia, the **Teatro Bastión del Carmen** is a theater building that incorporates part of the city's ancient fortifications.

## Real de San Carlos

At the turn of the century, naturalized Argentine entrepreneur Nicolás Mihanovich spent US$1.5 million to build an enormous tourist complex at the Real de San Carlos, five km west of Colonia, at a spot where Spanish troops once camped before attacking the Portuguese outpost. Among the attractions erected by Mihanovich, a Dalmatian immigrant, were a 10,000-seat bullring (Uruguay outlawed bullfights in 1912), a 3000-seat jai alai frontón, a hotel-casino with its own power plant (the casino failed in 1917 when the Argentine government placed a tax on every boat crossing the river), and a racecourse.

Only the racecourse functions today, but the ruins make an interesting excursion. There is also the **Museo Municipal Real de San Carlos**, focusing on paleontology, which is open daily (except Monday) from 2 to 7 pm.

## Places to Stay

As Colonia has become a more popular destination for Argentine and international travelers, hotel keepers have upgraded their accommodations and prices have risen, but there are still reasonable alternatives. The municipal tourist office on General Flores may help find accommodations in casas de familia. Some hotels charge higher rates on weekends (Friday through Sunday) than weekdays (Monday through Thursday).

**Bottom End** The *Camping Municipal de Colonia* (☎ 4444) sits in a eucalyptus grove at the Real de San Carlos, five km from the Barrio Histórico. Close to the Balneario Municipal, its excellent facilities are open all year and are easily accessible by public transport. Fees are about US$3.50 per person.

Except for camping, really cheap accommodations have nearly disappeared in Colonia. The cheapest in town is the *Hotel Español* (☎ 2314), Manoel Lobo 377, with large but dark rooms for US$8 single (if available), US$15 double with shared bath. The very central *Hotel Colonial* (☎ 2906), General Flores 440, costs US$13/20 a single/double without breakfast.

One of the best values is the very convenient but quiet *Posada del Río* (☎ 3002), on tree-lined Washington Barbot 258 near a pleasant sand beach, which charges US$15 per person with private bath. Another good choice is *Posada de la Ciudadela* (☎ 2683), Washington Barbot 164, where rates are US$20 per person.

**Middle** *Hotel Los Angeles* (☎ 2335), Av Roosevelt 203, is a modern, rather impersonal building on a busy street some distance from the Barrio Histórico, but service is good for US$25/38 a single/double weekdays, US$35/55 weekends, with breakfast. Upgraded *Hotel Italiano* (☎ 2103), Manoel Lobo 341, charges US$35 for doubles with shared bath, US$55 with private bath, breakfast included.

Friendly, usually quiet (despite occasional noise from a nearby bar on weekends) and very clean, with all rooms facing onto a central patio, *Hotel Beltrán* (☎ 2955), General Flores 311, is one of Colonia's oldest hotels. Since remodeling, rates are US$36 double with shared bath, US$45 with private bath, including breakfast, but rates rise to US$70 double on weekends.

Downtown *Hotel Natal John* (☎ 2081), General Flores 394, costs US$45/68 a single/double. *Hotel Esperanza* (☎ 2922), near the entrance to the Barrio Histórico at General Flores 237, charges US$55 double with breakfast, while double rates at *Hotel Leoncia* (☎ 2369), Rivera 214, are US$60 with breakfast.

**Top End** *Gran Hotel Casino El Mirador* (☎ 2004), distant from the Barrio Histórico on Av Roosevelt, is a high-rise hotel with every modern luxury and nothing of Colonia's unique personality. Rates are US$70 per person with half-board, US$80 with full board. Conveniently central at General Flores 340, *Hotel Royal* (☎ 3139) costs US$60/90 a single/double weekdays, US$80/120 weekends. Probably the most distinctive accommodations are at *La Posada del Gobernador* (☎ 3018), 18 de Julio 205 in the Barrio Histórico, but it's arguably overpriced for US$105 a double.

## Places to Eat

*Confitería El Colonial* (☎ 2906), General Flores 432, is an excellent and reasonably priced breakfast spot, serving enormous hot croissants. One of Colonia's best values is *El Asador*, Ituzaingó 168, a parrilla often jammed with locals. *El Portón*, General Flores 333, is a more upscale but appealing parrilla.

*El Suizo*, another parrilla at General Flores and Ituzaingó, appears to charge more because of its attractive colonial setting than for its food. Down the block at General Flores 229, the extensive menu at *Mercado del Túnel* (☎ 4666) varies in quality – there are some very good dishes, but choose selectively (try eyeing the dishes of neighboring patrons).

*Pulpería de los Faroles*, at Del Comercio and Misiones de los Tapes in the Barrio Histórico, has an upscale ambience but is not outrageously expensive for a good meal. *La Casona del Sur*, two doors away, is a good confitería that doubles as a handicrafts market. At night, it has live music.

At the tip of the Barrio Histórico is a good pizzería in a remodeled tower. A recent reader recommendation is *Arabella*, 18 de Julio 360.

## Getting There & Away

**Air** LAPA (☎ 314-1005) at MT de Alvear 790 in Recoleta, flies twice daily from Aeroparque to Colonia except Sunday (once only). The 15-minute crossing costs US$23 one-way.

**Boat** Buenos Aires has regular ferry and hydrofoil *(aliscafo)* services to Colonia. These sail from Dársena Norte, near downtown at Madero and Viamonte, or from Dársena Sur, Av Pedro de Mendoza 20 in La Boca. There is now a US$10 departure tax from these terminals. In Colonia, ferries land at the port at the foot of Av Roosevelt.

Ferrytur (☎ 315-6800, 300-1366 at Dársena Sur), Av Córdoba 699, sails the ferry *Ciudad de Buenos Aires* twice daily weekdays, and daily on weekends, to Colonia (2½ hours) and back. These depart weekdays at noon and 8 pm, weekends at 7:30 pm only. Regular fares are US$10 one-way, US$7 for children ages three to nine. One-way fares for automobiles start at US$40.

Buquebus (☎ 313-4444), Av Córdoba 867, has two daily ferry sailings to Colonia on the *Eladia Isabel* and *Silvia Ana*, except weekends when there is only one crossing. Ferries depart at 4 am and 8 pm. Cars weighing up to 1200 kg pay US$60 exclusive of passenger fares, while those over 1200 kg pay US$70. A Buquebus colectivo leaves the Av Córdoba offices for Dársena Sur 1½ hours prior to every departure.

Ferrytur's hydrofoil *Sea Cat* goes to Colonia (one hour) three times daily, Monday to Saturday, and twice Sunday for US$25 one-way, US$45 return; children ages three to nine pay US$15/25. Fares may be higher on selected peak days and in summer. Aliscafos (☎ 314-2473), Córdoba 787, also runs several hydrofoils (one hour, US$21) daily to Colonia. This is faster but more crowded, and there's a luggage limitation.

Passengers departing from the ferry terminal in Colonia pay a US$3 departure tax.

# MONTEVIDEO

Uruguay's capital dominates the country's political, economic and cultural life even more than Buenos Aires does Argentina's. Nearly half of Uruguay's 3.2 million citizens live here. There is a certain logic to this: The capital's superb natural port links the country to overseas commerce, and the almost exclusively rural economy hardly requires a competing metropolis for trade and administration.

In many ways, economic stagnation has left modern Montevideo a worn-out city where key public buildings are undistinguished, utilitarian constructions that would not be out of place in Eastern Europe – according to one graffito, it's 'un necrópolis de sueños rotos' (a necropolis of broken dreams). Still, the municipal administration is sprucing up public spaces like Plaza Cagancha and promoting restoration of the Ciudad Vieja, the colonial core that is the city's most appealing feature.

# History

Spain's 1726 founding of Montevideo was a response to concern over Portugal's growing influence in the River Plate area; it was in turn a fortress against the Portuguese as well as British, French and Danish privateers who came in search of hides on the Banda Oriental, the 'Eastern Shore' of the Río de la Plata.

The city's port, superior to Buenos Aires in every respect except its access to the Humid Pampa, soon made it a focal point for overseas shipping. An early 19th century construction boom resulted in a new Iglesia Matriz, cabildo (town hall) and other neoclassical monuments, but after independence Uruguayan authorities demolished many of these buildings and planned a new center east of Ciudad Vieja (Old City) and its port.

During the mid-19th century, the city endured an almost constant state of siege by the Argentine dictator Rosas, who was determined to create a small client state to Buenos Aires. After Rosas' fall in 1851, normal commerce resumed and, between 1860 and 1911, the British-built railroad network assisted the capital's growth.

Like Buenos Aires, Montevideo absorbed numerous European immigrants in the early 20th century, when construction of the city's first locally financed meat-freezer plant was followed by two similar foreign-backed enterprises, closely linked to the export trade. Growth has continued to stimulate agricultural intensification near Montevideo to feed the rapidly increasing urban population. Much of this population consists of refugees from rural poverty who live in *conventillos*, large older houses converted into multi-family slum dwellings. Many of these are in the Ciudad Vieja, but even this population is being displaced as urban redevelopment usurps this picturesque but valuable central area.

# Orientation

Montevideo lies on the east bank of the Río de la Plata, almost directly east of Buenos Aires on the west bank. Most visitors from Buenos Aires will arrive by ferry or hydofoil at the Ciudad Vieja, the colonial grid on a small peninsula near the port and harbor, an area once surrounded by protective walls. The city's functional center is Plaza Independencia to the east and around Plaza Cagancha. Across the harbor to the west, the 132-meter Cerro de Montevideo was a landmark for early navigators and still offers outstanding views of the city. To the east, the Rambla or riverfront road leads past attractive residential suburbs with numerous public parks and sandy beaches.

MAP 4

**Bahía de Montevideo**

Muelle B

Dársena

Muelle A          Dársena 1

Paro

Muelle
de Escala

Dársena
Fluvial

Muelle de
Contenedores

Rambla 25 de Agosto

Mercado
del Puerto

Ped
Mall

Piedras

Cerrito

Treinta y Tres

Ituzaingó

JC Gómez

Plaza
Constituc

Cuareim

Guaraní

Maciel

Pérez Castellano

Colón

Solís

Bartolomé Mitre

Misiones

11
10
8
6

12
14
13

15
16
17

9
Plaza
Zabala

25 de Mayo

Washington

Buenos Aires

Reconquista

Alzaibar

40

38
39

Sarandí

Escollera
Sarandí

Parque

Rambla Francia

**Montevideo**

0      150     300 m

| PLACES TO STAY | PLACES TO EAT | OTHER |
|---|---|---|
| 4 Hotel Arapey | 2 Club Libanés | 1 Ferry Port |
| 5 Residencial Acevedo | 3 Club Alemán | 8 Casa Garibaldi |
| 6 Hotel Mediterráneo | 7 La Camargue | 10 Palacio Taranco, |
| 9 Hotel Capri | 13 Natura | Museo de Arte Decora |
| 20 Hotel Palacio | 18 Olivier | 11 Casa Lavalleja |
| 24 Hotel Victoria Palace | 26 Oro del Rhin | 12 Museo Romántico |
| 25 Hotel Internacional | 35 Pizza Bros | 14 Casa Rivera |
| 27 Hotel Ideal | 40 Confitería de la Corte | 15 Banco La Caja Obrera |
| 32 Hotel Aramaya | 41 Confitería La Pasiva | 16 Cabildo, Museo y Arch |
| 34 Hotel Ateneo | 45 Mercado Central, | Histórico Municipal |
| 36 Hospedaje El Aguila, | Restaurant Morini | 17 Iglesia Matriz |
| Pensión Catalunya | 47 Oriente | 19 Mercado de los Artesa |
| 37 Hotel Alvear | 49 Las Brasas | 21 Museo Torres García |
| 39 Hotel City | 51 La Suiza | 22 Puerta de la Ciudadela |
| 43 Hospedaje Solís | 55 El Fogón, La Vegetariana | 23 Mausoleo de Artigas |
| 50 Hotel Español | 61 Ruffino | 28 Ferryturismo |
| 52 Albergue Juvenil | 62 Vida Natural | 29 Free Way Viajes |
| 53 Hotel Casablanca | 63 Taberna Vasca | 30 Ministerio de Turismo |
| 54 Gran Hotel América | 68 La Genovesa | 31 Buquebus |
| 56 Hotel London Palace | 69 La Vegetariana | 33 Mercado de los Artesa |
| 57 Hotel Nuevo Ideal | 70 Mesón del Club Español | 38 Correo Central |
| 58 Hospedaje del Centro | 74 El Horreo | (Main Post Office) |
| 64 Hotel Oxford | | 42 Manos del Uruguay |
| 65 Hotel Lafayette | | 44 Teatro Solís |
| 66 Hotel Libertad | | 45 Fun Fun (Tango) |
| 67 Hotel Windsor | | 46 Palacio Estévez |
| 71 Hotel Embajador | | 48 Palacio Salvo |
| | | 60 Manos del Uruguay |
| | | 72 La Cumparsita |
| | | (Nightclub) |
| | | 73 La Cumparsita |
| | | (Tango) |

Valparaiso
Old Train Station

To Palacio
Legislativo

La Paz
Julio Herrera y Obes
Rio Negro
Paraguay
Florida

Galicia
Cerro Largo
Andes
Convención
Rio Branco
Paysandú
Mercedes
Colonia
Av Uruguay

Barrios Amorín
Eldó
Yaguarón
Yí
Cuareim
Florida
Ciudadela

3
2▼
4■
5■
6■
7■

36■

To Tres Cruces Bus Terminal,
Parque José Batlle y Ordóñez

▼37■

30■⊕

34■
33■
35■

▼69■
70▼

Santiago de Chile

25■
26
Colonia
27■
29■
28
31■

Plaza
del
Entrevero

Plaza
Cagancha

24▼
Plaza
Independencia

Av 18 de Julio

53■
54●
55▼
56■

60●
61
62▼▼
63■
67■
66■

▼68■

▼50■
23■
22■

49▼
48▼
San-José
47

51
52

57■
59■
58■
64■
65■

46■
44■
45▼

Soriano

Canelones
Julio Herrera y Obes
W F Aldunate
Paraguay

Maldonado
Rio Branco
Durazno

Gutiérrez Ruíz
Zelmar Michelini
Carlos Quijano
Eldó
Yaguarón
Santiago de Chile

74▼

71■
Parque
Rambla Gran Bretaña
Convención
Carlos Gardel

72■
73■

Av Gonzalo

Río de la Plata

Cementerio
Central

Rambla República Argentina

To Parque
Rodó

WAYNE BERNHARDSON

Bas-reliefs in Ciudad Vieja

# Information

The Ministerio de Turismo (☎ 90-4148) has a cubbyhole information office on the ground floor at Av Libertador General Lavalleja 1409; it's open from 9 am to 6:30 pm weekdays. The Oficina de Informes (☎ 41-8998) at Terminal Tres Cruces, the new bus station at Bulevar Artigas and Av Italia, is open from 7 am to 11 pm daily and is better prepared to deal with visitor inquiries. The very useful weekly *Guía del Ocio*, which lists cultural events, cinemas, theaters and restaurants, comes with the Friday edition of the daily *El País*.

There are many exchange houses around Plaza Cagancha and on Av 18 de Julio.

# Walking Tour

To orient yourself in downtown Montevideo, take a walk from **Plaza Independencia** through the Ciudad Vieja to the port. On the plaza, an honor guard keeps 24-hour vigil over the **Mausoleo de Artigas**, which is topped by a 17-meter, 30-ton statue of the country's greatest hero. The 18th-century **Palacio Estévez**, on the south side, was the Government House until 1985. On the east side, the Baroque, 26-story **Palacio Salvo**, was the continent's tallest building when it opened in 1927 and is still the tallest in the city. Just off the plaza is the **Teatro Solís** (see below).

At the west end of the plaza is **La Puerta de la Ciudadela**, a modified remnant of the colonial citadel that dominated the area before its demolition in 1833. Calle Sarandí, part of which is now a peatonal, leads to **Plaza Constitución**, also known as Plaza Matriz, where a central sculpture, by the Italian Juan Ferrari, commemorates the establishment of Montevideo's first waterworks. On the east side of the Plaza Constitución, a historical museum is housed in the cabildo (finished in 1812), a neoclassical stone structure designed by Spanish architect Tomás Toribio. Begun in 1784 and completed in 1799, the **Iglesia Matriz**, on the corner of Sarandí and Ituzaingó, is Montevideo's oldest public building, the work of Portuguese architect José de Sáa y Faría.

Detour one block north of Plaza Constitución to see the outstanding bas-reliefs by Edmundo Prati on the **Banco La Caja Obrera** (1941), 25 de Mayo at Ituzaingó. Returning to Calle Rincón, continue west to the Casa Rivera at Rincón and Misiones, the Museo Romántico at 25 de Mayo 428, and the Casa Lavalleja at Zabala and 25 de Mayo, all part of the **Museo Histórico**

**Nacional** (see below). See also the **Palacio Taranco** (1910), at 25 de Mayo and Primero de Mayo, built in an 18th-century European style by French architects commissioned by a wealthy merchant; it houses the **Museo de Arte Decorativo**, open weekdays from 2 to 6 pm. From there, visit **Plaza Zabala**, site of the colonial governor's house until its demolition in 1878; there is a statue to Bruno Mauricio de Zabala, Montevideo's founder, by Spanish sculptor Lorenzo Coullant Valera. From the plaza, continue west along Washington and north to Colón and 25 de Mayo, where the **Casa Garibaldi** once housed the Italian hero, and then to Piedras and the **Mercado del Puerto** (see below).

## Museo Histórico Nacional

The national history museum actually consists of four different houses, most of them former residences of Uruguayan national heroes in the Ciudad Vieja. Built in the late 18th century, the **Casa Lavalleja**, Zabala 1469, was the home of General Lavalleja from 1830 until his death in 1853; in 1940, his heirs donated it to the state. The **Casa Rivera**, a 19th-century building at Rincón 437, belonged to General Fructuoso Rivera, Uruguay's first president and founder of the Colorado Party. The **Casa Garibaldi**, at 25 de Mayo 314, belonged to the Italian patriot who commanded the Uruguayan navy from 1843 – 1851; it now contains many of his personal effects. All the houses are open Tuesday through Friday from 12:30 to 6:30 pm, Sundays and holidays from 2 to 6 pm.

The 18th-century **Museo Romántico**, 25 de Mayo 428, is full of paintings and antique furniture, but its exterior has been modified from the original colonial style. It keeps the same hours as the rest of the museum.

## Museo Torres García

This museum in the Ciudad Vieja, on the peatonal at Sarandí 683, displays the works of Uruguayan artist Joaquín Torres García, who spent much of his career in France producing abstract and even cubist work like that of Picasso, as well as unusual portraits of historical figures such as Columbus, Mozart, Beethoven, Bach and Rabelais. Open weekdays from 3 to 7 pm and Saturdays from 11 am to 1 pm, it also has a small gift shop and bookshop. Admission is free.

## Palacio Legislativo

At the north end of Av Libertador General Lavalleja, the
neoclassical legislature, bril-
liantly lighted at night, is one
of the city's most impressive
landmarks. Guided tours
(available in English) take
place every half hour between 1:30 and 4:30 pm on
weekdays only.

WAYNE BERNHARDSON

## Teatro Solís

Named for the first Spaniard to set foot in what is
now Uruguayan territory, Montevideo's leading theater
opened in 1856, delayed by Rosas' siege of Montevideo
(construction actually began in 1842). Performers who
have appeared here include Caruso, Toscanini, Pavlova,
Nijinski, Sarah Bernhardt, Rostropovich and Twyla
Tharpe. See Entertainment for more details.

WAYNE BERNHARDSON

## Mercado del Puerto

At its opening in 1868, Montevideo's port was the continent's finest, but its market survives on personality and
atmosphere. No visitor should miss the old port market
building at the foot of Calle Pérez Castellano, where
an impressive wrought-iron superstructure shelters a
gaggle of reasonably priced parrillas (choose your cut off
the grill) and some more upmarket restaurants with

outstanding seafood. About 40 years ago, local entre-preneurs began to add more sophisticated restaurants to the grills that even then fed the people who brought their produce to the market, and the market gradually became a local phenomenon.

Especially on Saturdays, it is a lively, colorful place where the city's artists, craftsworkers and street musicians hang out. *Café Roldos*, at the same site since 1886, serves the popular medio y medio, a mixture of white and sparkling wines.

## Organized Tours

Free Way Viajes (☎ 90-8931), Colonia 994, runs a recommended city tour (US$13) and another by night for US$24 (US$35 with dinner included). It organizes additional tours throughout the country and has guides available in several languages.

## Special Events

Much livelier than that of Buenos Aires, Montevideo's late summer Carnaval is well worth the trip for those who can't make it to Rio de Janeiro. Semana Criolla festivities, during Semana Santa (Holy Week), take place at Parque Prado, north of downtown.

## Places to Stay

Prices for accommodations have risen faster than inflation at large in recent years, so that many former bottom-end hotels are now mid-range. Bottom-end hotels are often dark and rundown, but there are a few exceptions.

**Bottom End** For budget travelers, the most reasonable and central lodging is the *Albergue Juvenil* (☎ 98-1324), the official youth hostel at Canelones 935, which costs about US$8 per night, including breakfast, with a hostel card; linen costs US$1.20 additional. It has kitchen facilities, a lounge and information. Its 11 pm curfew could restrict your night life, though it's not impossible to arrange a later arrival with the caretaker. It's closed from noon to 7:30 pm daily.

In the Ciudad Vieja, a new and good choice is the simple but friendly *Hospedaje Solís* (☎ 95-0437), Bartolomé Mitre 1314, which charges only US$8 for spacious singles with shared bath; those with private bath cost US$20.

*Hotel Nuevo Ideal* (☎ 98-2913), Soriano 1073, has mildewy singles/doubles with private bath for US$13/18, but its central location is a strong point. *Hospedaje del Centro* (☎ 90-1419), at Soriano 1126 next to the Peruvian Consulate, charges US$10/13 with shared bath, US$14/17 with private bath; once a luxurious single family residence, it's clean but declining, and some rooms are very dark. *Hospedaje El Aguila*, an old and funky but friendly place at Colonia 1235, has rooms with shared bath for US$11/16. *Pensión Catalunya*, nearby at Colonia 1223, is very clean and slightly cheaper, but room size varies greatly. Recommended *Hotel Windsor* (☎ 91-5080), Zelmar Michelini 1260, charges US$10/15 for singles/doubles with shared bath, US$13/18 with private bath.

Friendly, appealing *Hotel Libertad*, Carlos Quijano 1223, charges US$14 double with shared bath, US$20 with private bath. *Hotel Ideal* (☎ 91-6389), Colonia 914, is clean and friendly with good bathrooms; singles/doubles with shared bath are US$15/20, with private bath US$18/25.

One of Montevideo's best budget accommodations has been *Hotel Palacio* (☎ 96-3612) at Bartolomé Mitre 1364, but it seems to be living on its reputation after unwarranted price increases. Singles with brass beds (some of them sagging), antique furniture and balconies cost US$17 with shared bath – but ask for the 6th-floor rooms, where the balconies are nearly as large as the rooms themselves and provide exceptional views of the Ciudad Vieja. Still a good place, but it's not the value it once was.

**Middle** A good choice is *Hotel Arapey* (☎ 90-7032) at Av Uruguay 925 with rooms for US$20/25. At *Hotel Ateneo* (☎ 91-2630), Colonia 1147, rates are US$20/26 with private bath and television, but some rooms are a bit dark. *Residencial Acevedo*, Av Uruguay 1127, has rooms for US$20 with shared bath or US$25 with private bath, single or double.

*Hotel Casablanca* (☎ 91-0918), conveniently central at San José 1039, charges US$25 per double with private bath. *Hotel Capri* (☎ 95-5970), in the Ciudad Vieja's red-light district at Colón 1460, charges US$26 for singles or doubles with private bath and color TV; there's a 20% discount Monday through Thursday. Recommended *Hotel City* (☎ 98-2913), Buenos Aires 462, is comparably priced.

Probably the best mid-range value is *Hotel Mediterráneo* (☎ 90-5090), Paraguay 1486, which charges US$30/40 for well-kept rooms with breakfast and excellent service. Pleasant, comparably priced *Hotel Aramaya* (☎ 98-6192) is at Av 18 de Julio 1103. *Hotel Español*

(☎ 90-3816) at Convención 1317 charges US$25/40 for interior rooms, US$35/50 for those facing on the street.

**Top End** Montevideo's top-end hotels lack the luxury of those in Buenos Aires, but there are some decent values. All of them include breakfast in their rates. *Gran Hotel América* (☎ 92-0392), Río Negro 1330, charges from US$48/62, while the *Hotel London Palace* (☎ 92-0024), Río Negro 1278, costs US$47/64. Comparable places, for about US$50/67, include *Hotel Alvear* (☎ 92-0244) at Yí 1372 and *Hotel Internacional* (☎ 90-5794) at Colonia 823. *Hotel Embajador* (☎ 92-0009), San José 1212, is slightly dearer at US$54/73.

Refurbished *Hotel Oxford* (☎ 92-0046) at Paraguay 1286 costs US$70/85, which includes an outstanding breakfast. *Hotel Libertador* (☎ 92-0079), Florida 1128, is an upscale hotel that also houses US Peace Corps volunteers when they're in town. The recently built *Hotel Lafayette* (☎ 92-2351), Soriano 1170, is Montevideo's only real luxury hotel, charging US$98/113, though the *Hotel Victoria Palace* (☎ 98-9565), Plaza Independencia 759, makes an effort to be one.

## Places to Eat

Montevideo falls short of Buenos Aires' sophistication and variety, but its numerous restaurants are unpretentious and offer excellent values. Reasonably priced, worthwhile downtown restaurants include *Morini* (☎ 95-9733), Ciudadela 1229, and *Mesón Viejo Sancho* (☎ 90-4063), San José 1229. *La Genovesa* (☎ 90-8729), San José 1262, has good seafood with abundant portions, but note that IVA is not included in the listed prices, nor is the cubierto or service.

Uruguayans eat even more meat than Argentines, so parrillada is always a popular choice. Central parrillas include *El Fogón* (☎ 90-0900) at San José 1080, *Las Brasas* (☎ 90-2285) at San José 909, and the many stalls at the Mercado del Puerto. If you've OD'd on meat, there are several vegetarian restaurants: *La Vegetariana* at Yí 1334 (☎ 90-7661) and San José 1056 (☎ 91-0558), *Natura* (☎ 95-7047) at Rincón 414, and *Vida Natural* at San José 1184.

Seafood is another possibility. *La Posada del Puerto* (☎ 95-4279) has two stalls in the Mercado del Puerto, while *La Tasca del Puerto* is outside on the peatonal Pérez Castellano. *La Proa* (☎ 96-2578), a sidewalk café on the peatonal Pérez Castellano, has entrees from about US$8; with drinks, dinner for two should cost about US$20. It serves as many as 800 people per day, but the service is still friendly and personal. Another popular place in the Mercado is *El Palenque* (☎ 95-4704).

As in Argentina, Italian immigration has left its mark on the country's cuisine. For pizza, try *Emporio de la Pizza* (☎ 91-4681), Río Negro 1311; less traditional is *Pizza Bros*, Plaza Cagancha 1364, a lively place with good pizza and bright but not overpowering decor. For more elaborate dishes, visit *Ruffino* (☎ 98-3384) at San José 1166.

*Olivier* (☎ 95-0617), at JC Gómez 1420 just off Plaza Constitución, is a very highly regarded but expensive French restaurant. *La Camargue* at Mercedes 1133 likewise has an outstanding reputation but is not cheap. Spanish food is available at *Mesón del Club Español* (☎ 91-5145), Av 18 de Julio 1332, and *El Horreo* (☎ 91-7688), Santiago de Chile 1137, which has flamenco shows Fridays. For Basque food, visit *Taberna Vasca* (☎ 92-3519) at San José 1168.

Other European places include the *Club Alemán* (☎ 92-2832) at Paysandú 935 for German food, while Swiss specialties including fondue can be found at *La Suiza*, Soriano 939. There's Middle Eastern food at the *Club Libanés* (☎ 90-1801), Paysandú 898. *Oriente*, Andes 1311, has a good Chinese menu, but some dishes are expensive.

*Confitería La Pasiva*, on Plaza Constitución at JC Gómez and Sarandí in the Ciudad Vieja, has excellent, reasonably priced minutas and superb flan casero in a very traditional atmosphere (except for the digital readout menu on one wall); the 'pasiva entrecote' has been highly recommended as sufficient for two.

Other decent confiterías include *Oro del Rhin* (☎ 92-2833), at Convención 1403 (the oldest in the city), and *Confitería de la Corte*, at Ituzaingó 1325 just off Plaza Constitución, which has very good, moderately priced lunch specials.

# Entertainment

Gardel spent time in Montevideo, where the tango is no less popular than in Buenos Aires. The very informal *Fun Fun* (☎ 95-8005), Ciudadela 1229 in the Mercado Central has a good mix of young and old. *La Cumparsita* (☎ 91-6245) has two locations – one is a general nightclub on Carlos Gardel near Gutiérrez Ruiz, the other features tango, two blocks away on Carlos Gardel near Zelmar Michelini. The tango club gets very crowded, so make reservations; it also features candombe (Afro-Uruguayan) dancing. Prices for show and dinner run about US$20 per person.

At the southwest corner of Plaza Independencia, at Buenos Aires 678, *Teatro Solís* (☎ 95-9770) has superb acoustics and offers concerts, ballet, opera and plays throughout the year. It is also home to the Comedia Nacional, the municipal theater company. Get tickets at least a few days before events.

Soccer, an Uruguayan passion, inspires large and regular crowds. The main stadium, the *Estadio Centenario* in Parque José Batlle y Ordóñez off Av Italia, opened in 1930 for the first World Cup. Later declared a historic monument, it also contains the Museo del Fútbol.

## Things to Buy

For attractive artisanal items, at reasonable prices in an informal atmosphere, visit Mercado de los Artesanos, which has branches on Plaza Cagancha and at Bartolomé Mitre 1367 in the Ciudad Vieja. Manos del Uruguay, at San José 1111 (☎ 90-4910) and Reconquista 602 (☎ 95-9522, is famous for its quality goods. The daily crafts market in Plaza Cagancha is a hangout for many younger Uruguayans.

## Getting There & Away

**Air** Many international airlines serve Montevideo from Ezeiza. Commuter airlines also provide international services between the two countries. Pluna and Aerolíneas Argentinas 'Puente Aéreo' (Air Bridge) offers a US$52 one-way fare between Aeroparque and Montevideo. Líneas Aéreas Privadas Argentinas (LAPA) runs a bus-plane combination from Buenos Aires' Aeroparque Jorge Newbery to Montevideo via Colonia (US$30.50). Aerolíneas Regionales Uruguayas (☎ 93-1608), Yí 1435, flies from Aeroparque. For contact information, see the Getting There & Away chapter.

**Bus** There is regular service from Buenos Aires' main bus station. One company to try is General Urquiza (☎ 313-2771), which has nightly service to Montevideo (US$25, nine hours). See the Bus section of the Getting There & Away chapter for more details.

Still reasonably close to downtown, Montevideo's long-overdue Terminal Tres Cruces (☎ 41-8998), at Bulevar Artigas and Av Italia, is a big improvement on the individual bus terminals that once cluttered Plaza Cagancha and nearby side streets. It has decent restaurants, clean toilets, luggage check, public telephones, a casa de cambio and many other services.

**Boat** Most services across the Río de la Plata from Buenos Aires are bus-boat combinations via Colonia, but the so-called 'Aviones de Buquebus' are high-speed ferries that arrive at the port at the foot of Pérez Castellano. These take only about 2½ hours (US$37). Users of the new hydrofoil port at Dársena Norte pay US$10 to travel to Montevideo.

Ferrytur's ferries and hydrofoils to Colonia make bus connections to Montevideo. Ferrytur (☎ 315-6800 or ☎ 300-1366 at Dársena Sur), Av Córdoba 699 at Maipú in Retiro, runs the ferry *Ciudad de Buenos Aires* weekdays at noon and 8 pm, and weekends at 7:30 only to Colonia (2½ hours). Their bus-hydrofoil combination to Montevideo (four hours, US$35 on peak weekends, US$25 weekdays) via Colonia departs three times daily except Sunday, when it runs only twice. There are slight discounts for round trips. Fares may be higher on selected peak days and in summer.

Buquebus (☎ 313-4444), Av Córdoba 867 in Retiro, runs 'Aviones de Buquebus' (high-speed ferries) that reach Montevideo in 2½ hours and cost US$37 in turista, US$49 in primera; children ages two to nine pay US$19/32. There are four sailings daily. A Buquebus colectivo leaves the Av Córdoba offices for Dársena Sur 1½ hours prior to every departure.

Cacciola runs a bus-launch service from the Buenos Aires suburb of Tigre four times daily. In Tigre they're at the Terminal Internacional, Lavalle 520 (☎ 749-0329); tickets are also available at their downtown Buenos Aires office (☎ 322-0026) at Florida 520, 1st floor, Oficina 113. In Montevideo, Deltanave (☎ 91-5143) at Plaza Cagancha 1340 runs launches from Tigre to Nueva Palmira.

Most of the boat services across the Río de la Plata maintain offices at Terminal Tres Cruces in Montevideo as well.

# Getting Around

**To/From the Airport** For US$4, there is a special airport bus from Pluna's downtown offices; see the schedule posted there. The D-1 Expreso bus from the Ciudad Vieja also goes to Carrasco.

**Bus** Montevideo's improving fleet of buses less frequently leaves you gasping for breath with noxious diesel fumes, and still goes everywhere for about US$0.45. The *Guia de Montevideo Eureka*, available at bookshops or kiosks, lists routes and schedules, as do the yellow pages of the Montevideo phone book. As in Argentina, the driver or conductor will ask your destination. Retain your ticket, which may be inspected at any time. This is not Buenos Aires, however – most routes cease service by 10:30 or 11 pm.

**Taxi** Taxis have meters and drivers correlate the meter reading with a photocopied fare chart. Between midnight and 6 am fares are higher. There is a small additional charge for luggage, and riders generally round off the fare to the next higher peso.

# Glossary

**ACA** – Automóvil Club Argentino, an automobile club that provides maps, road service, insurance and other services, and operates hotels, motels and campgrounds throughout the country. It's a valuable resource even for travelers without motor vehicles.

**albergue transitorio** – not to be mistaken for an *albergue juvenil* (youth hostel), this is very short-term accommodations normally utilized by young couples in search of privacy. Some places cater exclusively to this trade, while some lower-end hotels rely on it in part to remain financially viable. An alternative euphemism, used in Uruguay, is *hotel de alta rotatividad*.

**aliscafo** – hydrofoil, from Buenos Aires across the Río de la Plata to Colonia and Montevideo, Uruguay.

**argentinidad** – rather nebulous concept of Argentine national identity, often associated with extreme nationalistic feelings.

**asado** – barbecue, often a family outing in summer.

**autopista** – freeway or motorway.

**banda negativa** – low-cost air tickets in Argentina, for which limited seats on particular flights are available for discounts of up to 40% off the usual price.

**bandoneón** – accordion-like instrument used in tango music.

**barras bravas** – violent soccer fans, the Argentine equivalent of Britain's 'football hooligans'.

**barrio** – neighborhood or borough of the city.

**boliche** – a nightclub, but the word usually implies informality and even rowdiness.

**cabildo** – colonial town council.

**cachila** – in Uruguay, an antique automobile, often beautifully maintained.

**cajero automático** – automatic teller machine (ATM).

**calle** – street.

**cambio** – see 'casa de cambio'.

**característica** – telephone area code.

**carapintada** – in the Argentine military, extreme right-wing, ultranationalist movement of disaffected junior officers, responsible for several attempted coups during the Alfonsín and Menem administrations.

**carne** – while this word generally means 'meat', in Argentina it specifically means 'beef'. Chicken, pork and the like may be referred to as *carne blanca* (white meat).

**cartelera** – discount ticket agency offering great bargains on cinemas, tango shows and other performances.

**casa de cambio** – foreign exchange house, often simply called a 'cambio'.

**casco** – 'big house' of a livestock estancia.

**caudillo** – in 19th-century Argentine politics, a provincial strongman whose power rested more on personal loyalty than political ideals or party organization.

**certificado** – registered mail.

**coima** – a bribe. One who solicits a bribe is a *coimero*.

**conventillo** – tenements that housed immigrants in older neighborhoods of Buenos Aires and Montevideo. On a reduced scale, these still exist in the San Telmo barrio of Buenos Aires and the Ciudad Vieja of Montevideo.

WAYNE BERNHARDSON

A Montevideo conventillo

**cospel** – token used in Argentine public telephones in lieu of coins. There are different types of cospeles for local and long-distance phones.

**costanera** – seaside, riverside or lakeside road.

**criollo** – in colonial period, an American-born Spaniard, but the term now commonly describes any Argentine of European descent. The term also describes the feral cattle of the Pampas.

**DDI** – Discado Directo Internacional (International Direct Dialing), which provides direct access to home-country operators for long-distance collect and credit-card calls. This is a much cheaper alternative to the rates of the Argentine companies Telecom and Telefónica.

**démedos** – literally 'give me two', a pejorative nick-name for Argentines who travel to Miami, where everything is so cheap that they buy things they don't need.

**Dirty War** – in the 1970s, the violent repression by the Argentine military of left-wing revolutionaries and anyone suspected of sympathizing with them.

**estancia** – Historically speaking, an extensive grazing establishment, either for cattle or sheep, under a domi-nating owner (estanciero) or manager with a dependent resident labor force of gauchos. Many Argentine estancias, often very luxurious, have opened themselves to tourists for recreational activities such as riding, tennis and swimming, either for weekend escapes or extended stays.

**facturas** – pastries.

**ficha** – token used in the Buenos Aires subway system (Subte) in lieu of coins.

**Gardeliano** – fan of the late tango singer Carlos Gardel.

**gas-oil** – diesel fuel.

**gasolero** – motor vehicle that uses diesel fuel, which is much cheaper than ordinary petrol in Argentina.

**Gran Aldea** – the 'Great Village'; Buenos Aires prior to the massive European immigration of the late 19th and early 20th centuries.

**guita** – in lunfardo, money.

**hacer dedo** – to hitchhike, literally 'to make or do thumb'.

**hoteles de categoria** – top-end hotels, usually recom-mended by tourist offices and travel agencies to foreign visitors no matter what their economic status.

**ida** – one way.
**ida y vuelta** – roundtrip.
**iglesia** – church.
**interno** – extension off a central telephone number or switchboard, often abbreviated 'int'.
**IVA** – *impuesto de valor agregado*, value added tax (VAT); often added to restaurant or hotel bills in Argentina and Uruguay. If there is any question, ask whether IVA is included in the bill. In some instances, IVA is refundable on tourist purchases taken out of the country.

**literatura gauchescha** – 'gauchesque' literature, a romantic literature *about* as opposed to *by* the usually illiterate gauchos of the Pampas.
**locutorio** – private long-distance telephone office, which usually also offers fax services.
**lunfardo** – street slang of Buenos Aires, with origins in immigrant neighborhoods at the turn of the century.

**maqueta** – stage set model for a given production at the Teatro Colón, from which sculptors refer to in creating the actual performance out of Styrofoam.
**mercado paralelo** – 'parallel market', a euphemism for the black market in foreign currency, which does not exist at present.
**minuta** – in a restaurant or confitería, a short order such as spaghetti or milanesa.
**museo** – museum.

**nafta** – gasoline or petrol.
**ñoqui** – a public employee whose primary interest is collecting a monthly paycheck. So-called because potato pasta, or ñoquis (from the Italian *gnocchi*), are traditionally served in financially strapped Argentine households on the 29th of each month, the implication being that the employee makes his or her appearance at work around that time.
**novela** – television soap opera.

**pampero** – South Atlantic cold front that brings dramatic temperature changes to northern Argentina.
**parada** – bus stop.
**parrillada, parrilla** – respectively, a mixed grill of steak and other beef cuts, and a restaurant specializing in such dishes.
**pasaperros** – professional dog walker in Buenos Aires.
**peatonal** – pedestrian mall, usually in the downtown area.
**peña** – club that hosts informal folk music gatherings.

**piropo** – sexist remark, ranging in tone from complimentary and relatively innocuous to rude and offensive.
**porteño** – inhabitant of Buenos Aires, a 'resident of the port'.
**primera** – 1st-class on a train.
**Proceso** – in full, 'El Proceso de Reorganización Nacional', a military euphemism for its brutal attempt to remake Argentina's political and economic culture between 1976 and 1983.
**propina** – a tip; for example, in a restaurant or cinema.
**puchero** – soup combining vegetables and meats, served with rice.
**pucho** – in lunfardo, a cigarette or cigarette butt.
**puerta a puerta** – express mail, literally 'door to door'.
**puesto** – 'outside house' on a livestock estancia.
**pulpería** – rural shop (often also serving as a saloon) or 'company store' on a cattle or sheep estancia.

**quilombo** – in lunfardo, a mess. Originally a Brazilian term describing a settlement of runaway slaves, it came to mean a house of prostitution in Argentina.

**recargo** – additional charge, usually 10%, which many Argentine businesses add to credit-card transactions because of high inflation and delays in payment.
**recova** – a colonnade, very common in colonial and neocolonial Argentine architecture.
**río** – river.
**RN** – Ruta Nacional, a national highway.
**RP** – Ruta Provincial, a provincial highway.
**ruta** – highway.

**SIDA** – AIDS.
**sobremesa** – after-dinner conversation, an integral part of any Argentine meal.
**Subte** – the Buenos Aires underground railway.
**sudestada** – a southeasterly storm out of the South Atlantic that often combines with high tides and heavy runoff to flood low-lying barrios like La Boca.

**tarjeta telefónica** – magnetic telephone card, a convenient substitute for cospeles (see above).
**técnico** – specialist in theater skills such as scenery or makeup.
**tenedor libre** – literally, 'free fork', an 'all-you-can-eat' restaurant. Also known as *diente libre* ('free tooth').
**tercera edad** – 'third age', a Spanish language euphemism equivalent to 'senior citizen' in English. Travelers over the age of 60 are eligible for some discounts in Argentina.

**trasnochador** – one who stays up very late or all night, as do many Argentines.

**trucho** – bogus, a term widely used by Argentines to describe things that are not what they appear to be.

In an apparently sycophantic fit, Argentina's National Mint Director caused a minor scandal when he arranged the printing of the 'Menem trucho,' closely resembling Argentine currency but really political propaganda crediting President Carlos Menem with an economic miracle.

**turista** – 2nd-class on a train, usually not very comfortable.

**tuteo** – use of the pronoun *tú* in Spanish and its corresponding verb forms.

**valizas** – triangular emergency reflectors, obligatory in all Argentine motor vehicles.

**villas miserias** – shantytowns on the outskirts of Buenos Aires and other Argentine cities.

**voseo** – use of the pronoun *vos* and its corresponding verb forms in the River Plate republics of Argentina, Uruguay and Paraguay.

**yerba mate** – 'Paraguayan tea' *(Ilex paraguariensis)*, which Argentines consume in very large amounts. Drinking mate is an important everyday social ritual.

# Index

# MAP LEGEND

## ROUTES

▬▬▬▬ ▬▬ Freeway

───── ── Major Road

───── ── Minor Road

──⟩  ⟨── Tunnel

▬▬▬▬▬▬ Pedestrian Mall

ᴵᴵᴵᴵᴵᴵᴵᴵᴵᴵᴵᴵ Stairs

## AREA FEATURES

◼ Garden, Zoo, Golf Course

◼ Park

◼ Plaza

## WATER FEATURES

Coastline
Ferry
Beach
River

## SYMBOLS

✈ Airport

❻ Bank

▯ Bar/Nightclub

◖ Bus Station

☕ Café

⊞ Cathedral

✝ Church

⚑ Embassy

❖ Garden

↑ Golf Course

✪ Hospital

⌂ Hostel

■ Hotel

⛩ Lighthouse

♪ Live Music

▲ Monument

🏛 Museum

☀ Overlook

◳ Post Office

▼ Restaurant

❖ Shopping Mall

🏨 Stately Home

❶ Tourist Information

🐘 Zoo

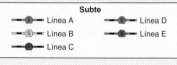

### Subte

──Ⓢ── Línea A

──Ⓢ── Línea B

──Ⓢ── Línea C

──Ⓢ── Línea D

──Ⓢ── Línea E

# Map Index

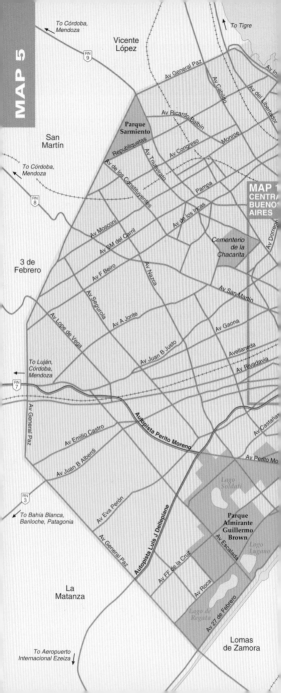

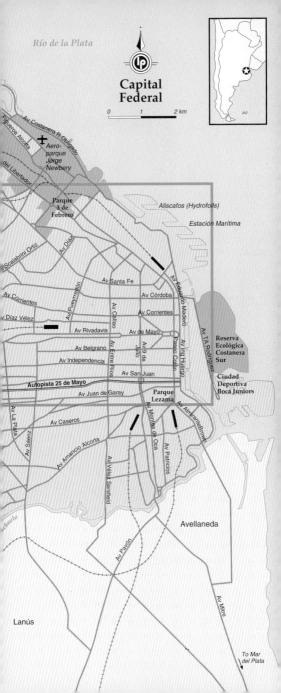

Río de la Plata

Capital
Federal

0    1    2 km

Av Costanera R. Obligado

Figueroa Alcorta

Aero-
parque
Jorge
Newbery

del Libertador

Parque
3 de
Febrero

Aliscafos (Hydrofoils)

Estación Marítima

J Scalabrini Ortiz

Av Díaz

Av Santa Fe

Av Pueyrredón

Av Eduardo Madero

Av Córdoba

Av Corrientes

Av Corrientes

Av Callao

J Díaz Vélez

Av Rivadavia

Av de Mayo

Av 9 de Julio

Paseo Colón

Av Ing Huergo

Av T.A. Rodríguez

Reserva
Ecológica
Costanera
Sur

Av Belgrano

Av Entre Ríos

Av Independencia

Av San Juan

Ciudad
Deportiva
Boca Juniors

Autopista 25 de Mayo

Av Juan de Garay

Parque
Lezama

Av La Plata

Av Caseros

Av Sáenz

Av Amancio Alcorta

Av Vélez Sarsfield

Av Montes de Oca

Av Patricios

Av Almirante Brown

Avellaneda

achuelo

Av Pavón

Lanús

Av Mitre

To Mar
del Plata

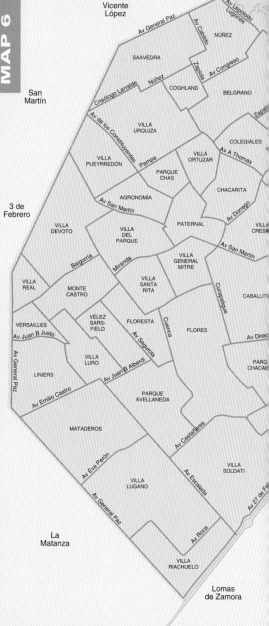

MAP 6

Vicente López

San Martín

3 de Febrero

La Matanza

Lomas de Zamora

Av Leopoldo Lugones
Av General Paz
NÚÑEZ
Av Cabildo
Zapiola
Av Congreso
SAAVEDRA
Crisólogo Larralde
Núñez
COGHLAND
BELGRANO
Zapa...
Av de los Constituyentes
VILLA URQUIZA
COLEGIALES
Pampa
VILLA ORTUZAR
Av A Thomas
VILLA PUEYRREDÓN
PARQUE CHAS
CHACARITA
AGRONOMÍA
Av San Martín
PATERNAL
Av Dorrego
VILLA CRES...
VILLA DEVOTO
VILLA DEL PARQUE
Av San Martín
Baigorria
VILLA GENERAL MITRE
Miranda
Curapaligüe
CABALLIT...
VILLA REAL
MONTE CASTRO
VILLA SANTA RITA
VERSAILLES
VÉLEZ SARSFIELD
FLORESTA
Cuenca
FLORES
Av Direc...
Av Juan B Justo
Av Segurola
PARQ CHACA...
Av General Paz
VILLA LURO
Av Juan B Alberdi
LINIERS
PARQUE AVELLANEDA
Av Emilio Castro
MATADEROS
Av Castañares
VILLA SOLDATI
Av Eva Perón
Av Escalada
VILLA LUGANO
Av 27 de Feb...
Av General Paz
Av Roca
VILLA RIACHUELO

Río de la Plata

## Barrios of Buenos Aires

0    1    2 km

Av Costanera R Obligado

PALERMO

Av Díaz

Córdoba

RECOLETA

Montevideo

RETIRO

Av Córdoba

Av Eduardo Madero

ALMAGRO

BALVANERA

Av Callao

SAN NICOLÁS

Av Rivadavia

MONSERRAT

Chile

Av Independencia

Av La Plata

BOEDO

Av Loria

SAN CRISTÓBAL

Av Juan de Garay

Av Entre Ríos

CONSTI-
TUCIÓN

SAN
TELMO

Av Caseros

Av Pedro de Mendoza

LA
BOCA

Av Caseros

PARQUE
PATRICIOS

Av Patricios

NUEVA
POMPEYA

Mirave

BARRACAS

Riachuelo

Avellaneda

Lanús

MAP 7

Quesada
To Nuñez
■ 1
Av Congreso
Manuel Ugarte
Dr P I Rivera
Franklin D Roosevelt
Plaza Alberti
Moldes
▼ 3
🏛 4
Blanco Encalada
▼ 2
10
11 🏛
12 ▼
13 ▼
17 ▼
Olazábal
Vuelta de Obligado
Mendoza
Cuba
Arcos
16 🏛
🏛 18
14 ▼
Av Cabildo
Juramento
Plaza General Manuel Belgrano
15 ▼
Plaza Noruega
20 †
Echeverría
22 ▼
23
24 ▼
Amenábar
Ciudad de la Paz
Antonio José de Su
Vidal
Moldes
L Pampa
To Villa Urquiza
Av Cabildo
Conesa
Zapiola
R Freire
José Hernández
Virrey del P
Plaza Castelli
■ 29
Virrey del Piño
Plaza Portugal
Virrey Olaguer
Plaza Juan J Paso
Av de los Incas
Av El Cano
FCG B Mitre
To Colegiales

PLACES TO STAY
1   Hotel Majale
29  Hotel de la Rue
32  Key's Hotel

PLACES TO EAT
2   Munich Belgrano
3   L'Altro Cesare
5   Mis Raíces
6   Tía Teresa de Belgrano
7   Chinatown
8   Buffet Libre
9   Tomasso
10  Antiguo Belgrano
12  Gabbiano
13  Cloé
14  La Chaya
15  Casita Suiza
17  Heladería Freddo
21  2020 Restaurant

22  Cien Años
23  Al Shawarma de Aladino
24  Yinyang
26  Furchi
28  El Ceibal
30  Coto

OTHER
4   Museo Casa de Yrurtia
11  Merlyn Café
16  Museo de Arte Español
    Enrique Larreta
18  Museo Histórico Sarmiento
19  Museo Líbero Badii
20  Iglesia de la Inmaculada
    Concepción (La Redonda)
25  Australian Consulate
27  Automóvil Club Argentino (ACA)
31  Instituto Geográfico Militar

**Belgrano**

To Costanera

0   150   300 m

Av del Libertador

Miñones

Arribeños

Juramento

11 de Septiembre

Zavalia

5▼
7▼
▼8
9▼
6▼

FCG B Mitre

19

Barrancas
de
Belgrano

Golf Club
Lagos de
Palermo

Av Valentín Alsina

Av del Libertador

Av Luis M Campos

Arribeños

11 de Septiembre

3 de Febrero

O'Higgins

Arce

Arredondo

Villanueva

25

Plaza General
Morazán

Virrey Loreto

Virrey Arredondo

6▼

27
28

To Palermo

Zabala

Céspedes

Aguilar

Pampa

Teodoro García

Av Federico Lacroze

Olleros

Gorostiaga

▼30   Maure

Av Cabildo

To Palermo

Zapata

Jorge Newbery

31

B. Matienzo

32   S Dumont

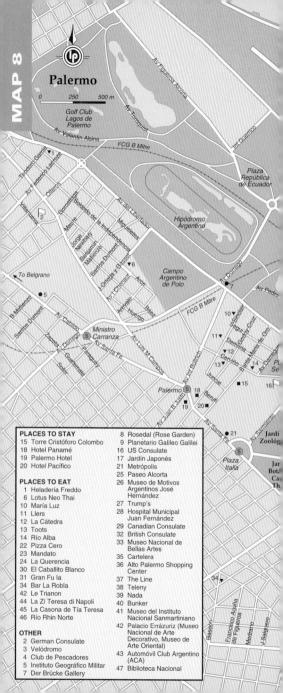

MAP 8

# Palermo

0    250    500 m

Golf Club Lagos de Palermo

Av Valentín Alsina

FCG B Mitre

Av Figueroa Alcorta

Intl Guerico

Teodoro García

Av F Federico Lacroze

Olleros

Gorostiaga

Av F Federico Lacroze

Villanueva

Jorge Newbery

Batiaguez

Matienzo

Santos Dumont

Soldado de la Independencia

Migueletes

Av del Libertador

Plaza República de Ecuador

Hipódromo Argentino

To Belgrano

B Matienzo

Av Cabildo

Santos Dumont

Av Dorrego

Zapiola

Guatemala

Paraguay

Soler

J Ortega y Gasset

Arce

J Cramaut

Arévalo

Huergo

Campo Argentino de Polo

Av Dorrego

FCG B Mitre

Av Pedro

Ministro Carranza

Av Santa Fe

Av Luis M Campos

Av Int Bullrich

Av Sinclair

Sinclair

Seguola Cruz

Godoy Cruz

Clemente

Cerviño

Santa Maria de Oro

Av Cabrera

Pl Se

Jurcall

Palermo

Berutti

Av Juan B Justo

Metrópolis

Jardí Zoológ

Jar Bot Ca Th

Plaza Italia

## PLACES TO STAY
15 Torre Cristóforo Colombo
18 Hotel Panamé
19 Palermo Hotel
20 Hotel Pacífico

## PLACES TO EAT
1 Heladería Freddo
6 Lotus Neo Thai
10 María Luz
11 Llers
12 La Cátedra
13 Toots
14 Río Alba
22 Pizza Cero
23 Mandato
24 La Querencia
30 El Caballito Blanco
31 Gran Fu Ia
34 Bar La Robla
44 Le Trianon
44 La Zí Teresa di Napoli
45 La Casona de Tía Teresa
46 Río Rhin Norte

## OTHER
2 German Consulate
3 Velódromo
4 Club de Pescadores
5 Instituto Geográfico Militar
7 Der Brücke Gallery

8 Rosedal (Rose Garden)
9 Planetario Galileo Galilei
16 US Consulate
17 Jardín Japonés
21 Metrópolis
25 Paseo Alcorta
26 Museo de Motivos Argentinos José Hernández
27 Trump's
28 Hospital Municipal Juan Fernández
29 Canadian Consulate
32 British Consulate
33 Museo Nacional de Bellas Artes
35 Cartelera
36 Alto Palermo Shopping Center
37 The Line
38 Teleny
39 Nada
40 Bunker
41 Museo del Instituto Nacional Sanmartiniano
42 Palacio Errázuriz (Museo Nacional de Arte Decorativo, Museo de Arte Oriental)
43 Automóvil Club Argentino (ACA)
47 Biblioteca Nacional

**Río de la Plata**

Costanera R. Obligado

Aeroparque Jorge Newbery

Av. Leopoldo Lugones

Belisario Roldán

● 3

Av. Casares

Parque de la Raza de Bosque Alegre

9 ⊙

Av. Casares

**Parque 3 de Febrero**

Int Isabel

Av. Iraola

Av. Sarmiento

Av. Adolfo Berro

Parque M Belgrano

Pier

○ 4

### Inset map

Plaza Grand Bourg
41 🏛

Elizalde

Castilla

Plaza República de Chile

Av. del Libertador

Tagle

Plaza República del Uruguay

42 🏛
43 ●

Pereyra Lucena

José Rateno

▼ 44

▼ 45

▼ 46

Av. Las Heras

Austria

Plaza R Darío

47 ●

---

Av. del Libertador

17 ✷

Av. Casares

Av. Figueroa Alcorta

Plaza Alemania

Plaza República del Perú

U F

Segui

Hume

Republica Arabe Siria

Av. Las Heras

Ugarteche

Cervino

Scalabrini Ortiz

Cabello

Callao

Castex

26 🏛

Plaza Grand Bourg

Plaza República de Chile

Plaza República del Uruguay

Plaza Naciones Unidas

29 ▪

J Gutierrez

22 ▼

R. Peña

Salguero

25 ✷

J. Salguero

27 ✷

28 ○

Sinclair Bulnes

Diaz

Plaza Alferez Sobral

23 ✷
24

30 ▼

Cnel Ho Campo

Plaza JJ de Urquiza

33 🏛

Plaza Mitre

32 □

31 ●

Plaza Francia

Plaza R Darío

Galileo

Newton

Copernico

Gelly

A. Pacheco de Melo

Juan Gutierrez

Ayacucho

Av. Pueyrredón

*see inset map*

Cementerio de la Recoleta

**Parque Las Heras**

Calabrini Ortiz

Araoz

Canning

Julián Alvarez

J. Salguero

35 ●

Vidt

Bulnes

36 ✷

Bulnes

37

Plaza E Mitre

Diaz

Billinghurst

S. de Bustamante

French

Peña

Agüero S

Av. Pueyrredón

Paraneta

José Hernández

Ayacucho

Uriburu

Azcuenaga

Junín

Laprida

38 ●

Agüero S

Guemes

Charcas

Mansilla

Paraguay

Soler

Austria

Agüero

Larrea

TM. del Anchorena

Jumal

Berutti

Beruti

Almagro

39 ●

Arenales

Pueyrredón S

Av. Santa Fe

Ecuador

40 ●

To Recoleta

Av. Callao

Tango musicians working the street
in La Boca

A peaceful moment in the Iglesia Nuestra Señora
del Pilar in Recoleta

A tomb in Recoleta Cemetery depicting life, death and
everything in between

MAP 9

**PLACES TO STAY**

3 Hotel Plaza Francia
12 Alvear Palace Hotel
18 Residencial Hotel Lion D'Or
25 Guido Palace Hotel
30 Caesar Park Hotel
31 Park Hyatt Buenos Aires
38 Ayacucho Palace
41 Wilton Palace Hotel
48 Hotel Versailles
52 Alfa Hotel
53 Residencial El Castillo
60 Hotel Rich
64 Hotel Presidente
68 Etoile Hotel

**PLACES TO EAT**

3 Restaurant Schiaffino
5 Café de las Flores
7 Plaza del Pilar
11 Pizza Cero
13 El Sanjuanino
15 Heladería Freddo
16 La Rueda
19 Robertino
20 La Gomería
22 Bar Rodi
23 Patio López
24 Au Bec Fin
29 Los Inmortales
30 Midori
32 Kugenhaus
33 Restaurant Ruso
34 French Bistro
37 Watani
39 Restaurant del Club Sirio
40 Pizza Banana
42 Guadalest
44 Cantabria
45 Los Inmortales
46 Romanaccio
56 Sorbera Sola
62 La Esquina de las Flores
65 La Biela
66 Estilo Munich
67 La Tasca de Germán
69 Don Juan
70 Sensu
71 Cabaña Las Lilas
72 Lola
73 Café de los Angeles
74 Heladería Freddo
75 Clapper's Café
76 Hippopotamus
77 Clark's
78 Harper's
79 Henry J Bean's
80 Gato Dumas Cocinero

**OTHER**

1 Museo Nacional de Bellas Artes
2 Centro Municipal de Exposiciones
4 Salas Nacionales de Cultura
6 El Sol
8 Centro Cultural Ciudad de Buenos Aires
9 Iglesia de Nuestra Señor de Pilar
10 Café de la Paix
12 Afrika
14 Municipal Tourist Kiosk
17 Facultad de Ingeniería
21 Uruguayan Consulate
27 Spanish Consulate
28 Shampoo
28 Le Club
35 Gallery
36 La Polara
47 Artesanías Argentinas
47 Rossi y Carusso
49 Mexican Consulate
50 Librerías Turísticas
51 Area
54 Contramano
55 La Comedia
57 Caño 14
58 Italian Consulate
59 Clásica y Moderna
63 Teatro Coliseo
61 Clásica y Moderna
63 Teatro Cervantes (Museo Nacional del Teatro)
76 Hippopotamus

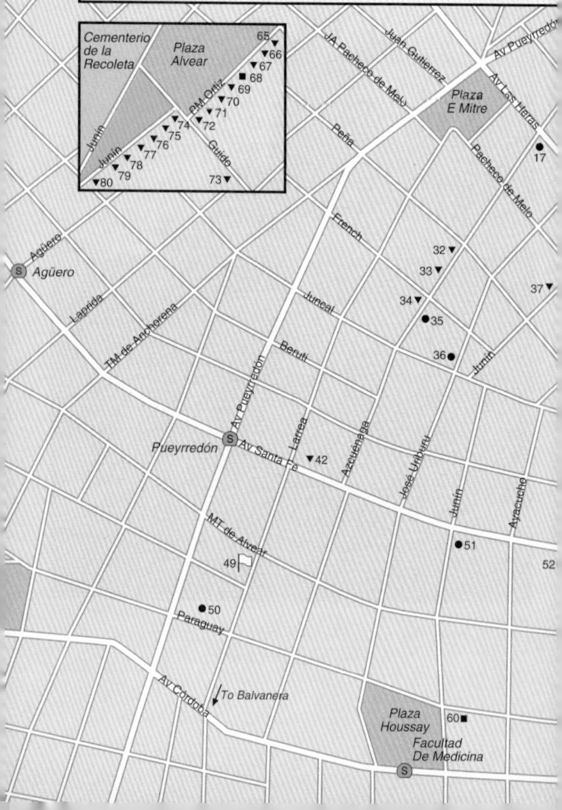

Parque Las Heras

Cementerio de la Recoleta

Plaza Alvear

Plaza E Mitre

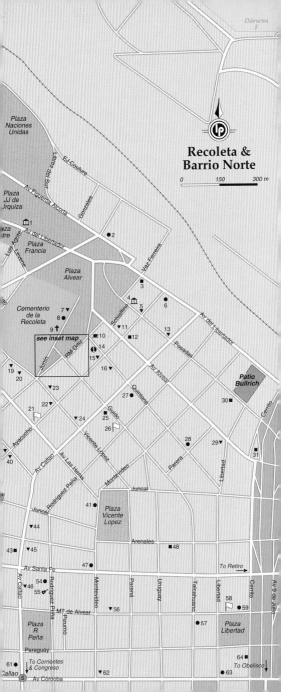

# Recoleta &
# Barrio Norte

Dársena F

Plaza Naciones Unidas

Plaza JJ de Urquiza

Plaza Francia

Plaza Alvear

Cementerio de la Recoleta

see inset map

Patio Bullrich

Plaza Vicente Lopez

Plaza R Peña

Plaza Libertad

0      150      300 m

E J Couture

Av Figueroa Alcorta

Av del Libertador

Yrigoyen Ferreira

Schiaffino

Posadas

Av Alvear

Quintana

Guido

Vicente Lopez

Las Heras

Montevideo

Juncal

Arenales

Av Santa Fe

Rodríguez Peña

Montevideo

Paraná

Uruguay

Talcahuano

Libertad

Cerrito

Av 9 de Julio

MT de Alvear

Pizurno

Paraguay

Av Córdoba

Callao

Av Callao

Ayacucho

Junín

RM Ortiz

To Retiro

To Corrientes & Congreso

To Obelisco

MAP 10

**PLACES TO STAY**
- 10 Sheraton Hotel
- 21 Crillón Hotel
- 26 Plaza Hotel
- 27 Hotel Central Córdoba
- 35 Elevage Hotel
- 44 Promenade Hotel
- 63 Hotel Diplomat
- 65 Gran Hotel Orly
- 68 Hotel Waldorf
- 70 Hotel San Antonio

**PLACES TO EAT**
- 6 Dolli
- 8 La Mosca Blanca
- 12 Alicia
- 17 Las Nazarenas
- 20 Los Chilenos
- 29 Dora
- 30 China Doll
- 34 La Cantina China
- 36 A'Mamma Liberata
- 43 Filo
- 46 Parrilla al Paso
- 47 El Salmón
- 48 La Chacra
- 49 Macau
- 50 Giardino
- 52 Yinyang
- 64 Alimentari
- 69 Catalinas

**OTHER**
- 1 Instituto Nacional de Enseñanza Superior en Lenguas Vivas
- 2 Correo Internacional (Parcel Post)
- 3 Brazilian Consulate
- 4 Irish Consulate
- 5 Museo Municipal de Arte Hispano-americano Isaac Fernández Blanco
- 7 American Express
- 9 Torre de los Ingleses
- 11 Dirección Nacional de Migraciones
- 13 Vermeer Gallery

**Retiro**

0    50    100 m

To Recoleta

Estación Retiro

To Barrio Norte

Plaza Libertad

Plaza Libertador General San Martín

San Martín

To the Microcentro

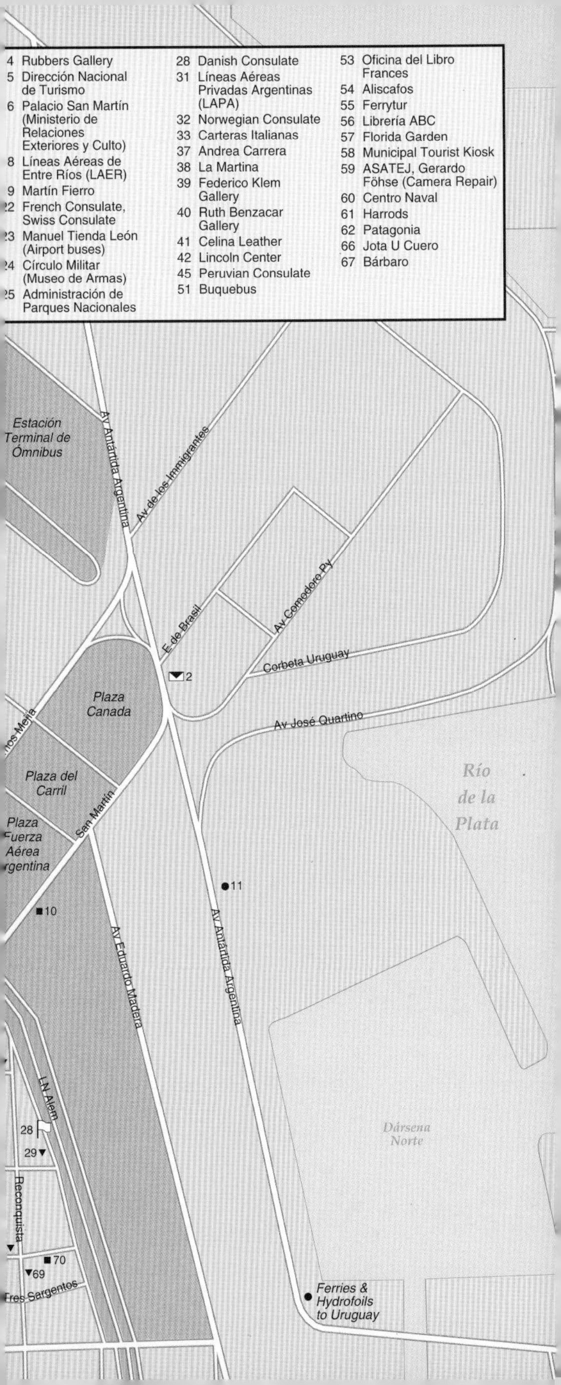

Estación Terminal de Ómnibus

Av Antártida Argentina

Av de los Inmigrantes

Av Comodoro Py

F. de Brasil

Corbeta Uruguay

▼2

Plaza Canada

Av José Quartino

Río de la Plata

Plaza del Carril

Plaza Fuerza Aérea Argentina

chos Mena

San Martín

Av Antártida Argentina

■10

●11

Av Eduardo Madero

L.N. Alem

28
29▼

Reconquista

■70

Dársena Norte

▼69

Tres Sargentos

● Ferries & Hydrofoils to Uruguay

# Microcentro & Monserrat (Catedral al Sur)

Río de la Plata

Dársena Norte

0    150    300 m

Av Amanda Argentina

Ferries & Hydrofoils to Uruguay

Bouchard

Av Eduardo Madero

●57

Av La Rabida

●109

Av Ing Huergo

Acapardo

## PLACES TO STAY
- 5 Petit Hotel Goya
- 9 Hotel Maipú
- 10 Hotel Libertador Kempinsky
- 12 Hotel Phoenix
- 19 Hotel Carsson
- 21 Claridge Hotel
- 24 Hotel Regidor
- 25 Hotel Italia Romanelli
- 26 Gran Hotel Colón
- 30 Hotel Regis
- 32 Hotel O'Rei
- 37 Tucumán Palace Hotel
- 51 King's Hotel
- 56 Hotel Plaza Roma
- 63 Liberty Hotel
- 75 Hotel Continental
- 77 Gran Hotel Argentino
- 83 Novel Hotel
- 88 Gran Hotel Hispano
- 88 Hotel Avenida
- 91 Astoria Hotel
- 92 Gran Hotel España
- 94 Turista Hotel
- 99 Hotel Nogaró

## PLACES TO EAT
- 7 Broccolino
- 16 La Posta del Gaucho
- 22 La Posada de 1820
- 25 Cicerón
- 27 La Estancia
- 28 Giardino
- 29 La Casona del Nonno
- 31 El Palacio de la Papa Frita
- 33 Oriente
- 34 McDonald's
- 35 ABC
- 36 El Pulpo
- 39 McDonald's
- 40 El Palacio de la Papa Frita
- 41 Los Idolos
- 42 Los Inmortales
- 43 La Rural
- 44 Pumper Nic
- 45 La Lecherísima
- 52 Granix
- 55 Verde Esmeralda
- 61 Pumper Nic
- 71 Cabaña Blanca
- 73 Restaurant Islas Malvinas
- 76 Granix
- 97 Swedish Club
- 103 Restaurant San Francisco

## OTHER
- 1 Municipal Tourist Kiosk
- 2 Centro Naval
- 3 Alianza Francesa
- 4 Hachette
- 6 Young Men's Bar
- 8 Federal Express
- 11 Celine
- 13 Equipo Teatro Payró
- 14 Campanera Dalla Fontana
- 15 Asociación Ornitológica del Plata
- 17 Fondo de Cultura Económica
- 18 Instituto Cultural Argentino-Norteamericano
- 20 Le Lab
- 23 Swan Turismo
- 38 Rancho Grande
- 46 Laboclick
- 47 Teatro Esmeralda
- 48 Tanguería Corrientes Angosta
- 49 Telefónica, Encotel
- 50 Richmond
- 53 Chilean Consulate
- 54 Austral Líneas Aéreas
- 55 Instituto Goethe
- 57 Luna Park
- 58 Dinar Líneas Aéreas
- 60 Buenos Aires Visión
- 62 Cotton Club de Buenos Aires
- 64 Delgado
- 65 El Ateneo
- 66 Museo Mitre
- 67 Museo de la Policia Federal
- 68 Swedish Consulate
- 69 Correo Central (Main Post Office)
- 70 Guante
- 72 Archivo y Museo Histórico del Banco de la Provincia de Buenos Aires Doctor Arturo Jauretche
- 74 Laboratorio de Idiomas de la Facultad, Universidad de Buenos Aires
- 78 Municipal Tourist Kiosk
- 79 Banco de Boston
- 80 Edificio Menéndez-Behety
- 81 Banco de la Nación
- 82 Chiche Farrace
- 85 Academia Nacional del Tango
- 86 Café Tortoni
- 87 Israeli Consulate, Dutch Consulate
- 89 Casa Rosada (Casa de Gobierno)
- 90 El Dorado (Tango lessons)
- 93 Morocco
- 95 Aerolíneas Argentinas
- 96 Cabildo
- 98 Asociación Argentina de Polo
- 100 DHL International
- 101 Belgian Consulate
- 102 Bar del Museo
- 104 Aerolíneas Argentinas
- 105 Museo de la Ciudad, Farmacia de la Estrella
- 106 Fundación Vida Silvestre Argentina
- 107 Capilla San Roque
- 108 Japanese Consulate
- 109 Edificio Libertador

MAP 12

**LP**

# Corrientes & Congreso

0    150    300 m

To Almagro

Pueyrredón

Av Pueyrredón

Av Corrientes    Pasteur

25●

🏛 24

50
Potosín

Paso    Larrea    Azcuénaga    Pasteur    Uriburu    Junín    Ayacucho    63■

Alberti    Pasco

79▼
78●

Plaza
1 de
Mayo

92

Pichincha    Sarandí

To San Cristóbal

101
▼

## PLACES TO STAY
- 18 Columbia Palace Hotel
- 26 Sarmiento Palace Hotel
- 29 Bauen Hotel
- 49 Hotel Bahía
- 51 Gran Hotel Sarmiento
- 52 Hotel Lyon
- 55 Hotel Callao
- 57 Normandie Hotel
- 58 Hotel Americano
- 60 Cardton Hotel
- 63 Hotel Ayamitre
- 64 Hotel Molino
- 65 Savoy Hotel
- 69 Gran Hotel Oriental
- 73 Hotel Lourdes
- 73 Hotel Mar del Plata
- 74 Hotel Parlamento
- 75 Hotel Plaza
- 76 Hotel Europa
- 77 Hotel Sportsman
- 82 Hotel Roma
- 83 Hotel Napoleón
- 85 Chile Hotel
- 86 Nuevo Hotel Mundial
- 87 Hotel Marbella
- 90 Castelar Hotel
- 91 Hotel Reina
- 94 Hotel Central
- 98 Hotel Cevallos
- 100 Hotel Palace Solís
- 106 Hotel Carlos I
- 108 Hotel La Casita

## PLACES TO EAT
- 4 Bar La Robla
- 5 Coto
- 6 La Casa China
- 14 Heladería Cadore
- 20 Los Inmortales
- 23 Lin Lin
- 28 El Toboso
- 31 Han Kung
- 36 El Palacio de la
  Papa Frita
- 37 Chiquilín
- 41 Pippo
- 42 La Fronda
- 43 Supercoop
- 44 Güerrín
- 45 Pizzería Serafín
- 46 Los Teatros
- 50 Casa de Corea
- 53 Cervantes II
- 54 Ratatouille
- 56 La Continental
- 68 Bar La Robla
- 69 Vecchio Unione
- 71 Confitería del Molino
- 72 La Americana
- 79 Yong Bin Kwan
- 80 Quorum
- 84 Villarosa
- 89 El Hispano

- 92 La Casa de Orihuela
- 95 La Fonda de Montserrat
- 97 Restaurant Status
- 101 Yuki
- 102 La Cabaña
- 104 Laurak Bat
- 107 Chez Moi

## OTHER
- 1 La Casa de Carlos Gardel
- 2 Palacio de las Aguas
  Corrientes
- 3 Paraguayan Consulate
- 7 Templo de la Congregación
  Israelita
- 8 Blakman Video No
  Convencional
- 9 Sapse Líneas Aéreas
- 10 Instituto de Lengua Española
  para Extranjeros (ILEE)
- 11 Palacio de Justicia (Tribunales)
- 12 Conventillo de las Artes,
  Escuela Presidente Roca
- 13 Alquileres Lavalle
- 15 Teatro Presidente Alvear
- 16 Café La Paz
- 17 Foro Gandhi
- 19 Buenos Aires Tur
- 21 Platero
- 22 Teatro Blanca Podestá
- 24 Museo del Cine Pablo
  D Hicken
- 27 Complejo Cultural Ricardo
  Rojas
- 30 Bookstore
- 30 Teatro Fundación Banco
  Patricios
- 32 Teatro El Vitral
- 33 Teatro Suizo
- 34 Café Pernambuco
- 35 Paseo La Plaza (Cartelera
  Vea Más, Café Homero,
  Teatro Complejo La Plaza)
- 38 Centro Cultural San Martín,
  Dirección General de Turismo
  de la Municipalidad de
  Buenos Aires
- 39 Teatro General San Martín,
  Museo de Artes Plásticas
  Eduardo Sívori, Museo de
  Arte Moderno
- 40 Oliverio

- 44 Galería Teatro Lorange
  (Cartelera Baires)
- 47 Oficina del Libro Francé
- 48 Cooperación, Informació
  y Ayuda al Enfermo de
  SIDA (COINSIDA)
- 59 Tradfax
- 61 Asociación Argentina de
  Albergues de la Juventu
- 62 Kinefot
- 67 El Subsuelo
- 71 Confitería del Molino
- 78 Aquilanti
- 81 Palacio del Congreso
- 88 Teatro Avenida
- 93 Biblioteca del Congreso
- 96 Mercado del Congreso
- 99 Automóvil Club Argentir
  (ACA)
- 103 Bolivian Consulate
- 105 Teatro del Sur

S Av Córdoba

Callao

3

To Recoleta

Viamonte

Carmen

Del 4

▼5

7

Plaza
Lavalle

Teatro
Colón

Tucumán

Tribunales

S

▼6

11

12
13

Lavalle

10

Callao

14

16 17 18

19

21

23

Pellegrini

Obelisco

S

S Av Corrientes

15

Uruguay

S

▼20

22

To the
Mircrocentro

Plaza
de la
República

9 de
Julio

27 ▼28

29

30

31

32
33

34 35 36

40
38 41

39 42

44

▼45

47

46 ▼

49

48

S

Sarmiento

51 54 55
52
▼53 56

58

37

59

60

43

61

62

Perón

64 65

57

▼66

67

▼68

Bartolomé Mitre

69

71 ▼

72

Rodríguez
Peña

74

Montevideo

Paraná

76

Uruguay

Talcahuano

Libertad

Cerrito

Av 9 de Julio

Av Callao

73

75

77

Lima

S

Rivadavia

Congreso

81

Plaza
del Congreso

Sáenz
Peña

S

82

Av de Mayo

83

▼84

85

86

87

88 ●

89

90 91

Av de
Mayo

S

Hipólito Yrigoyen

Riobamba

Combate de los Pozos

Av Entre Ríos

Solís

Virrey Cevallos

Luis Sáenz Peña

San José

Santiago del Estero

Salta

Lima

Bernardo de Irigoyen

Alsina

93

94

▼95

96

97▼

98

Moreno

99

100

To San
Telmo

Moreno

S

Av Belgrano

▼102

103

▼104

Venezuela

105

México

Chile

Av Independencia

Independencia

S

Estados Unidos

Carlos Calvo

106

Humberto Primo

Entre
Ríos

San
José

107▼

San
Juan

S Av San Juan

Autopista 25 de Mayo

Cochabamba

To Constitución

108

Constitución

MAP 13

San Telmo

To Congreso

To Microcentro

Manzana
de las
Luces

San Telmo

0    150    300 m

Adolfo Alsina

Av Julio A Roca

Moreno

Defensa

Balcarce

Peru

Bolivar

● 1
🏛 2

Av Belgrano

Belgrano

3 ●

5 de Julio

† 5

♻ 6

Piedras

Chacabuco

4 ▼

Venezuela

México

▼ 7

● 8

9 ● ● 10

Chile

▼ 11

Av 9 de Julio

Bernardo de Irigoyen

Tacuari

🏛 12

13 ▼

14 ▼

■ 15

16 ●

▼ 18

▼ 19        20

Pasaje San Lorenzo

21 ▼ 22  23 ●

17 ●

Av Independencia

Independencia

24 ▼

Estados Unidos

■ 26

25 ▼

27 28 ●
Pasaje Giuffra

Plazole
Olazát

30 ▼

31 ●

32 ◆◆

33 ●

34 ●
▼ 35 ● 36

38 ▼

37 ● 39
▼

Carlos Calvo

▼ 44

▼ 45

Humberto Primo

Plaza
Dorrego
▼ 40

● 41  43 ●

▼ 42

46 ■

47 ▼

48 ■

49 ▼

† 51

▼ 50

● 52

San
Juan

Av San Juan

To Constitución

🏛 53

Autopista 25 de Mayo

54 ♻

Cochabamba

Bernardo de Irigoyen

● 55

Tacuari

Piedras

Chacabuco

Peru

Bolivar

Defensa

Balcarce

Av Juan de Garay

■
57

🏠 56

Av Brasil

▼ 59

† 58

60 ▼

Plaza
Constitución

Constitución

Av Caseros

61 ■

Parque
Lezama

🏛 62

Estación Constitución
(Transportes Metropolitanos
General Roca, Ferrocarril Roca)

Hornos

Av Martín García

Irala

Pilcomayo

Av Patricios

Ruy Diaz de Guzman

Pi Y Margall

Liberti

Herrera

To Barracas

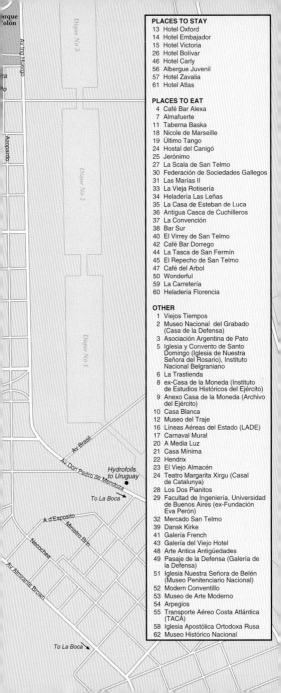

Parque Colón

Av Ing Huergo

Azopardo

Dique No 3

Dique No 2

Dique No 1

Av Brasil

Av Don Pedro de Mendoza

Hydrofoils to Uruguay

To La Boca

A. d'Esposito

Ministro Brin

Necochea

Av Almirante Brown

To La Boca

# MAP 14

## La Boca

Av Brasil

Hydrofoils
to Uruguay

Dársena
Sur

0    150    30

Guayaquay

A d'Esposito

Azobispo
Espinosa

20 de Septiembre

Av Pedro de Mendoza

M Galvez

MC Victorica

Juan M Blanes

Gustavino

To San
Telmo

Guayaquil

Arzobispo
Espinosa

20 de Septiembre – P Zenta Briano

Caboto

Bdjito Pérez Galdós

1

Ministro Brin

Necochea

Agustín R Caffarena

Av Almirante Brown

Wenceslao Villafañe

Aristóbulo del Valle

Martín Rodríguez

Pinzón

Del Valle Iberlucea

Zolezzi

Palos

Brandsen

▼ 5
▼ 6

Plaza
Solís

Suárez

▼ 7
▼ 8

3
2

To Barracas

Olavarría

Aráoz de Lamadrid

Av Pedro de Mendoza

Moreau

Garibaldi

4

▼ 9

20

Puente
Nicolás
Avellaneda

AVELLANE

10 ▼

13
14

19

Caminito

12  15       16

17 �📍 18

Aráoz

11

Magallanes

21 ▼

Rocha

Carlos F Melo

Benito Quinquela Martín

22 ▼

Alvarado

Av Pedro de Mendoza

Riachuelo

Ponce

La Pasta

Frías

Las Heras

Pinzón

Espejo

Zapiola

Carlos F Melo

Carboni

3 de Febrero

Vieytes

Alberti

### PLACES TO EAT
3  La Cancha
5  Spadavecchia
6  Il Piccolo Vapore
7  Tres Amigos
9  Gennarino
9  Helados Sorrento
10  La Orquesta
13  El Lunfa
14  El Samovar de Rasputín
20  El Viejo Puente de Mario
21  La Barbería
22  Puerto Viejo

### OTHER
1  Casa de Almirante Brown
2  Estadio Doctor Camilo Cichero
   (La Bombonera), Boca Juniors
   soccer team
4  Mercado y Frigorífico
   Benincasa-Mazzello
11  Siglo XX Cambalache
12  Via Caminito
15  Museo de Cera
16  La Vuelta de los Tachos
17  Museo de Bellas Artes de La Boca
18  Teatro de la Ribera
19  La Barca bas reliefs

ESTE ES EL
ATELIER
del Pintor
TERRONES
ACUNA
Entrada por
CALLE
MAGALLANES 847

La Boca street scenes

MAP 15

Av A Thomas

Av Dorrego

Av Federico Lacroze

Av Forest

FEDERICO
LACROZE
(S)

Jorge Newbery

(S) DORREGO

Av Warnes

Av Corrientes

(S) MALABIA

Av Dr Honorio Pueyrredón

Av San Martín

Av Patricias Argentina

Av Juan B Justo

Av D Alvarez

Av Gaona

Av Acoyte

Av Boyacá

ACOYTE (S)

Avellaneda

(S) PRIMERA
JUNTA

Av Rivadavia

Av Juan B Alberdi

Av Pedro Goyena

JOSÉ M
MORENO (S)

EMILIO
MITRE (S)

Av Eva Perón

Av Varela

Av Castañares

MEDALLA
MILAGROSA

VARELA (S)

(S) PLAZA DE LOS VIRREYES